Also by Christopher Byron

> *Skin Tight: The Bizarre Story*
> *of Guess v. Jordache*

> *The Fanciest Dive: What Happened*
> *When the Media Empire of Time/Life*
> *Leaped Without Looking into*
> *the Age of High Tech*

> *Foreign Matter*
> (A Novel)

deleteyourbroker.com

*Using the Internet
to Beat the Pros
on Wall Street*

>> Christopher Byron

a fireside book
published by simon_&_schuster

new_york

london

toronto

sydney

singapore

FIRESIDE
Rockefeller Center
1230 Avenue of the Americas
New York, NY 10020

First Fireside Edition 2002
FIRESIDE and colophon are registered trademarks
of Simon & Schuster, Inc.

For information about special discounts for bulk purchases,
please contact Simon & Schuster Special Sales:
1-800-456-6798 or business@simonandschuster.com

Designed by Sam Potts
Manufactured in the United States of America

10   9   8   7   6   5   4   3   2   1

The Library of Congress has cataloged
the Simon & Schuster edition as follows:
Byron, Christopher.
      DeleteYourBroker.com / Christopher Byron.
            p.   cm.
      Includes index.
            1. Electronic trading of securities—United
      States.   2. Investments—United States—
      Computer network resources.   I. Title: Delete
      your broker.com.   II. Title.
      HG4515.95.B97 2001
      332.64'0285—dc21   00-045009

ISBN 0-684-85468-6
      0-684-85469-4 (Pbk)

Acknowledgments

No book of this sort would be complete without an acknowledgment of at least some of those to whom the author owes a debt of gratitude. To that end I would like, in particular, to express public appreciation to Arthur Carter, the publisher of the wildly irreverent—and equally wildly successful—New York *Observer* newspaper, for which I have had the surpassing honor of crafting a weekly Internet-syndicated Wall Street news column for more years now than I care to count.

Were Arthur's legacy to consist of nothing but his accomplishments as a publisher, it would be considerable. But only those who have known him for more than thirty years, as I have, know that he, more than any other individual alive today, is responsible for giving shape to the forty-year boom in investment banking that has dominated and defined Wall Street to this day. As a co-founder and name partner of Carter, Berlind & Weill, Arthur created the investment bank "boutique" that gave the go-go 1960s its name on Wall Street. It began in cramped digs on Wall Street, moved eventually to midtown Manhattan and the General Motors Building, and boasts a direct lineage that proceeded through Shearson, Hayden Stone and American Express, to become at century's end Salomon Smith Barney and, ultimately, Citigroup.

That's all quite humbling, to say the least. But for me, the most humbling thing of all is to have had Arthur as a mentor on my columns. For that I shall ever be as grateful as I can possibly express.

I would also like to thank my agent, Joni Evans of the William Morris Agency, (a) who encouraged me to wake up to the implications of the Internet when I don't think even *she* fully realized what she meant, (b) who thereafter has handled virtually every detail of my career and, maddeningly, has mostly refused to be paid for any of it, and (c) who had the foresight to look three years down the road and see a book when I was having trouble looking beyond my next deadline.

Finally, I would like to thank my editor at Simon & Schuster, Robert Bender, whose skillful guidance in discussing and shaping this book has been as valued and worthwhile on this occasion as it has been when I have had the honor to work with him on projects in the past. For the many others who have contributed time and effort to helping me with this book, I am sure they will greet my decision not to mention them by name with a sigh of relief. Read on and I suspect you will see why. Enjoy.

Weston, Connecticut
June 2000

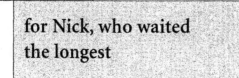

>>>

for Nick, who waited
the longest

Contents

deleteyourbroker.com

*Using the Internet
to Beat the Pros
on Wall Street*

chapter one

How the Internet Has Changed Investing

This is a book about investing on Wall Street. It's also about investing on the Internet and about investing *in* the Internet. This book won't make you rich—at least not in the Bill Gates scheme of things—but if you've already got a few dollars, it might help keep you from getting poor . . . as well as help you make your money grow. It should help you to match, or even beat, the broad market averages—and it may even show you how to have some fun while doing so. It is written from a perspective of thirty years as a financial writer and columnist covering Wall Street, as well as, from time to time, that of an investor.

It is written in the belief that, in numerous and important ways, the advent of the Internet and its graphical offspring, the World Wide Web, have fundamentally changed the way Wall Street operates, tipping the balance of power for the first time away from professional investors and speculators, and toward everyday individuals. Almost anything—and I mean anything—that a professional investor, hedge fund manager, mutual fund portfolio manager, or brokerage firm desk trader can do with his $12,000-per-year stock trader's terminal and his $100,000-plus research reports, can now be done by any individual with a personal computer, a modem, and a $20-per-month connection to the Internet.

But don't quit your day job just yet, because there is a second belief that underpins this book—namely, that no matter how much you wish it were otherwise, the odds are greatly, indeed impossibly, against your getting rich overnight and staying that way for any appreciable period of time. The structure of the market is against you, some of the cleverest card-counters on the planet are against you, the tax laws and technology are working against you, and on top of all that you've got the powerfully disruptive and unpredictable forces of human psychology working against you.

As I write these words in the spring of the year 2000, something approaching a kind of mini-panic seems to have gripped Wall Street. After years of rising stock prices—capped by six months of an unprecedented further surge that erupted when people thought prices could absolutely, positively go no higher—the market just as abruptly turned around and started dramatically dropping. It took nearly thirty years for the NASDAQ Composite Average to climb to the 4,000-plus level (and, briefly, 5000-plus) that the index reached by March of the year 2000. Then in scarcely a single sickening week, it lost 25 percent of those thirty years' worth of gains.

Some stocks—particularly in the technology and so-called dot.com sectors, which people had thought could only go up—went down so fast it became impossible to sell them. Many stocks lost 25 percent or more of their value in a single day—not just one day, but day after day after day as the slide progressed.

On the first trading day of the year 2000, ReSourcePhoenix.com, a California-based Internet company with more than 200 employees, sold for $25 per share and was worth $280 million on Wall Street. Investors who held the shares had watched themselves grow rich beyond their dreams, and many had pledged their shares as collateral on loans to buy yet more stock, or put additions on their homes, or take vacations, or buy sports cars. You name it.

Three months later, ReSourcePhoenix.com was selling for $1.65 per share, and the whole company was worth less than $19 million on Wall Street. In other words, 93 percent of its value had been wiped out, and investors have been taken to the cleaners. By the summer of 2001, the price had dropped to a mere one cent per share.

Obviously, no one can know what the future holds. Were it otherwise, the person with that knowledge would, in the end, wind up with all the money. But we can know what happened in the past, which means that, by slow and careful navigation, we can move forward by constant reference to the rearview mirror of life. And in the end, that is all that investing in stocks is about: trying to figure out where we are headed by looking at where we have been. As we'll see later in this book, the most important single lesson history teaches us in that regard is that, over time, stock prices always rise, but that they do not rise, over the long sweep of years, at more than about 10 percent to 15 percent annually. The corollary to that fact is this: When stock prices do rise beyond the norm, the day comes when they *fall* more than normally, so that, in the end, the growth rate returns to the norm.

This means that the mood of seeming panic that grips the market as I write these words could vanish tomorrow, and stock prices could begin soaring all over again. But *any* movement of prices—either up *or* down—outside the norm will eventually be offset by a counterbalancing move in the opposite direction.

Trying to anticipate when those moves are about to occur—in effect, to snatch the money and run—is what market timing is all about, and the odds are greatly against getting it right.

· · ·

The purpose of this book is not only to help you recognize and appreciate the difficulty of trying to time the market—to anticipate its ups and downs—but also to recognize other pitfalls and opportunities of the market—and to exploit them to your benefit. Some of these opportunities and pitfalls were once limited to Wall Street professionals, but thanks to the Web are now open to everyone.

This book will actually take you into the Web itself so you can look at and understand exactly what is being discussed in the text. Throughout this book you'll find what are known as hyperlinks. Just type these Web addresses exactly as you see them into your computer's Internet browser and you'll be transported directly to the Web site page that is being discussed in this book. Since the World Wide Web is like an enormous global library in which the librarians are constantly moving around the locations of the books and periodicals, some of these links may be out of date by the time you read this book. So just type the following: www.deleteyourbroker.com, and you'll be taken to a Web site that will list updated links for your convenience.

In this book we'll look at the risks and rewards of day trading—an activity that basically boils down to trying to anticipate minute-to-minute moves in individual stocks on the NASDAQ electronic stock exchange. Day trading has become an extraordinarily popular pursuit among individual investors in the last couple of years, not least because of the almost deafening level of promotion that has accompanied the growth of online investing itself.

Nonetheless, one of the conceits of this book is that you can lose your pants as a day trader, and that you should stay away from the activity. For one thing, the technology of home-based Internet connections just isn't reliable enough to be dependable on a minute-to-minute basis, and in day trading, minutes (and sometimes even seconds) can mean the difference between profit and ruin. What's more, as a day trader an individual gains no advantage whatsoever against professional traders at major investment firms like Goldman Sachs, who have been doing exactly the same thing for years.

Even so, as an online investor you should at least know what day trading is all about and how it works—if for no other reason than because you can sometimes profit greatly from the pricing distortions created in the market by the day traders. In short, you don't have to *be* a day trader to make money from day trading, but you do have to understand how it works and what drives it.

Thus, if you were to type the following hyperlink (known as a URL, which stands for something that we don't need to care about) into your browser—www.daytradingstocks.com/tradinglinks.html—you'd be taken to a Web site that lists over 100 different further hyperlinks to businesses and firms engaged in one aspect or another of day trading. You could spend the next four hours clicking from one link to the next, but this book will save you the trouble by identifying which links are the best, and why.

This book will also discuss the all-important topic of fundamental analysis. The hyperlinks in those chapters will show you precisely how to find the most valuable, up-to-the-minute information to undertake your own, independent, unbiased such research. Why is this important?

Because for generations fundamental research on individual companies has been the premier investment tool of every major brokerage house on Wall Street. But generally speaking, the highest quality reports have been almost completely unavailable to individuals—at least until after the investment firms that prepared them have shared their contents with their major institutional clients. This in turn means that the opportunity for individuals to profit from the buy or sell recommendations contained in the reports have all been exploited and leeched away by the brokerage firm's institutional clients by the time individual retail clients ever see them.

All the major brokerage houses have both institutional and individual retail clients (that's you)—and in every food chain, the individuals rank at the bottom.

In this book, I'll show you how to set up your browser so you will be alerted whenever one of these reports is distributed by an investment firm to its institutional clients.

For example, click on the following URL—

http://www.jagnotes.com

—and you'll be transported to the sign-up page for a service called JAGNotes. This service costs $9.95 per month and offers an early morning daily commentary on its Web site of just about everything that nearly every major Wall Street firm is telling its major institutional clients about the market, and individual companies within it, that morning. A lot of this information comes to JAGNotes via cable TV and various Web sites, so if you don't want to spend the money for the JAGNotes service, you can set up your computer to do many of the same things the JAGNotes people are doing.

Best of all, I'll show you how to produce your own reports on almost any publicly traded company using exactly the same raw information that the investment firms themselves use. What's more, because *you'll* be doing the research (which is surprisingly easy), you'll know it is being done correctly—which is something you cannot always be sure of in the work of investment firm analysts.

The best, most up-to-date fundamental research information on any company comes from its latest financial reports filed with the Securities and Exchange Commission. There's an astonishing array of information contained in those filings—from how much revenue the company has been collecting to how much it has been paying its top officials in the form of salaries and bonuses. You can even find out if the top executive gets free health insurance or a company car.

All this information, and more, is available for the taking from the forms and reports that publicly traded companies must file with the SEC on a regular basis. There are 10-K forms and proxy statements,

8-Ks and IPO registration filings . . . a torrent of arcane-sounding material that pours into the SEC every day of the year, covering just about every financial matter imaginable.

Up until about four years ago, you could get these documents in only one of three ways: either phone or write to the investor relations department of the company itself and ask to be mailed a copy (don't hold your breath waiting for it to arrive); go to the public reading room of the SEC's regional office in New York City (or its headquarters in Washington, D.C.) and make a photocopy; or hire a document retrieval and research firm like Disclosure Inc. to do it for you.

Whichever way you chose, you'd have been in for a long wait—and in one case a major expenditure of money—before you ever got your hands on a single document. Meanwhile, whatever useful information might have been contained in the reports would assuredly have already been discovered—and acted upon—by Wall Street's research analysis, leaving you with nothing in the end but a lot of wasted time and money for your efforts.

Thanks to the Web, you can now get these documents the very instant they are first filed with the SEC—and you can get them for free. Not only that, you can make watch lists to alert you when specific companies you are interested in submit their documents to the SEC—and that service is usually free too.

Since May of 1996, these reports have all been submitted to the SEC in computerized form and stored in the SEC's EDGAR database. (EDGAR is an acronym for something, but it doesn't matter what). In any case, you can get instant access to these reports from more than a dozen different Internet-based services, a number of which are now free to the user. Click on the following URL and you'll be taken to one of them: www.edgar-online.com.

But how do we make use of such copious information as investors? What's the difference between income and cash flow anyway—and does it really matter? What's the difference between short-term and long-term liabilities, and does *that* matter? Likewise for goodwill and intangibles? What is deferred revenue and why should we care?

These are the sorts of questions that form the grist of fundamental stock analysis, yet for generations on end, Wall Street has so jealously guarded the answers that you'd think they contained the formula for Coca-Cola. An entire vocabulary of befuddlement and confusion has evolved along the way—a language of obscurantism designed to suggest that only a high financial priesthood has been admitted to its secrets. For example, here is how a stock analyst for the Wall Street investment firm of FAC/Equities at First Albany Corp. described financially attractive investments in the Internet sector in the autumn of 1998:

> *[those that] . . . enable and optimize the commerce process for businesses by using technology as an enable.*

In this book, we'll demystify the terms—and the process—of fundamental analysis, exploring in detail, in everyday language that anyone can understand, how to use such reports without going crazy in the process. You can set bookmarks in your computer to be taken to sites that contain well-prepared, easy-to-use glossaries of these terms. For example, here is the address of one such glossary, maintained for free by Microsoft Corp.:

http://moneycentral.msn.com/investor/Glossary/glossary.asp.

We'll also show you where to find inexpensive—and even free—software tools that you can use to automate much of the research process itself. Here's one such link: www.spredgar.com. Click on it and you'll be taken to the Web site of a marvelous little program that will automatically process the raw financial data of any EDGAR-based quarterly filing or annual report into every ratio and chart conceivable. Securities analysts charge tens of thousands of dollars for this sort of thing, but you can do the same thing for the one-time cost of the program, which is $125 for students, and $250 for everyone else.

Yet other chapters in this book are devoted to what is known as technical analysis. Simply stated, technical analysis of stocks is an activity that could not exist in its present form without computers. Yet now that computers are ubiquitous throughout Wall Street, so too is technical analysis. Over the last two decades, this seemingly arcane pursuit has developed into what is arguably the single most important factor affecting the course of the market on a day-to-day basis.

For thirty years a war has waged on Wall Street between the technical crowd and the fundamental bunch over which side has the better approach to securities analysis. One goal of this book is to show you how to make use of *both* approaches. Institutions are, by their nature, political creatures, with the various people in them all protecting their perceived vested interests and arenas of power. The technical analysts thus think that they alone hold the key to making money in the stock market, whereas the fundamental analysts think it's just the opposite. Private individuals, not trapped by such prejudices, can use *both* tools with a flexibility that large institutions lack.

The fundamental analysts make investment decisions based on the historical record of a company's performance (how much money did it make last year, and was it more, or less, than the year before? . . . questions like that). Their approach boils down to the assumption that, over the long haul, profitable companies will always turn out to be better investments than unprofitable ones. As a result, the fundamental analysts say that the historical record of a company's profitability is as good an indicator as any for predicting a company's future performance.

That's where they lose the tekkies, who say that a company's past results are absolutely no guarantee of its future performance. They argue that just because General Electric, under its chairman and CEO, Jack Welch, keeps racking up quarter after quarter of rising earnings doesn't mean anything regarding what the company will do in the future. All the tekkies are interested in is how G.E.'s stock price is likely to perform at particular times—as for example, when the company is preparing to report its latest quarterly numbers. Does trading volume go up in anticipation—and push the stock price up with it? And if so, where does it stop (what the technical folks call a "resistance point")? Technical analysts ask questions like, "Is there support for this stock at $50?" and "What's the on-balance volume trend?" (These concepts will be explained later in the book.)

To understand this quarrel between the fundamentalists and the tekkies, think of the two ways medical science approaches cancer research. The first way is to get down to the cellular—and subcellular level—and try to learn what it is within the organism itself that causes the cells to mutate and divide uncontrollably. We may liken this approach—which is what a biotech company like Amgen follows—to fundamental research.

The second approach to cancer research is to collect huge amounts of social science research data on given populations of people, and try to find patterns that correlate incidences of cancer to various conditions in the environment. This approach, followed by the American Cancer Society, the National Institutes of Health, and others, may be likened to technical analysis on Wall Street—the difference of course being that instead of using statistical evidence to identify at-risk populations of people, technical analysts are trying to spot trends in stocks on Wall Street.

As with anything on Wall Street, there are risks inherent in investing on the basis of technical analysis, and in this book we'll spell them out in detail. But you can also make a lot of money using technical analysis if you do things right—and the Internet puts every tool you'll need right at your fingertips.

For example, click on the following URL and you'll be looking at one of the tekkies' main tools—a stock chart—in this case for General Motors:

http://finance.yahoo.com/q?s=gm&d=b.

There's a lot you can do with a chart like that, and in this book we'll help you do it. Or, just type this URL into your computer: http://moneycentral.msn.com and you'll be taken to an investing Web site maintained by Microsoft. Once you get there you'll have to register as a user, but registration is free and you only have to do it once. This site has more—and more sophisticated—technical analysis tools than you can possibly imagine, and we'll discuss many of them in this book. For example, you can create a one-year chart of Dell Computer, the PC assembler and retailer, complete with ten-day and fifty-day moving average trends, a twenty-period Bollinger Band, and an on-balance volume chart.

Never mind what those concepts mean right now. In Chapter 3 we'll get into them in detail; for now it's simply enough to know that the book will show you how to get access to the concepts quickly, and how to make use of them.

Because the Web is an enormous and ever-expanding thing (that is, I *think* it's a thing), any book about it runs the evident risk of being out of date before it even gets to the printer. Over time, some of the hyperlinks are bound to be changed by the operators of the Web sites referred to in the text, so the book will also show you how to find what you're looking for even without the aid of the links. More important, no matter how much the Web evolves and changes in the period ahead, the basic element that makes it revolutionary for our purposes will remain unaltered: the enormous quantity of information that is available to us, mostly for free, somewhere or another on its Web sites.

In this book, we are not really interested in technology itself. How the Web works is something I frankly don't understand—and frankly hope never to need to learn, any more than I want to understand the principles of aerodynamic flight. For me it's enough to know that if I show up at Kennedy Airport, ticket in hand, the chances are good that I'll get on the plane, we'll take off, and six hours later I'll be at LAX in Los Angeles. Why the plane actually stays aloft—or becomes airborne in the first place or doesn't fall out of the sky as soon as we start to slow down—is not a matter of great moment to me one way or another. Getting there is enough for me.

It's the same with the Internet. Why is it, for example, that when I turn on a computer that is connected to a telephone line I can see real-time live streaming video of clothing-optional beaches in Baja, California, but I can't hear what my teenage daughter in the next room is saying over the same phone line to her boyfriend? Anyway, maybe it's better that I can't hear what they're talking about . . . right now . . . in the next room . . . when she should be doing her homework but isn't.

All that really matters, so far as the Internet goes, is that most of the time it works—and when it does, I can learn almost anything I need to know to make a good investment decision better or avoid stumbling into a bad one.

Of course, we can't be right in these things all the time because, well, if we were, the game would end pretty quickly. But we can be right a lot of the time, and over a generous span of years—ten or fifteen is ample—being right a lot of the time can make you some decent money.

How much is that? Frankly, I don't know. I've been in this business of writing about Wall Street for thirty years now, and I've never met *anyone* able to say how much is "a lot." In the end, a lot always turns out to be more than you've got now. How much more is the tricky part, for as Mark Twain said of bourbon, so is it true with money: too much is never enough.

It's a bit beyond the scope of this book to suggest how you might dwell for a time on the issue of how much is enough in light of your own personal circumstances. But I do know that any time you spend on the matter will be time well spent. The stock market does, after all, have a way of revealing the inner person.

It is, as you'll soon enough see, a core belief of this book that if you are able to stand or sit upright and breathe, you *must* be "in the market." You have no choice. That's a painful truth for people of my generation and circumstances who grew into adulthood in the 1960s, took liberal arts majors in Ivy League colleges, and basically sneered at and disdained "business" and "Wall Street" as the fountainhead of all that was most vile and corrupt in the world. Didn't Wall Street bring us Dow Chemical? And didn't Dow bring us napalm? And didn't napalm . . . well, you can just continue on from there.

What we didn't know, and didn't care to hear about or learn, was that Wall Street's ability to raise and deploy capital was also the reason why there were jobs for us when we graduated, and why, from that day to this, life for most of us has gotten better and better, year in and year out—no matter what the headlines have suggested to the contrary.

But now there are 70 million of us—and millions more right behind—who are marching into middle age, and we all know what comes after *that!* And that's where things will stop getting better and better unless we plan and act accordingly. So let me tell you about my nightmare. It's got to do with money and children, and millions and millions of miserable old people. Consider it a warning—a wake-up to what lies ahead if you don't *force* yourself to put money in the market. If you don't you may not die poor, but you'll certainly wind up less well off than you are today.

My dream is about generational warfare in the twenty-first century—a subject that is just about as taboo at the dinner table as, say, graphic descriptions of man-boy love. In my dream, I am thirty or maybe even forty years older than I am today—that is, eighty or ninety, somewhere around there . . . the *old* old, as we have learned to say. In my dream I remember that there was a time—back when I was pushing fifty—when good-looking women half my age would come up to me in the gym, look at me admiringly, and tell me I had a body like their younger brother's. But that stopped happening decades ago   in my dream. In my dream I don't lift weights anymore, the last of my teeth have long since fallen out, and I hobble along with a walker, listening as children make jokes behind me. And guess what, I haven't even gotten to the nightmare part yet.

The nightmare part is that, wherever I look, wherever I go, all I see are people just like me—millions of them. They are my generation, the baby boomers, the 77 million of us who were born between 1945 and 1964, now depleted by age and entropy to 43 million tottering, decrepit oldsters—every one of us seventy years of age or older. We are leaving, not singly or even by the hundreds, but by the tens of thousands every week.

In my dream I am living in the Time of Dying. It is worse than anything the country has ever before known—worse than World War II, when 300,000 died, worse even than the Civil War, when the totals on both sides approached one million. What's happening in my dream is more like some biblical plague. In my dream, nearly *10 million* die in a mere five years—a Vietnam War every week and a half— and every one of the dead is a member of my generation, the boomers. Like I said, this is a nightmare. Obits fill entire sections of the daily newspapers, and "In Memoriam" becomes a nightly feature on the evening news.

But it gets worse, for it turns out that, when all is said and done, we are just not dying fast enough. In my dream, a desperate national quarrel rages, shouted in code words and euphemisms. On one side are the kids—the Generation Xers—now middle-aged and muttering of "personal choice" and "individual rights." On the other side are me and my friends, the boomers, croaking back through saliva-parched voices that the hidden agenda of our children is all too obvious—that their *real* objective is simply to get us out of the way before the task of keeping us alive bankrupts the whole nation.

Which is more or less when I wake up, to be reminded, in a thousand subtle ways, that this really wasn't a dream at all, just a quick— and slightly out of focus—look at the future itself. If my fears are well founded, America faces a struggle—not all that many years from now either—when the boomers and their children begin literally a fight to the death over money. We're not talking inheritance here, we're talking the wealth of the nation itself.

It's pretty grim, this future of mine, but the weight of available research says the odds favor its coming true. Start with demographics. One way to look at the history of America in the twentieth century is through the lengthening life expectancy of its citizens—from 46.3 years for a male born in 1900, to 72.3 years for one born today. According to the U.S. Census Bureau, this rising trend will continue, with the result that a male born in the year 2035 will be able to look forward to at least 75.8 years of life.

But that number doesn't give you the true picture; it only tells you what the long-term prospects are for someone who has yet to run the full gauntlet of life, starting at birth. If you've actually run most of that gauntlet—from car accidents as a teenager, to heart attacks, breast cancer, and all the rest of it in middle age—and actually survived, the longevity picture in fact *brightens*. You become, as I said, a member of the old old. That is, if you somehow manage to reach eighty, you get to look forward, according to U.S. Census Bureau actuarial data, to somewhere around seven *more* years of life. The good news, in other words, is that if you live to be eighty you'll probably live to be eighty-seven. The bad news is you won't be able to afford it.

For one thing, the wealth of the nation just isn't growing as fast as its population is aging. America's long-term economic growth rate has been slowing since the 1950s. But the number of elderly has been rising relentlessly. According to researchers Laurence Kotlikoff and Alan Auerbach, the U.S. economy is currently being driven by 3.2 productive workers for every elderly and retired person. By the year 2029, when the youngest boomers will be in their sixties with the oldest (like me) in their eighties, the ranks of the elderly will have swelled so much that there will be only 1.8 productive workers for every elderly and retired person.

In short, unless the nation magically undergoes a sudden, vaulting—and sustained—surge in productivity for decades on end, your children and your children's children will be faced with a Hobbesian choice: either support dramatically higher taxes on their own incomes, or sharply cut back—or maybe even eliminate—federal transfer payments like Social Security and Medicare to their parents and grandparents (that's you!). Now stop for a minute and think: If you were in their shoes, how would *you* vote? In fact, you *are* in their shoes—right now—which is why, throughout virtually the whole of the 1990s, you've been voting to cut spending *and* taxes—the dragon's teeth of intergenerational warfare.

And don't delude yourself into thinking that private pension plans and IRAs are going to bail you out either—at least not at the rate boomers are pumping money into them currently. Says B. Douglas Bernheim of Princeton University, a leading authority on savings trends, "The typical baby boom household is saving at one-third the rate required to finance a standard of living during retirement comparable with a standard of living that it enjoys before retirement."

Buried in the latest U.S. census data is the grim proof of what Bernheim is talking about: Only 25.8 percent of Americans between thirty-five and forty-four years of age—the very heart of the boomer generation—even *have* an IRA or Keogh account at all, let alone have any money in it. In fact, add up *all* financial assets of the thirty-five-to-forty-four group, from their homes to their bank accounts, mutual funds, stocks, bonds, everything, and their median net worth is only $31,148.

Now $31,148 is a lot more than zero, but for someone turning forty, it's not where you want to be, especially if you want to do more in retirement than eat cat food out of a can. According to the Social Security Administration, if you're forty years old today, and earning $40,000 annually, you'll be able to count on no more than about $1,178 per month, in inflation-adjusted dollars, if you retire at sixty-five in the year 2020 (assuming, of course, that the program's retirement age hasn't by then been shoved back to save money, and that the benefit payouts haven't been cut or taxed). According to the Employee Benefit Research Institute, a Washington think tank on the retirement issue, employer pensions currently contribute only about 18 percent of the income that those already in retirement now live on—and the number of workers covered by pension plans has been going down in recent years.

It's a generally accepted rule of thumb that any retiree who wants to continue with something even approaching his pre-retirement lifestyle will need, at a bare minimum, at least fifty percent of the income he or she enjoyed as a productive worker. For a family with $40,000 a year of income now, that means at least, oh, let's treat ourselves right and say $25,000 annually, in inflation-adjusted retirement income, beginning at around age sixty-five in the year 2020. But where will the money come from if, at most, you can count on only about $14,000 a year from Social Security (if that) and maybe nothing at all from a corporate pension plan? Life may not always be fair, but in this case at least, its lesson seems clear: You'd better start saving and investing like hell.

Warns Bernheim of Princeton, "The accumulated empirical evidence overwhelmingly supports the conclusion that, unless their behavior changes dramatically, baby boomers will be forced to accept a significantly reduced standard of living in retirement." That's a nice way of saying it'll be cat-food-out-of-a-can time. You don't want that.

Why is the investing part important? Because, generally speaking, investing in common stocks has historically proved to be the best and safest way to make accumulated capital grow. I once spent a couple of weeks in a high-powered capital market training course run by Citicorp for the bank's best and wealthiest private clients (not that I fell into that category—it was just that, as a journalist, you get invited to things like that). Anyway, one of the more interesting presentations in the course involved various things to do with $1,000 to make it grow. The options ranged from putting it in short-term U.S. Treasury bills, to buying bonds, to buying real estate and precious metals, to investing in common stocks.

Of those choices—which pretty much cover all the choices that matter—the common stocks option won hands down and going away. For example, during the thirty years between 1964 and 1993—a time frame that covers almost every economic and financial condition imaginable except perhaps a 1930s-style depression—the average American mutual fund returned an average price appreciation of 11.58 percent annually, or half again better than any other investment category in the ranking.

And the most surprising thing was how easy it was to pick the winners: just buy a lot of stocks in well-managed companies and sit there with them. In other words, forget about market timing—that is, buying at the bottom and selling at the top. Just "buy and hold" and in the end you come out ahead. Of course, if the company itself turns out to be a disappointment—management fails to deliver on its public utterances about growth, let us say—then by all means get rid of the stock as quickly as possible. But don't pay any attention to swings in the market because they'll drive you crazy and you'll gain nothing by trying to time the cycles.

Whatever your long-term investment goals may turn out to be, my own experience as a writer and investor suggests very powerfully that the Internet is really the only research tool you'll need. For many years I worked as a business editor at *Time* magazine, and after that at *Forbes*. My enduring memory of those days is just how many people we needed to put out the product. In the Business Section of *Time*, where I worked as an editor from 1975 to 1983, we had, as best as I can recall, the following:

> One senior editor
> Two associate editors
> Three staff writers
> Five researchers
> One photo researcher
> One maps and charts researcher
> One secretary

That's fifteen people to produce roughly 3,000 words of copy per week. And mostly what the people did was hunt around for facts out of which the writers could fashion their stories. We had people who did nothing all day but read newspapers. We had people in field bureaus who sent in more facts. We had filers, organizers, it just went on and on. And all of it was designed, at the end of the day, to place a manila folder with maybe fifteen newspaper clips and three correspondent files on a writer's desk—out of which he was expected to cobble together a ninety-line story on, say, the health of the West German economy . . . or the prospects for Exxon . . . or the troubles at Lockheed.

The Internet changed all that. As a columnist at the end of the

1990s I am still doing more or less what I did as a magazine writer twenty years earlier—only I am making more money, have more free time in my life, and—most important for our purposes here—I am doing it all with literally no research support whatsoever. So far as I personally am concerned, the research capabilities of the Internet mean that one man can now do the work of what used to take fourteen.

Remember when you were a kid in school and they taught you in Social Studies about how Cyrus McCormick's reaper revolutionized the American farm and made it the envy of the world? Well, that's what the Internet is—the reaper of Wall Street.

Since its arrival on the scene I have used that tool to research hundreds—indeed even thousands—of different companies, large and small alike. The goal has been to ferret out underpriced stocks that Wall Street has overlooked, and overpriced stocks with which investors have foolishly fallen in love.

As has anyone in this line of work, I've had a few misses—or at least what seemed to be misses for a time. I predicted Yahoo, the Internet search engine company, would be a loser. Instead it proved astonishingly successful, roaring out of the gate as an IPO. Yet it eventually cracked as I warned it would, and by the summer of 2001 had fallen by 90 percent from its all-time high—though the slide did take much longer than I had expected.

And for every Yahoo there's been a Boston Chicken and a Planet Hollywood International—to mention just two of dozens of preposterously overpriced stocks that crashed and burned when investors finally woke up to what had been obvious for all to see in the companies' financials all along. The Internet enabled me to see those problems coming *way* down the road. In this book we'll look at these companies and more, to see where the secrets to their future lurked.

chapter two

Asset Allocation—
At Least Get This Right

High above midtown Manhattan, in a building looking down upon what was, for a time, Donald Trump's Plaza Hotel, and northward from that edifice across the meadows and monuments of Central Park, is the cloud-level office of a man whose very name is (or at least was) redolent of the associations of Wall Street power and prestige in what is now the fast-fading era known as the 1980s.

The man in question is Mr. John Gutfreund, the former chairman of Salomon Brothers of Wall Street, who parted ways with his company at the start of the 1990s following a scandal in Salomon's bond trading department. Many will tell you that the scandal was the result of lax management, and worse, on the part of Mr. Gutfreund himself—and up to a point, that is certainly right.

But, as we'll see in a minute, the *real* scandal involving John Gutfreund—at least for our purposes here—is that the man simply didn't know how to manage his money . . . at least his own personal money.

35

In subsequent chapters of this book we'll delve into how to use the tools of the Internet to identify specific actual companies that, by most widely accepted standards of investment value, have been overlooked by Wall Street professionals and are undervalued by the market. Similarly we'll put the Internet to use to find overvalued stocks that have been run to preposterous heights by the market and are almost certainly headed for a fall sooner or later.

But there is no point in doing any of that if, as an investor, you wind up creating a personal stock portfolio that is itself out of kilter. Step one in responsible personal investing is thus to make sure—absolutely and unalterably certain—that the various stocks and bonds in which you've invested your money will work together to maximize your upside potential gain while limiting the downside risk—in other words, to see (a) that your holdings are allocated to the right classes of assets for your circumstances, and (b) that the individual stocks and bonds are properly diversified within each class. Do that and you've got 85 percent of the game won before you even start to play. Ignore it and . . . well, let us return to the story of Mr. John Gutfreund.

As the chairman and CEO of what was, at the time, the largest and most feared investment bank in the world, Gutfreund had at his disposal the most brilliant and effective money managers on Wall Street, and though he put their talents to good use for Salomon's clients—at least until the bond trading scandal engulfed the firm—he never applied, to his own personal financial circumstances, the principles of asset allocation and portfolio diversification that are the very foundation of prudent investing. The result proved to be a personal tragedy over which his friends still avert their gaze as if passing a panhandler during the holidays—and over which his enemies still gloat to this hour.

John Gutfreund's mistake—into which we'll delve more deeply in due course—is one that, thanks to the Internet, no one today need repeat. In an unsettled and unpredictable world, when instant global communications means that an earthquake in Taiwan can within seconds cause a plunge of stock prices in New York for semiconductor companies in Silicon Valley, California—well, when things like that can happen, no investor is safe from disaster. In the end the only lasting and genuine security available to anyone is to diversify the asset classes and individual assets of one's investments so that everything you own isn't at risk of annihilation minute to minute—a bit of obvious enough wisdom that John Gutfreund's firm preached ceaselessly to its clients but Mr. Gutfreund never applied to himself.

The Internet provides every tool you'll ever need to avoid that mistake. Later on in this chapter we'll explore in detail how to use the two best of those tools, both of which are free to anyone. But for the moment, simply click on the following Internet address and you'll get a taste of what's to follow: www.quicken.com.

This will take you to the home page of the Web site run by Intuit, the folks who make the Quicken and TurboTax software. The site is free to anybody, but you'll have to register with the service to use it. After that you'll be able to go anywhere within the Web site and use any of its many services.

The most important of those services, for our purposes here, is something known as an asset allocation tool. This is a software program that will break down your stock holdings into what are known as asset classes, then scientifically determine the risk that you're taking on by holding all of them simultaneously.

You might think, for example, that it's cool to have 80 percent of your retirement money shoveled into eBay and Amazon.com at $200 per share. But the Quicken.com asset allocation tool will tell you you're out of your mind. So too will a similar tool—also free—on the Microsoft MoneyCentral Web site at www.moneycentral.msn.com.

I think that if this type of service had existed on the Internet when John Gutfreund was riding high, and if he'd had the common sense to use them, he'd still be a wealthy man today. The asset allocation tools would have told him, John, the way you've got your money all tied up in the stock of just one company—Salomon—isn't smart. What if the business blows up in your face?

Who precisely is to blame for the bond trading chicanery that nearly toppled Wall Street's mightiest banking house need not absorb us greatly here—though we may be assured that Gutfreund himself has devoted a good portion of his time since then attempting to establish the case that, in the end, he was not fundamentally at fault for what seems to have transpired directly under his nose.

Maybe so, and maybe not, and maybe John Gutfreund's post-Salomon life has been nothing more than a decade-long exercise in denial. Whatever the case, the experience itself hasn't been grand. To see, let us thus return to the top floor portal that opened on to the world into which Gutfreund moved following his departure from what the cognoscenti of the era would refer to chummily as "Solly," to behold what can result when you don't diversify your portfolio.

That floor, as you may imagine, was—and I am sure, still is—the final elevator stop heavenward in this prestigious address, owned as it happens by a pal of Gutfreund. In any event, and not surprisingly, upon disembarking, one enters a marbled corridor with brass inlaid designs on the floor and polished stonework all around—at the far end of which chamber there looms (or at least loomed) into view, solitary and resplendent in its isolation and foreboding dominance, two double-hung oak doors, upon which is (or was) written, in raised gold lettering, the words "John Gutfreund & Co.," as if, when it comes to the drumrolls of power, nothing more need be said to reveal the occupant on the other side than simply his name.

But before turning the knob and entering this apparent inner sanctum of power, let us pause briefly in the public corridor just out-side to reflect upon the time, effort, and cost that went into setting the scene thusly for one to approach the presence of Mr. Gutfreund in suitably awed spirits.

History has set such scenes before, to be sure. It was said that visi-tors to the court of Kublai Khan were expected to crawl on their bel-lies through the dirt for the last half mile before entering the presence of the Great One. Similarly, few men emerged from an audience with Hollywood mogul Louis B. Mayer without remarking upon how domineering a presence he seemed while seated behind his desk—which was said to be large enough to fill Wembley Stadium.

And in that spirit, let us not forget Prince Grigory Potemkin, who, it may be said, has done more than even Madonna herself to push back the frontiers of illusion in the practice of performance art. It was of course Prince Potemkin who in 1787 welcomed czarist empress Catherine the Great to her newly annexed territories in the Crimea and, intent upon showing her that the whole of the Crimea was filled with happy peasants inhabiting neatly painted cottages, erected false-front villages similar to the sets Hollywood would make, along her entire processional route . . . from which gesture the good prince has bequeathed his name to the ages as history's greatest phony.

Thus, with our hand on the door handle, and the double-hung oak-panels giving way on their silent and well-oiled brass hinges, it somehow seems fitting to hold the thought in mind of old Prince Potemkin as we enter the post-Salomon world of John Gutfreund—whose name for a decade was heavy with the aromas of extravagance and power, whose blond wife, Susan, gave a whole new meaning to the phrase social climber as she showered outrageously expensive gifts on well-connected people she barely knew . . . the former Pan Am stewardess who once bought a Christmas tree for her Manhattan apartment and wound up making a big deal out of having it hoisted up the outside of the building by a crane when the tree turned out to be too big to fit through the lobby.

Indeed, as we approach John Gutfreund for a catch-up chat on five years of nursed wounds, what could be more fitting than the memory of Prince Potemkin and those miles upon miles of false-front villages erected to hide the truth just beyond, for as the door swings open and we step in . . . well, that's just it—one step and we're *in* . . . as in, actually In The Office . . . not in some deep-pile-carpeted antechamber with a serious-looking young woman behind the sliding glass pane of a reception window . . . not in a room with even a sofa and a faux Regency coffee table displaying recent issues of *Architectural Digest* and perhaps *Fortune* . . . No, we're in John Gutfreund's *actual office* . . . a space in which everyone within it, and every single thing that goes on inside it, are actually and completely visible the very second you walk in the door. Open the door and you walk right into . . . the middle of . . . his office. It's the whole thing . . . all there is . . . *The Entire Office.*

There are no rows of desktop computers, no Quotron terminals, no Bloomberg machines—no banks of telephones ringing madly off the hook, with frantic young men and women shouting into two receivers at once. Instead, in the midst of the greatest bull market of the century, an almost funereal calm fills the room.

It is broken by the only other person, besides Gutfreund, who can be seen on the premises. She is a thirtyish receptionist who seems to spend all her time talking to friends on the phone—a phone that rarely rings. In this case she looks up, sees me at the door, and offers me a seat. Over in the corner sits a pot of coffee on a credenza, a container of half-and-half sits next to it, along with some sugar and Sweet'n Low packets in a Dixie cup. Another cup holds some plastic stirrers.

"Want some?" she asks, gesturing toward an opened box of Pepperidge Farm cookies that sits nearby. "Make yourself comfy. John'll be right with you."

Yet it's not as if Gutfreund is tied up in urgent consultations in the conference room—or better still, at some conclave of the power elite across town . . . breakfast at the St. Regis or something like that. No, the reality is, he's standing right there, five steps from the secretary, waiting to say hello. He's dressed in a businesslike blue suit, with a neatly knotted four-in-hand tie. His horn-rimmed glasses frame his eyes a bit owlishly, and his thinning gray hair and full jowls give a slightly worn and tired look to the presentation.

From which the inevitable question arises: He's gotten dressed up this way for who . . . *me?* This is the man who, it was said in *Liar's Poker,* had once played a hand of poker with one of his Salomon colleagues and bet $1 million on the turn of a card. Five years later and he's breaking out the Brioni to put a shine on a reporter? Oh my.

I had come to learn the story of John Gutfreund's catastrophic fall from grace. But what was there to say? Didn't he put *anything* aside? Here was the man who, at the height of his fame, had graced the cover of *Business Week* magazine under the headline, "The Lion of Wall Street" . . . who had ruled for a decade as the head of the most profitable investment firm in the history of American capitalism . . . whose steadily rising annual compensation totals—by far and away the most lavish in American business—were chronicled each year in the press as if they were Mark McGwire or Sammy Sosa home run totals. And now it's come down to *this?*

The battlefield of Wall Street is littered with casualties from the wars of the 1980s, from Dennis Levine, to Ivan Boesky, to Michael Milken and the collapse of Drexel Burnham Lambert. But no Wall Street general fell further, faster than John Gutfreund, the central figure in the Salomon Brothers bond rigging scandal of 1991.

In part, Gutfreund's story was of human fallibility itself—the "look the other way" culture of tolerance that seems to spread through all of Wall Street in bull markets when big money is to be made. One heard it from Drexel Burnham Lambert chairman Fred

Joseph as prosecutors built their case against his junk bond chief, Mike Milken (*I* didn't know what he was doing—oh no, not me!). One heard it again from the brass at Kidder, Peabody when the firm's head of government securities trading was revealed to have manufactured a fortune in phony trades (My boss told me to do it, honest, he approved it every step of the way.). And from Gutfreund one heard the same exculpatory refrain—this time regarding his role in allegedly covering up for a subordinate accused of submitting what ultimately totaled more than $15 billion in phony bids in U.S. Treasury Department debt auctions.

That he didn't know what was going on right under his nose was hard for people to accept. For eighteen years, from 1973 to 1991, John Gutfreund ruled supreme as Salomon's chief executive officer and eventually its chairman as well. It was said he could hear a nickel drop anywhere on Salomon's trading floor—and now suddenly he couldn't hear $15 billion fly magically in the window?

Gutfreund's eyes had been everywhere. He had engineered what amounted to a palace coup in which he sold his company to Phillips Brothers, the South African–controlled oil-trading firm, in the 1970s, then stealthily took over the parent organization, seized its capital, ousted its management, and emerged in 1981 as head of the biggest and richest investment bank in the world.

From his trading desk on the seventh floor of One New York Plaza, Gutfreund recruited what eventually became a worldwide army of his own creation—9,000 of the toughest and most feared investment bankers in the history of high finance. This was no white-shoe firm like Dillon, Read or Lehman Brothers, this was a blue-collar firm of bright, aggressive, and insecure young men and women from state colleges—every one of them determined to make up for their perceived shortcomings by outsmarting every Ivy Leaguer they came across. Like a Wall Street version of the legendary mailroom at the William Morris talent agency, Salomon spawned a phenomenal array of talented money men under Gutfreund. There was William Simon, Peter Petersen, James Wolfensonn, Henry Kaufman, Sidney Homer, Lewis Ranieri, John Meriwether, Michael Bloomberg, and many, many more.

With Gutfreund in command, Salomon Brothers literally changed the face of investment banking, engineering the lightning-fast mega-deals—particularly for companies in trouble—that have come to dominate high finance around the world. It was Salomon Brothers that orchestrated the 1975 bailout of New York City for Felix Rohatyn and the Municipal Assistance Corp., opening the way for Solly-led urban rescue packages from Boston to Cleveland in the decade that followed. It was Solly, under Gutfreund, that put together the 1977 rescue of Washington, D.C., insurance giant GEICO, making billions for savvy investors like Warren Buffett who saw that GEICO would be saved and began buying its stock. Solly under Gutfreund did the same thing for Lee Iacocca and Chrysler in 1981, putting together the government loan guarantee deal that saved the automaker from bankruptcy.

In each of these cases and more, Salomon was willing to commit its firm's own capital, often in unheard-of amounts—sometimes almost instantaneously—to make a deal go through. "If some insurance company like the Hartford got whacked by a hurricane and needed $100 million fast, there were plenty of firms that would take an offering to market and see if it could be sold," says a Salomon old-timer. "But we were the only ones who would take the position for our own account quickly and worry about reselling it later."

One reason Solly was willing to assume such risks is that, under Gutfreund, the firm developed various tactics to limit the downside exposure to its portfolio. In other words, it hedged and diversified its risks—something that, as we'll see in a minute, Gutfreund never did when it came to his own personal finances.

Too bad, for in a mere sixteen weeks beginning in April of 1991,

John Gutfreund's world collapsed all around him as a scandal engulfed Salomon's U.S. Treasury operations—a scandal that appeared
to implicate Gutfreund in the regulatory violations of an employee
named Paul Mozer, three levels below him.

A firestorm of protest erupted, in the media, in Congress, and
most especially in the Treasury and the U.S. Federal Reserve, as regulators began accusing Salomon and its boss of conspiring to rig the
auction market for U.S. government debt. Irate regulators began talking of revoking Salomon's status as a "primary dealer" in federal
debt—a move that would have barred the firm from government
auctions, the very lifeblood of Salomon's business, and almost certainly would have bankrupted it.

Against this backdrop, Gutfreund decided to resign from Salomon
Brothers—as he put it to friends, "to save it." Few of those closest to
him agreed with the move. His lawyer, Martin Lipton, counseled
against it, and so did his wife, Susan. "You're ending your career on
Wall Street," she told him in a desperate plea that he reconsider before
it was too late.

But John Gutfreund didn't listen, and the words turned out to be
prophetic. Rather than applaud his action for the statesmanlike gesture he hoped it would be seen as, critics seized on it as proof that
Gutfreund really did have something to hide. Even the man whom
Gutfreund prevailed on to step in and take over as interim leader of
the firm—Warren Buffett—turned against him and began blaming
Gutfreund for Salomon's woes.

And therein lay the seeds of Gutfreund's ruin, for eventually Buffett succeeded in preventing Gutfreund from receiving his retirement
options in the firm, and though neither Buffett nor anyone else (except of course Gutfreund) realized it, these retirement options were
literally the only money Gutfreund had salted away. Like a drunken
sailor on shore leave, Gutfreund had blown nearly every dime he'd

made during his twenty-plus-year career at Salomon. He'd blown it on apartments and villas, on parties and chartered jets—assuming all the while that his unexercised stock options in Salomon would become the millionaire's nest egg on which he'd retire.

What a mistake, as Buffett wound up blocking him from getting access to any of what he'd socked away in the company, forcing Gutfreund to go to court in an attempt to assert his rights. In the process he racked up astronomical legal bills, which he had to pay out of his own pocket—at the end of which he lost on the merits anyway as the judge in the case ruled that his resignation had in fact amounted to a "constructive firing." In such a case, the court held, the retirement options should have been forfeited. Then came a shareholder derivative action, which named him in a claim for $300 million in damages, and ate up what little he had left.

A few old friends stuck by him. Real estate developer Alfred Taubman gave him his Potemkin Village broom closet office, rent-free, at 712 Fifth Avenue. And CBS chairman Laurence Tisch, a longtime client of Salomon's, continued to play tennis with him on Saturdays at the New York Athletic Club. But for most of Wall Street's machers, John Gutfreund became the man who wasn't there, shorn of his reputation and even his money by events that were murky, hard to follow, and recalled at most in a single, rhetorical indictment: If he hadn't done something wrong, then why did he quit?

Thereafter, John Gutfreund began counting his pennies and nursing his resentments at the hand fate wound up dealing him. "I figured when I retired I'd be able to put $1 million or $2 million of my own money into interesting deals that came along," he said to me at one point during an interview for a magazine article on his career in eclipse. "Now, $50,000 is a lot of money."

Gutfreund's contacts at the top tier of global finance remain considerable. But he lacks the capital to play in their league. "A number of centa-millionaires have asked me to manage $10 million or so of their money," he said. "But if I haven't got any of my own in the pot, it just doesn't seem right, so I've been turning them down."

When I last checked in on Gutfreund, he was spending his time "consulting" for smallish, up-and-coming companies that hope to catch an updraft on his expertise. There was a Colorado company involved in an obscure side road off the information superhighway. And up in Boston he'd become a partner, for $50,000, with two Indian businessmen looking to do mutual fund deals on the subcontinent.

The tragedy in all this is, of course, that if he'd put even a little aside, properly hedged in a diversified portfolio, he'd still be wealthy a decade later. It was more likely hubris than ignorance that caused Gutfreund's downfall, but it was a mistake that any investor on the Internet can avoid almost without thinking. Too bad the Internet hadn't been there to help him when he needed it most.

To avoid the pitfall that swallowed Gutfreund, investors need to begin with an understanding of what asset allocation is all about. The simplest way to think of it is in terms of the different classes of investment categories that are available to investors on Wall Street, and the risks and rewards that are inherent in each class. Here is how the Microsoft MoneyCentral Web site defines the concept. Just click on

http://moneycentral.msn.com/investor/

glossary/glossary.asp?TermID=860

and you'll be taken directly to the glossary entry for the concept. Note the sentence that says asset allocation choices are "the single biggest factor that determines your long-term investment outcome."

The Quicken.com Web site goes even further and argues, based on historical evidence, that more than 90 percent of the long-term return from a portfolio is determined not by the stocks someone picks but by the asset classes he or she chooses to invest in. That is an amazing statement when you think about it: Nine tenths of your performance as an investor has utterly nothing at all to do with which specific securities you invest in but, rather, which *classes* of securities you select—stocks, bonds, or some combination of both. Want to know how the Quicken folks put it? Then click on

www.quicken.com/glossary

and see for yourself.

Here's how asset allocation works in practice. Assuming you have now registered as a Quicken.com user, then click on the following address and you'll be taken to a Quicken.com page where you can start to create a portfolio: www.quicken.com. There's a little tab on the page called "My Portfolio," and if you click on it and then follow the directions, you'll be able to set up a make-believe (or even real) list of stocks that you own.

Let's say you created a portfolio called "Make Believe," and in it you put 100 shares of General Motors, 100 shares of IBM, 100 shares of eBay, 100 shares of TheStreet.com, the Internet financial Web site operator, and $1,000 in cash. Let's further say, to make this easy, that each security sold for $30 per share and that you bought each stock on January 1, 1999. If you were to enter those transactions and then click on the tab named "Evaluate Portfolio," a screen would pop up revealing that your portfolio, as of early November 1999, was 86.6 percent comprised of large cap stocks (stocks in companies with market valuations in excess of $3.5 billion on Wall Street), 8.4 percent in small cap stocks, and 5 percent in plain old cash. The screen would further tell you that, over time, you could be reasonably certain that this portfolio is likely, in two out of every three years, to produce a yield on your money ranging from a 4.7 percent loss to a 26.1 percent gain, with the average being somewhere around 10.7 percent per year.

Do you want to lower your risk and still come up with the same average return? Of course you do! And that's where computerized asset allocation tools come in. By sorting through the almost infinite range of possibilities for groupings of asset classes in a portfolio, the computer can come up with a portfolio consisting of asset classes much more likely to hit our investment return target of a roughly 10.5 percent average annual return, but with much less risk and volatility. Specifically in the case of our portfolio, the Quicken.com Portfolio Evaluator screen will tell us, based on an enormous amount of historical performance data of almost every asset class you can think of, that we need to rebalance our portfolio so that only 44 percent consists of large cap stocks, whereas 10 percent is now devoted to small cap stocks, 30 percent is given over to international stocks, and 16 percent consists of bonds. Were we to do that, we'd have a portfolio that would produce a yield ranging from a 3.3 percent loss to a 24.3 percent gain in two out of every three years, with the average ranging somewhere around a 10.5 percent gain per year. In other words, by diversifying the classes in our portfolio, we'd come up with a package that would yield us a much more stable and predictable return without even bothering to select our first actual stock or bond. Not bad, huh?

There was a time not so long ago when advice like that cost $1,500 a pop from a financial plan consultant, who would invite you to his office twice a year, prepare a plan with lots of fancy charts and graphs, then hand you the whole shebang in a faux leather binder (inside of which was also your bill). Now you can get the same thing, twenty times a day if you wish, and it's totally free on the Web.

The concept of asset allocation is an outgrowth of what is known on Wall Street as Modern Portfolio Theory. The theory turns out to be the brainchild of one Harry Markowitz, who wrote a scholarly paper in 1952 arguing that you can reduce a portfolio's risk, and maximize its returns, by putting lots of different kinds of assets in it—in other words, a portfolio consisting of more than just Salomon Brothers stock options.

By the way, if Gutfreund had been able to use the asset allocation tools now available for free on the Quicken.com site when planning for his millionaire's retirement, he would have found that his risk-reward prospects were horrifying. By putting everything into a single class of large cap stocks, he faced the prospect of possibly losing 5 percent of his money every two out of three years just through concentration in one asset class. Then of course he compounded the problem by having every dollar within that class invested in just one security, meaning that he faced the moment-to-moment peril of being totally wiped out—which is exactly what wound up happening.

Portfolio diversification sounds pretty obvious today—even if the logic of it appears to have escaped Mr. Gutfreund—but don't forget, it wasn't so long ago when financier Bernard Baruch said that the best way to make a lot of money on Wall Street was for a fellow to put all his eggs in one basket and then "watch the basket."

Now I'll be the first to agree that when you're young and/or reckless, there's a certain allure to betting everything on the black, as they say in Las Vegas, just like John Gutfreund did. And in the spirit of full disclosure, I should tell you that I myself have had some success—and at least once—using Baruch's strategy.

Asset allocation? As they say in New York, fuggedaboudit. I was young, so what did I know! What I did was allocate *everything* on a single bet—just in the way Gutfreund did . . . a bet not on the future of Salomon Brothers but rather on the likelihood that precious metals prices would collapse, interest rates would fall, and bond prices would rise, exactly the opposite sort of bet from what asset allocation counsels investors to make. And as luck would have it, things worked out.

It happened in 1980 when, as some among us may still recall, in-

flation stood at 13.5 percent, interest rates were approaching 18 percent, and gold and silver were headed for the moon. It was, in a word,
an unusual moment—in fact, an utterly unsustainable moment—
and I remember it well, for it remains to this day the one and only
time in my career when I readily and even eagerly bet the ranch that
the world was out of step with its own history. Well, to be precise,
what I bet was all my wife's and my wedding presents and various
things like that.

I went through my house, from attic to basement—through cup-
boards and closets I hadn't looked through in years—and rounded
up every bit of sterling silver and gold that I could find. I looked
through kitchen drawers, through the credenza in the dining room,
everywhere you could think.

And out came the silverware. We had tons of it (well, not tons, but
actual whole pounds) . . . more, at any rate, than I'd have guessed.
You probably have a lot more lying around than you'd think too.
There was crud from our wedding (candlesticks and what-have-you).
I found a sterling silver cocaine spoon that some wafer-thin fashion
model had given my wife and me as a kind of ultra-hip wedding present more than a decade earlier. I found sterling silver picture frames,
a sterling silver ashtray, a sterling silver teething ring, a sterling silver
hairbrush . . . oh, it just went on and on. I never knew I had any of it,
but there it was—a lifetime of stuff that was suddenly worth ten and
twenty times its value when we'd originally acquired it. I found a gold
filling that had belonged to my great-grandfather, gold rings and
bracelets that had belonged to my wife's grandmother—just whole
shoeboxes full of the stuff.

And what I did was, I threw the whole lot of it into two pillowcases
and, looking oddly like a second-story artist who'd just burgled some
estate in Greenwich, I went down to a local gold and silver broker on
a Saturday morning, dumped it all out on his counter, and said,

"What'll you give me?" The man put it all on a scale, toted up the weight (nearly $800 per ounce for the gold, $30 per ounce for the silver), and ten minutes later I was walking out with a bank check for $30,000.

Which I took immediately to my broker and bought what were known in those days as "Bo Dereks"—newly issued long-term U.S. government bonds that weren't due to mature until the year 2010. I bought them on 95 percent margin. Not long afterward, gold and silver prices collapsed, and interest rates began a fifteen-year slide that sent my Bo Dereks into orbit. I was in my thirties at the time, and having a lot of money—or at least what seemed like a lot—I felt a rush of liberation. My wife and I took trips, we put an addition on our house, we had another child, and I quit my job and began writing full time.

I was lucky. My bet had been made on a hunch—nothing more than raw common sense. I simply could not see how the conditions then prevailing in the money markets of the world could continue much longer. It seemed to me that interest rates had gotten so high that all those billions of dollars held in corporate and government bond accounts by people who had yachts the size of my neighborhood were in danger of being wiped out before our eyes. It seemed to me that rich people just weren't going to sit still for that—that the pain had by then gotten so bad that they were going to come leaping out of their lawn chairs any minute now and say, See here, this has gone far enough (or some such), and that Washington would do whatever was necessary (whatever that was) to get rates headed back down again.

No research whatsoever went into this analysis—it was, as I said, all just a hunch, a sense that the United States was simply not going to become the biggest banana republic on earth, with people in the grip of Weimar Republic–like inflation and rushing out to buy sofas and refrigerators with their paychecks, then exchanging them for groceries, like what was supposedly taking place in Brazil.

But I could have been wrong—just like John Gutfreund turned out to be wrong—and, to be sure, there were many people who thought I was. I remember one night, just after I'd sold all the family silverware and bought the Bo Dereks, sitting in front of the tube and watching some guy on the news being interviewed as he stood in a long, curling line outside a currency exchange office in Brooklyn. The reporter stuck a mike in his face and asked him what he was doing and he looked straight at the camera and said that silver was going to $100 per ounce and he was there to cash in on the opportunity. What the man had done, it seemed, was sell a bunch of utility stocks that had gotten hammered in the interest rate spike. Then he'd taken the cash, and now he was standing in line to exchange the cash for (are you ready?) $10,000 worth of dimes! The dimes supposedly had a certain silver content, and as silver prices rose, they were said to be disappearing from circulation because investors were hoarding them for their bullion content. The man explained how each dime was already worth 11 or 12 cents (I forget exactly how much), and how it wouldn't be long before they'd be worth 20 or 30 cents each and his bag of dimes would be worth $30,000.

I couldn't believe it—and neither, for that matter, could the incredulous reporter. "Isn't that a little risky?" he asked, but the man said that he knew "exactly" what he was doing and the interview ended.

As things worked out, I made a killing while that guy in the interview may still be sitting with a bag of dimes in the back of his closet twenty years later. Like I said, I was lucky. In every transaction, there is always a seller for every buyer, which means, in the end, you've got a 50-50 chance of being right (or wrong).

Those aren't great odds. It's like, would you bet your life on the flip of a coin?

In fact, of course, a lot of people do. It's why we have Las Vegas and Atlantic City, and the coast-to-coast spread of Indian- and state-sponsored gambling casinos. We like the lure of easy money, it's got a very strong appeal.

There's a scene in Tom Stoppard's play *Rosencrantz and Guildenstern Are Dead* when one or the other of them is flipping a coin at the start of Act One. And every time it's flipped, it comes up heads. Time after time, flip after flip, it keeps coming up heads while Rosencrantz and Guildenstern, who are supposed to represent the comic relief antimatter in the tragedy of *Hamlet,* become more and more confounded at the apparent suspension of temporal reality into which they've wandered. They're in the two-dimensional world of the Langoliers, where everything has only one side . . . where no matter how many times you flip the coin, it always comes up heads. You can make a lot of money in a world like that.

At least you can if, like Tom Stoppard, all you want to do is write about such a place—that happy Valhalla where trees really do grow to the sky and a tossed coin always comes up heads. I personally don't know why I never succumbed to its lure. Maybe it's that I was raised a Catholic and taught to believe in the redemptive power of misery—and that if something came too easy, it wasn't worth having. In any case, when I hit the jackpot on the turn of the bullion market, I felt as if I'd gotten away with something and decided to stop playing.

Maybe it's my tough luck that I didn't keep rolling the dice. All this happened, after all, during the early stages of what eventually developed into the longest and strongest bull market in American history. Maybe if Ms. Derek and I had simply kept doubling up on the black . . . But I didn't do that. Instead, I just took the money and ran.

Like I said, I was lucky. Plenty of people—in fact, *most* people—aren't lucky like that even one time, let alone over and over again. For them, the party invitation never arrives in the first place—and those who do wangle an invitation wind up staying too long, ending up with nothing to show for the merrymaking but the inevitable hangover and feelings of self-loathing.

Asset allocation helps protect you against that very outcome, the bet-the-ranch approach to investing that pays off and pays off until suddenly it doesn't pay off anymore and you're left in wipeout-ville.

Such has been the too-often-told fate of people who struck it rich in the Internet IPO frenzy of 1998–99—the brilliant young heroes who pushed their life savings (or maybe just their parents' life savings) into Internet initial public offerings at twenty times any reasonable price, only to see the stocks quadruple all over again on opening day. They remind me of that guy with the bag of dimes in front of the currency exchange office in how confident they seemed in what the future held. Well, at least he didn't sink it all into silver futures, so maybe he still has his dimes instead of nothing at all.

Granted, Modern Portfolio Theory and its asset allocation offspring cannot protect you from disaster if you are bound and determined to keep doubling up on the black. But Modern Portfolio Theory and asset allocation can at least help ensure that the disasters don't spread out to bring ruin to your entire portfolio. That's because Modern Portfolio Theory requires diversification, preventing one from betting the ranch on any one stock.

The essence of the concept is that historical rates of return for various securities—and classes of securities—should be incorporated in any properly diversified portfolio so that investment risk can be calculated for the portfolio as a whole. Armed with such information, an investor can then maximize his rate of return for any given level of risk by adjusting the balance of the portfolio's various classes of assets.

For example, over any five-year or longer time frame, statistical research has shown that two particular classes of securities—international stocks and small cap growth stocks—have outperformed every other class studied, rising by an average of 12 percent annually. Large cap stocks have risen by 11 percent, bonds have risen by just under 6 percent, and money market funds have risen by around 3.8 percent.

Further research has shown that, if you hold a diversified portfolio of securities within any given class, your odds are at least nine in ten of hitting the historical performance results for the class *no matter what individual stocks you select.* In other words, 90 percent of your portfolio's performance will be determined simply by what class you're invested in. Everything else—from market timing, to fundamental research, and everything in between—will account for only 10 percent of the outcome.

That's why I say, if you get absolutely nothing else right, get the part about asset allocation nailed down and you're 90 percent of the way to success before you even get going.

chapter three

What Is Technical Analysis and Why Should You Care?

There is a fellow I know named Ray Dalio who works in an office by a lake in Connecticut, managing more billions of dollars than either you or I can imagine for a group of investors halfway around the world in the Middle East. Ray does this by means of technical analysis, a fancy term for trying to make predictions about future stock and bond prices based on the behavior of investors in the past.

In the last twenty years, technical analysis has become one of the driving forces of Wall Street; in fact, there are those who will tell you it has become *the* driving force. In this chapter we'll look at the conceptual underpinnings of technical analysis and come to some conclusions about what it can do for you as an investor and what it can't. Then in the next chapter we'll explore technical analysis in action, drawing on the vast—and ever-growing—array of Internet Web sites that are devoted, one way or another, to using technical analysis as a guide for buying and selling stocks.

You can make a lot of money at technical analysis if you are good at it, and Ray Dalio is. He is as near to a money genius as anyone I've ever encountered. He's also richer than God, lives in a Greenwich mansion overlooking Long Island Sound (my own house would fit in his garage), has homes in Vermont and Mexico, and some sort of castle-type thing in Spain—and when things get slow at the office he has a habit of packing up and taking his family on African safaris. Life's tough, huh?

Yet for all that, Ray is also what we mean by a Regular Guy. He's a big, strapping fellow with a hearty laugh, a fabulous jack-o'-lantern smile, and a handshake that could crush a fifty-five-gallon oil drum. It's just that when you get him on the subject of numbers, investing, and finance, his eyes develop a kind of laserlike intensity and begin burning a hole in the ether somewhere over the horizon as he starts talking about things that neither you nor I will ever understand.

The last time I saw him—for a cup of coffee in a local Starbucks— Ray was absorbed in something he called "capturing the excess al- pha." Now I wouldn't know excess alpha if I stepped in some of it, but Ray put it this way, "What we're working on at the moment is figuring out how to buy funds, sell the market against them, and capture the excess alpha in the trade." Got that?

As you might have guessed, Ray lives in a world of his own. He isn't interested in what products a company makes or distributes, or how much money it earns for those activities. He doesn't care who runs the company or how well management does its job. Ray is interested in something bigger, broader, and more daunting than that. Ray is interested in the biggest Big Picture of them all: the economy of the entire world—and what drives it: the cost of a dollar to the U.S. government, and how it makes people behave.

When it comes to investing, the value of money—and most espe- cially, the U.S. dollar—is where everything begins, and Ray is the kind of fellow who by nature likes to begin at the beginning. There is a terrific moment in the movie *Nine 1/2 Weeks* when Kim Basinger asks Mickey Rourke what he does for a living, and he answers, "I buy and sell money." It's one of those throwaway lines that says a lot more than one might think, for just in the same way that soy beans are the basic grain crop of agriculture, money is the basic crop of investing—and like everything else in life, money comes at a price . . . the price, in the case of money, being the interest rate you have to pay in order to borrow it.

Listening to Ray talk about money is to approach the whole subject on the plane of metaphysics—an entire philosophy of human experience seems to underpin what he says. Inflation, depression, war, peace, affluence, poverty—one way or another the whole march of human history can be told through the relentless struggle between those who've got the money, and those who want it. Want to know why Argentina once had one of the highest living standards in the world, and now is, well, what it is? Whole libraries have been filled with treatises on the ruinous effects of Peronism. But to Ray it's all so much simpler: too much money in the economy to make saving it worthwhile.

Like land or other property, money is something that you can own for a time, or even for a very long time—in fact, even for as long as you live. But sooner or later, you as an individual will be gone, yet the money you possessed will still be there, possessed by somebody else. That's why the Germans refer to interest rates as the *renten* of money—meaning how much it costs to rent it for a while, since, philosophically speaking, you can never possess it forever.

To a man like Ray, it is the rental cost of the money—that is, its interest rate—that determines everything, for the interest rate of money is the pressure relief valve that keeps the value of money more or less in balance with the value of what it's supposed to be able to buy. Simply put, interest rates control the availability of the one thing that everyone on Wall Street wants more than anything else: money.

And since all the different kinds of money there are in the world—at least all the different kinds that matter—are ultimately exchangeable into U.S. dollars (of which there are more loose in the world than any other currency), the easiest—and surest—way to stand back and get a truly Big Picture of the value of everything there is in the world is to keep your eye constantly on the rental cost of a dollar . . . which is what people like Ray do, day and night, 365 days a year.

To do this, Ray has a big office, with dozens of young men and women dressed in 1990s-era casual Friday garb five days a week, rushing all over the place, keeping track of "the numbers." And the eerie thing is, Ray seems to know everything they know as soon as they know it—as if he were somehow wired into every brain in the office.

One thing the little Ray-lettes are constantly watching is whether more money from overseas is flowing into the United States—and especially Wall Street—than out of it, which fact they want to know because, in the aggregate, there are more dollars outside the United States than in it, which means that foreigners can have an enormous influence on stock and bond prices: When foreign-owned (or should we more properly say "rented") dollars start pouring into Wall Street, the prices of what they are seeking to buy tend to go up. If the prices go up too high—or too rapidly—investors start borrowing money against the rising value of their stock holdings and buy even more stock with the borrowed money—which goes up in price, and against which they borrow yet more money, and, well, you get the idea: A bubble develops.

That's when the government steps in (or at least is *supposed* to step in) and starts reducing the supply of money in the economy. (One easy way: print less of it.) And just as happens with, say, the housing supply (when you reduce the number of apartments for rent, and demand stays constant, rental prices rise), so too with money: When you reduce its availability, people will pay more to acquire it and the rental price of money will rise. That means borrowing it will become more expensive and, eventually, demand for dollars will abate and the run-up in stock prices will slow.

Ray has been following these in-and-out flows for years—decades even—and he's been putting it all in his computers by the lake there in Connecticut. When exactly it was I do not know, but long ago the time came to pass when Ray had so much information and data—and all of it cross-referenced digitally with everything else the Ray-lettes were tracking—that it became possible to ask the computer what would happen to stock and bond prices in the United States if, say, the Thai bhat (their currency) weakened a bit against, say, the Japanese yen, and get back what would turn out to be a pretty reliable answer.

As I said, Ray is a technical analyst, and his whole game (at least this part of it) is to predict human behavior based ultimately on a single variable—the course of interest rates. Other technical analysts look at things like the course of stock prices, or the ebb and flow of money in and out of the market, or, believe it or not, even the phases of the moon. All such data can be reduced to digital information on a computer screen and as such (one hopes) give a clue to the biggest question of them all: What will happen next?

Ray doesn't take accounts for less than $5 million, and most of what he manages is in much bigger slices even than that. But you don't have to sign him a check with six zeros on it to get access to the same sort of information that he—and other technical analysts—use to make forecasts every day of the week. There's even a Web site—www.neatideas.com—run by a Texas research institute that uses an artificial intelligence software program to predict the future course of any stock price you might be interested in—all based on technical analysis modeling of how the stock has behaved in the past.

For some of the wildest forecasting of all, click on a Web site bearing the name www.stock100.com. This site, run by the ex-head of the

State of California's Office of Foreign Investment and his partner, a Chinese mathematician from the University of California at Berkeley, uses advanced artificial intelligence algorithms, adapted from commodities futures contract trading, to make constantly updated five-day-ahead forecasts of price movements for 200 widely traded stocks—100 each on the upside and the downside for the five days ahead. If you had bought—and sold—every stock forecasted by the site for a five-day-ahead price change beginning on October 6, 1999 (to pick an arbitrary though typical date), you would have made 7 percent on your money in the five-day period.

Or, if you want to stay more in the mainstream, even Microsoft's MoneyCentral site has an array of technical analysis forecasting tools. Click on the following address—

http://moneycentral.msn.com/investor/finder/predefstocks.asp

—and you'll be taken to a page within MoneyCentral that offers several different, predefined stock-screening programs to find stocks with prices that technical analysts expect will be heading higher. Yet another Web site—www.dailystocks.com—offers links to an almost overwhelming array of technical analysis tools for stock picking. Go to this address: http://www.dailystocks.com/volume_alerts.htm, and you'll find more than a dozen further links to sites providing technical analysis tools related to price and volume trends alone.

So okay, there's plenty of technical analysis stuff available on the Web, right? But what actually *is* technical analysis anyway? Here is how a textbook on the subject defines what people like Ray actually do:

> *Technical analysis is a method of predicting price movements and future market trends by studying charts of past market action which take into account price of instruments, volume of trading, and, where applicable, open interest in the instruments.*

Here is an easier way to say the same thing: Technical analysis is what you do in order to try to figure out what everyone else is doing—so that you can do it first.

Technical analysis, simply put, is the social science of investing. The idea behind it is that if you can discern patterns in the performance history of a stock (or a sector, or even the whole stock market), you can project those patterns into the future, invest accordingly, and thereby make a lot of money.

There is an old saying on Wall Street: "The trend is your friend," and it is based on the belief that, indeed, technical analysis enables one to glimpse the future. In hopes of doing just that, presumably sage individuals have been sacrificing nubile virgins to vengeful gods since man first emerged from the primordial slime and asked the aforementioned Big Question (Okay, so what happens next?). But only in the twentieth century has technical analysis come into its own—and only in the last couple of decades has it gained wide acceptance as an authentic social science discipline with a knowable internal logic.

By general agreement, the man who invented technical analysis was Charles Henry Dow, a late-nineteenth-century newspaperman with a big, scruffy beard that made him look like one of the Smith Brothers of cough drop fame. One day Dow and a pal, Edward D. Jones, got the idea that you could add up the latest quoted prices of a basket of typical Wall Street stocks and thereby create a kind of proxy index, or average, for the whole of the stock market.

So Dow and Jones came up with a list of a dozen such stocks, added up their closing prices on a day back in late May of 1896, and without further ado pronounced the birth of the "Dow Jones Industrial Average."

Over the years, nearly all the original twelve companies in the Average either went out of business or were merged into other companies, leaving only one—Connecticut-based General Electric Co.—that is still in the Average to this day. Meanwhile, more and more new companies got added until the total reached its present level of thirty.

There is a Web site (http://averages.dowjones.com) that will give you quite a lot of information about the Average, including, for example, what it was on any given day from 1896 to the present. Another Web site (www.e-analytics.com) lists every change in the composition of the Average over its life (that is, which companies were added, which were dropped, and when), as well as provides obscure little factoids and tips, like how a one-point change in any given stock in the Average affects the value of the overall Average itself. If it's rainy outside and you're bored at your desk, you can kill an hour or two just on this site. (If you're *still* bored, then click on the following and proceed as directed:

http://www.pagetutor.com/idiot/idiot.html.)

We may think of the Dow Jones Industrial Average as ushering in the age of technical analysis not because the Average itself was complex or particularly technical (it wasn't, and isn't—as we'll see in a minute), but simply because, over time, it became widely accepted in the popular mind as being synonymous with the trend of the market itself. When the Average moves up from one day to the next, the market itself is thought to be "trending higher." When the Average moves down, the trend for the overall market is thought to be down.

That at least is the uncritical, shorthand way the matter is handled in the media, particularly on TV. Since the days of Huntley-Brinkley and Walter Cronkite, all three broadcast networks have routinely reported the closing price of the Dow Jones Industrial Average to viewers, typically illustrated with a convenient little up or down arrow to indicate which way the trend moved from the closing price of the day before.

As a result, it seems a reasonably safe bet that by now almost everyone in America—maybe even the whole world—knows that the "Dow Industrials" and the "stock market" are, in some fundamental way, the same thing. And because of that, they have learned, over time, to believe that movements in one are mirrored by movements in the other.

In fact, the two are not really linked at all. Sometimes the Dow Industrials go up while the rest of the stock market goes down. In fact, that happens quite a lot. Over the course of the 1990s, the Dow Industrials have roughly quadrupled in value, and at millennium's end stood at somewhere around 11,000. But a different measure of stock market performance—the Russell 2000 Index, which tracks companies smaller than those in the Dow Industrials—has risen barely half as much. In both cases, the clear trend was upward—but the Dow Industrials rose almost twice as fast, over the period, as did the broader-based Russell 2000.

Nonetheless, it is the broad trend that matters, and in this we may say that the Dow Industrials have proven, over time, to be a reasonably good forecaster of the direction of the market as a whole: UP. And it is that upward trend, reflected in the Dow and embedded in the post-Depression American consciousness, that matters so far as technical analysis is concerned. Generally speaking, and over time, people expect the stock market to rise, and when the Dow goes up it tends to confirm and reinforce that expectation.

Just click on the following address:

http://moneycentral.msn.com/investor/charts/
charting.asp?Symbol=$indu

It will take you to a page on the Microsoft MoneyCentral Web site, depicting the Dow's performance since 1932. Or look at the chart below, showing a more detailed view of the same data, for the Dow Average during just the 1990s. Is it any wonder people have learned to expect the stock market to rise? Mostly, that's all it does! The chart it-

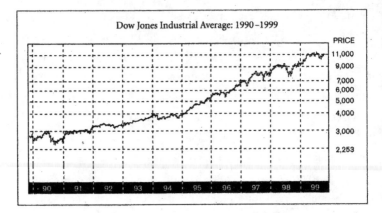

Dow Jones Industrial Average: 1990–1999

self comes from a Web site known as Wall Street City, which can give you similarly customized charts on any stock, or any index you can name, for almost any time period for the last thirty years. The address is: www.wallstreetcity.com.

Now, if you want to drive yourself crazy very quickly, think of what you'd have today if you'd simply invested $10,000 in the Dow—not all the way back in 1932 but as recently as August of 1982 when the latest long-term bull market advance began. The task wouldn't have involved any research whatsoever—just picking the thirty stocks of the Index, and holding them through the following eighteen years. Why, you'd have wound up with $130,000, give or take. Indeed, if you'd refined the task only slightly, and each year bought only the ten *worst*-performing stocks in the Dow for the year just ended, then sold them twelve months later for the new patch of losers—what's known as the "Dogs of the Dow" strategy—you'd be holding a portfolio worth maybe $350,000, pre–taxes and fees, for your trouble—and all because the Dow Average, for no other reason than a universally shared perception that it somehow *is* the market, has tended to benefit from everyone's expectation that the stocks in the Index will simply keep going up because that is the American Way.

. . .

There are, in fact, even bigger and grander trends than the century-long upward trend of the Dow Industrials. If you really want to get the Big Picture, there's the Kondratieff long wave, named for a nineteenth-century Russian economist, Nikolai Kondratieff, who seemed to spend his every waking minute tracking commodity prices, wages, and other economic statistics.

From those labors, Kondratieff discovered fluctuations in cycles of fifty to sixty years—a fact that infuriated Marxists because it implied that every capitalist downturn would be followed by a rebound. Why the fluctuations in the first place? According to Kondratieff, they occurred because businesses tend to overinvest at the top of each cycle, causing innovation-stifling shortages that bring about collapse. Kondratieff's theory is going strong even in the age of baby boomers and are debated endlessly on Internet message boards.

Here's what a Kondratieff long wave looks like:

```
      1814            1864            1920            1974
       /\              /\              /\              /\
      /  \            /  \            /  \            /  \
     /    \          /    \          /    \          /    \
    /     |        /     |        /     |        /     |
   /      |      /      |      /      |      /      |
  /       |    /       |    /       |    /       |
 /        |  /        |  /        |  /        |
/         | /         | /         | /         |
/         |/          |/          |/          |
/         |/          |/          |/
```

Be that as it may, a trend is just that—a *trend*—and as the Kondratieff long wave cycles suggest, just because the general trend is up, doesn't mean that you can't have plenty of downward movements along the way. So if you want to drive yourself not-so-crazy, think of what you'd have wound up with if you had invested $10,000 in the Dow back in the trough of the 1932 depression, then sat with it patiently for the next twenty years, until the start of the Eisenhower 1950s: only $36,000. And if you want to feel downright terrible about things, here's what you'd have wound up with had you invested $10,000 at the peak of the 1960s bull market (January 1966) and hung on through the Nixon-Ford-Carter years until the market exploded under Ronald Reagan in August of 1982: a mere $9,300—in other words, a 7 percent loss for your trouble.

The trouble with mega-trends is they're too big to be helpful. As a result, it's never very easy to know whether you're at the start of one, in the middle of one, or the world is about to drop out from under you at the end of one. Were the Romans all standing around in A.D. 470 saying, Oh my God, there's only a couple of years left before the whole place goes to hell?

Not only that, but it is also not that easy to get very worked up about things that might not happen for another half century. Who gets up in the morning and says, Egads, time is running out—I'd better start planning for the year 2050! In America, nearly everyone has a lifetime seat to whatever is playing at the Short Attention Span Theater, and it doesn't do much good to keep reminding ourselves, in the words of T. S. Eliot, that your whole life can be shoveled away, a teaspoonful at a time, before you ever realize what's been happening. Generally speaking, we seem to prefer the sentiment of Eliot's contemporary, economist John Maynard Keynes, who summed things up thusly when it came to the long wave view of life and investing: In the long run we're all dead anyway.

Figuring out when the long run ends for each of us, individually, is of course a critical question—and it is why technical analysis, over the last two-plus decades, has become focused on ever shorter time frames. When I was beginning as a financial writer on Wall Street at the start of the 1970s, stock price charts typically covered five years of a security's performance, and it was easy to find charts that covered ten and even twenty years of data. Today, charts mostly range from a year down to a day, and almost every major financial site on the Web provides chart data for intraday movements ground as finely as a minute at a time.

Charts are, indeed, the basic building blocks of technical analysis, which is why technical analysts were known on Wall Street until recently, somewhat derisively, as "chartists." What they do is study charts—every kind of bizarre, weird-looking chart you can think of, some of which predate even Wall Street itself.

In the chartists' pantheon of heroes, there's a special and reserved pedestal for an eighteenth-century Japanese rice trader named Munehisa Homma, the inventor of the candlestick chart. You can learn all about him and his strange obsession by visiting a Web site called www.altavest.com.

To purists in the art of chart reading, the invention of the candlestick chart ranks right up there with the discovery of penicillin and screen doors—the rough equivalent of figuring out that by sticking an odometer inside a dashboard speedometer, you could simultaneously see both a vehicle's speed and the distance it had traveled without having to move your eyeballs more than once. Think of candlesticks as the chartists' answer to a head-up display of flight instruments in an F-14 Tomcat and you've got the basic idea.

Here's what a sixty-day candlestick chart of Dell Computer looks like, available on a Web site called www.siliconinvestor.com, which you can access and use all you want for free:

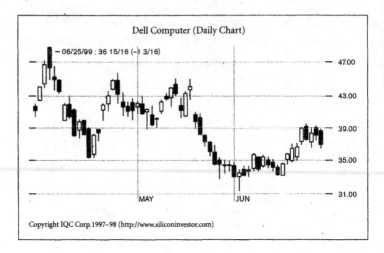

Dell Computer (Daily Chart)

— 06/25/99 : 36 15/16 (–1 3/16)

Copyright IQC Corp. 1997–98 (http://www.siliconinvestor.com)

This type of chart shows a lot of information all at once. Each vertical line/box represents a single day's trading activity. The thin little lines running vertically out each end of each box mark the stock's high and low price of that day. The box itself marks the opening and closing of the day. If the box is colored, it means that the stock closed lower than it opened; if the box is hollow, it means the stock closed higher than it opened.

Armed with all that information, you can glance at one of these charts and see in an instant whether the stock is trending higher or lower: If you see more black boxes than hollow ones, it means the stock has mainly been closing lower than it opened, which means more people are selling than buying. If a particular box has long lines sticking out of the top and bottom (they're referred to by the cognoscenti as "wicks"—as in a candlestick's wicks, get it?), it means the stock was really volatile that day.

For example, check out the chart for Dell. It shows that June 2, 1999, was a real rock-and-roll day for the computer maker. The stock had traded down for the nine previous sessions, then abruptly on

June 2 it sold off even more sharply, dropping nearly to $31 per share but recovering and closing *up* on the day at nearly $34.

As we'll see eventually, chartists make a big deal out of reversals like that, and typically regard them as a short-term buying opportunity. Check out the next two weeks of trading history and you'll see that they weren't wrong—though you would have been hard-pressed to see it if you'd been living through events as they unfolded day to day and were trying to figure out which way things were moving on, say, June 14. On that date the stock had once again traded down for three days in a row, and nothing in the chartists' goat entrails suggested the trend wouldn't continue—but it instead reversed course and started heading upward again. Go figure.

When the seemingly unexplainable manifests itself in a chart, technical analysts look for explanations in, what else, but more charts. One of their favorites are charts dressed up with something called Bollinger Bands. It has been Mr. Bollinger's special contribution to the betterment of mankind to figure out that Newton's Second Law of Motion applies to stock prices as well as falling apples . . . that is, that prices tend to trade within an upper and lower range (i.e., band) of their values, and that when they break out of those bands they tend to keep ripping along for quite a while until something intervenes to stop them.

Not only does Bollinger have an investment tool named after him (Bollinger Bands), but there's even a book called *Understanding Bollinger Bands,* by Edward D. Dobson, to help the uninitiated get up to speed on the whole subject. And, of course, there's a Web site, www.bollingerbands.com, for further exploration of Bollingerisms. Bollinger himself now runs an investment fund, Bollinger Capital Management, from whence he ventures forth regularly for appearances on CNBC, where he expounds to the public concerning what his Bollinger Bands are telling him.

Here's what the chart for Dell looks like when Bollinger Bands are added to it:

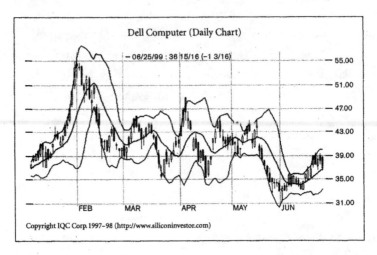

Dell Computer (Daily Chart)

— 06/25/99 : 36 15/16 (–1 3/16)

55.00
51.00
47.00
43.00
39.00
35.00
31.00

FEB   MAR   APR   MAY   JUN

Copyright IQC Corp. 1997–98 (http://www.siliconinvestor.com)

The line in the middle is a twenty-day "moving average" of the stock's price. You calculate a stock's moving average by taking any given number of trading days (in this case, twenty) and averaging them up. Then you move to the next, or twenty-first day, add *it* to the average, and remove the first day. Then you just keep moving on through the calendar in that fashion, creating a—you guessed it—moving average. This smooths out the peaks and valleys in day-to-day price fluctuations and gives you a more gracefully rolling trend line.

Bollinger Bands are plotted off these trend lines. The top line in the chart above is the upper band of the Bollinger Band, the bottom line is the lower band. The two lines are plotted as standard deviations off the moving average.

Now don't worry, we're not going to go into probability theory and the concept of standard deviation—at least not much. All you need to know is that in any given population of anything—from people, to farm animals, to stock prices—you can come up with an average: the average weight of free range chickens, the average height of Belgian dwarfs, the average price of a stock on Tuesdays—it makes no difference; two or more of anything and you can figure out an average.

When you plot those measurements on a piece of graph paper, you'll see that most of the things you're plotting wind up being clustered around the middle, or average, of the population that you're plotting, with fewer and fewer reaching out toward the edges. If you've got 1,000 people and their average height is five foot eight, most of the thousand will be around five foot eight, with fewer and fewer people in the group as you move toward four-foot-tall midgets and seven-foot-tall basketball freaks.

That is what is called a bell curve. Standard deviation is a measure of how much of the bell curve is needed to cover roughly 68 percent of the population in the sample (one standard deviation from the mean), how much is needed to cover 95 percent of the population (two standard deviations), and how much is needed to cover the rest (three standard deviations).

A high standard deviation means that more of the population is out there at the sloping edges of the bell curve, whereas a low standard deviation means the opposite: that most of the population is clustered near the middle.

What Bollinger did was take the moving average of two standard deviations off the central moving average (got that?) of the stock being plotted, and drew upper and lower bands marking the limits within which the stock in question tends to move 95 percent of the time. Then he came up with all sorts of theories about what it means when the prices move this way and that within the bands.

Nearly every major financial site on the Web now includes Bollinger Bands, or something like them, in their charts. The best—which is to say easiest to use—are available, once again, on the Microsoft MoneyCentral Web site,

http://moneycentral.msn.com/investor/charts/charting.asp

But chartists have more tools at the ready than just Bollinger Bands and candlestick charts. For example, there's the Fibonacci Ratio. This refers to the brainchild of a thirteenth-century Italian mathematician named Leonardo Fibonacci, who became absorbed with the question of how many pairs of rabbits could be produced as offspring by a single pair in one year. If you assume—as Lenny apparently did—that a rabbit will reach reproductive maturity in two months' time, and that each reproductive litter will consist of two rabbits, then if you put an adult male and female rabbit in a room with plenty of whatever it is that rabbits need to get it on (which is apparently not much), a certain sequence of events will automatically follow.

Within a month's time you'll have *two* pairs of rabbits—the original pair of adults plus two offspring. By the end of the second month the original pair will have reproduced again, but since the offspring from the first litter will still be too young to reproduce, the total rabbit population in the room will number three pairs: the original adults and two litters of offspring.

But after that the pace picks up. In the third month you'll have 5 pairs, in the fourth month, 8 pairs, and by the end of the twelfth month, 377 pairs—which is to say 754 rabbits. (Of course, genetic inbreeding being at play in all this, we may also assume that we're talking about 754 hemophiliac rabbits with sloping foreheads and a penchant for being kidnapped by visitors from outer space.)

In any case, what's interesting about this is not simply how quickly you can fill up a room with retarded rabbits, but rather the progress of the growth: Each new generational total turns out to be precisely the sum of the previous two generational totals. Month one: two pairs. Month two: three pairs. Month three: five pairs. Month four: eight pairs.

That's the Fibonacci Number Sequence, which can in turn be reduced to a growth ratio of 1.618 to one—or, inversely, a *reduction* ratio of 0.618 to one.

Together, these have come to be known in mathematics as Fibonacci's Golden Ratio, and mathematicians have spent centuries documenting its appearance in everything from geometry to the structure of the human body and the architecture of ancient Egypt. Now, inevitably, they've gotten around to Wall Street.

Here's the idea: Since no stock price moves in a straight line forever, the reversals that take place from time to time might well be expected to unfold in Fibonacci-like sequences. Thus, if a stock doubles, for example, you might expect it, according to the Golden Rule of Lenny and his rabbits, to give back more or less 38.2 percent of those gains before moving up any further.

Does it work? Sometimes. On October 10, 1998, Dell Computer closed in the midst of a panicky sell-off of nearly all technology stocks, ending the day at just under $25 per share. Thereafter it rallied to just over $50 by the first of February 1999. Fibonacci's Golden Ratio would have held that any subsequent sell-off from that level would have bottomed out at somewhere around $40, and sure enough, on February 2 the stock fell apart, dropping all the way back to just over $40 per share by February 17. Time to buy for the next leg up? Not quite, for, as things turned out, the stock continued to weaken and by the summer of 1999 was selling for barely $37 per share.

But what's a few dollars (or rabbits) among friends? Besides, if neither Mr. Homma nor Messrs. Bollinger or Fibonacci can glimpse tomorrow, there's always the Stochastics Oscillator. I won't even try to explain this one, but a chart of same is shown on page 76.

Or how about the on-balance volume, shown on page 77. The premise behind this charting technique, developed by a stock trader named Joe Granville, who was popular in the 1970s, is that stocks

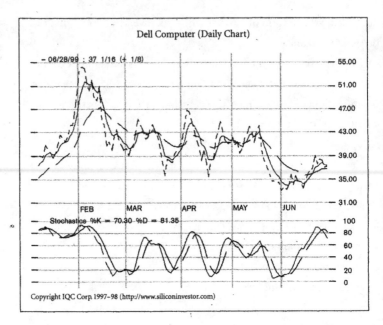

Dell Computer (Daily Chart)

– 06/28/99 : 37 1/16 (+ 1/8)

55.00
51.00
47.00
43.00
39.00
35.00
31.00

FEB   MAR   APR   MAY   JUN

Stochastics %K = 70.30 %D = 81.35

100
80
60
40
20
0

Copyright IQC Corp. 1997–98 (http://www.siliconinvestor.com)

tend to move up, over time, when money is flowing into them, and down when money is flowing out. Duh!

On-balance volume is tracked on a chart that treats volume on a day in which the stock closes *up* from its previous day's close, as being positive volume, while volume on a *down* day is treated as negative volume. On-balance volume is then computed by adding up all the positive and negative daily volume numbers and seeing whether, on any given day, you're in positive or negative territory for a particular stock.

As with nearly all technical indicators, the chartists don't pay so much attention to the actual volume level, but rather to which way the trend is heading: Is negative volume improving? Is positive volume weakening? Those are the sorts of questions chartists ask.

Collectively, what all these charts and analytical theories (and we are only scratching the surface here) try to do is allow an investor to see backward into the future. In their charts and graphs, chartists

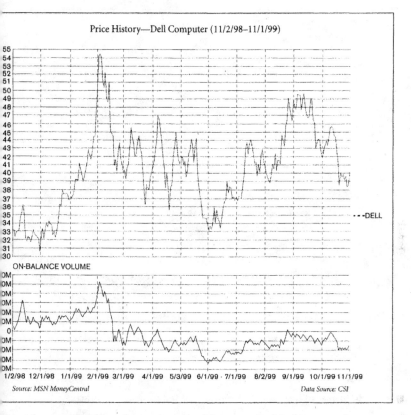

Price History—Dell Computer (11/2/98–11/1/99)

Source: MSN MoneyCentral

Data Source: CSI

are forever searching for patterns and images: double bottoms, for example, or double tops, or heads and shoulders, or Elliot Waves, or cups and handles . . . it just goes on and on—for each and every one of which there are more Web sites than you can visit in a month.

Take the double top pattern, which occurs when a stock's price climbs to the same level (give or take 3 percent, then can't go any further and falls back—*two times in a row.* When this happens, the stock is said to have hit "resistance" at that level, and that a top has therefore been "confirmed." Here's what a double top looks like in the price history of Yahoo, the search engine company, during the winter of 1998–99:

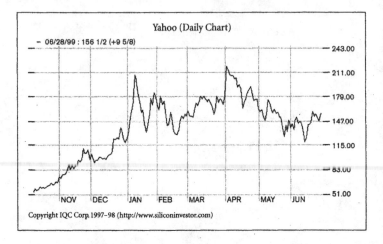

See those two little pointy peaks in January and then again in April? It's the April peak, at about $214 per share, that is said to have confirmed the January top of just under $208. See what happened thereafter—how the stock fell apart all the way down to $119 in the middle of June? According to technical analysis, this happened because of that resistance that the stock had encountered at $214—all those people who for one reason or another had either decided not to sell, or not to buy, with the result that the price came apart.

Seeing all that, a smart technical trader would have sold his Yahoo at its all-time high of $214 and taken his profits. But the fact is, no one needed a double top confirmation chart to be smart that way.

That's because virtually the whole of the Internet sector fell apart that April, and for a reason that no chart could anticipate, no matter how artfully drawn its double tops and head and shoulder patterns: Fears had begun to spread through Wall Street that interest rates were about to rise, threatening a financial squeeze on companies with weak balance sheets and earnings. As a result, people everywhere just woke up one day in early April and said, Thanks but I think I'll cash in right now . . . and nary a double top confirmation could be found anywhere as a result. Amazon.com, the online bookseller, didn't undergo a double top, and neither did Lycos or America Online, or almost any of the others. They all just "sold off."

What gives technical analysis its greatest predictive strength—the habitual nature of human behavior—is always at peril to the greatest strength of man himself: his free will and capacity for doing precisely the opposite of that which is expected of him.

When George Bush sent American troops into the Persian Gulf in Operation Desert Storm, virtually the whole world (or at least that portion of it able to get CNN) was convinced that Iraqi strong man Saddam Hussein had some sort of rope-a-dope scheme afoot when, night after night, U.S. forces pounded Baghdad, then pounded Iraqi troop fortifications—and the Iraqis did nothing to respond. They just stood there, day after day, then week after week, taking it, reinforcing the suspicions of everyone that crafty old Saddam was lulling the West for some spectacular sucker punch. But no sucker punch ever came— just night after night of bombing and shelling, then a steamrolling U.S. assault over the Iraqi emplacements, through all of which the Iraqi leader just stood there (as it were) getting his brains beaten in.

No one expected he could be *that* dumb, but he was . . . just as no one ever imagined that Hitler would invade Russia (but he did), or— to reel in the scope of things a bit—that the president of the United States, at the peak of his popularity, would get caught hitting on the office help; or that Hugh Grant and Eddie Murphy would get pinched whistling up mustache rides on Rodeo Drive; or that . . . oh, why do people do things like that?

Why, when everything is going great—when inflation is under 1 percent and there's nothing but smooth sailing, economy-wise, for as far into the future as the mind of man can foresee—does the chairman of the U.S. Federal Reserve turn up in front of a congressional committee to mutter about the inevitable necessity of raising interest rates—and thereby knocks 50 percent off the price of every stock on Wall Street with a ".com" in the name?

In the theater arts, it's called the McGuffin—what Alfred Hitchcock referred to as the device or plot element that drives the logic of the action, as, for example, the mixed-up identities at the start of *North By Northwest,* or the Janet Leigh subplot in *Psycho,* or that bit at the start of Tom Stoppard's play when Rosencrantz and Guildenstern stand there flipping the coin, time after time, and it keeps coming up heads. The difference is, on Wall Street the McGuffin can turn out to be Rosencrantz grabbing the coin in midflight, kicking Guildenstern in the shins, and running offstage shouting, "I'd rather have it in T-Bills if you don't mind!"

Just because a stock trades up (or down) for eight straight days in a row is no guarantee that it will do so again on the ninth, no matter how many charts say so. There are only two directions in which a stock can move: up or down—and statistically speaking, there is a 50-50 chance of either . . . and no amount of charting can ever account for every human variable that gets processed in that snap instant of decision when, against all expectations, investors everywhere conclude that Ronald Perelman isn't an asset to Revlon but a downright *liability,* and begin bidding Revlon's shares *up* in the belief that he's about to call it quits and sell the business.

Nonetheless, we don't live in a totally chaotic world, with the Queen of Hearts running all over the place randomly cutting off people's heads. For the most part, for most people—and most companies—and most countries—one day is pretty much like the next. When unexpected events intervene, people, countries, companies soon adjust and life once again resumes its familiar rhythms—which is why technical analysis does have a certain predictive value a fair amount of the time. People are fundamentally creatures of habit, meaning that what they've done in the past is often a good indication of how they'll behave in the future. In the next chapter we'll see how money can be made from that fact on the Web.

chapter four

Day Trading: The Risky Offspring of Technical Analysis

You can definitely make money as a technical trader—even if you trade stocks on a minute-to-minute basis as a day trader—and in this chapter we'll examine a couple of strategies that seem to work at least some of the time. But before getting into the details, I think it only proper to put a big red flag on day trading itself. We'll call it the financial equivalent of the Surgeon General's Warning: Caution, Trading Stocks in This Way Can Be Very Hazardous to Your Financial Health and Emotional Well-being. Be Careful!

The risks derive from the fact that day trading is really no different from playing musical chairs with your money. The whole objective of technical analysis is, as we've seen, somehow to figure out how to get a jump on everybody else, and then to make sure that you don't rush instantly off a cliff while trying to capitalize on your "opportunity." In the end, that's really all the charts and trends and inflection point analyses are about—to help you figure out how to do what everyone else is doing . . . before *they* figure out what *you're* doing (which is, of course, figuring out what *they're* doing).

But there's more to it than that because, given the fact that every other technical analyst and trader in the world is looking at basically the same charts and trend data that you're looking at, what confidence can you possibly have that you'll be seeing what's in that data before anyone else sees it? Are you really the smartest person on earth?

That's not the smart-alecky question it might seem to be. The stock market is lots of things: It's the second largest (after the U.S. Treasury market) storehouse of value for the capital markets of the world; it's a major employer in New York City and several other cities; and it's also lately become a big TV advertiser on Super Bowl Sunday.

But beyond all that, the stock market is also something else. Thanks to the Internet and the proliferation of momentum trading, the stock market has now become the biggest gambling casino on the planet.

As a result, the entire country now seems to be transforming itself into a nation of Gordon Gekkos, blissfully celebrating how much we made on Yahoo before lunch. War? Peace? Social justice? Forget all that—it seems that the only thing Americans really want to know anymore . . . the thing that really gets them up and gets them going . . . basically comes down to this: What will Maria Bartiromo or David Faber say next on CNBC and how can I make a buck from it?

One industry research group figures that online retail investing has more than tripled since 1996 and will triple again by the year 2002. By 1999, already online trading accounted for 14 percent of all equity transactions on Wall Street, and the way things are going it is easy to suppose that the percentage will just keep growing and growing.

I know people—lots of them—who have by now quit their jobs

and begun Day Trading For A Living. I know a fellow in Boston who has now resigned from his position as headmaster of a prestigious private school, taken out a jumbo second mortgage, and pushed it all into eBay and Dell. He says that not long ago he made "just short of a million dollars" in a single ten-day period. I know people in Europe (lots of them) who rush home from work at mid-afternoon every day to catch CNBC's pre-game festivities over satellite TV from Fort Lee, New Jersey, before trading starts in New York at 9:30 A.M. People do this on the islands of Greece. They do it in India. I get e-mail from people who do it in Shanghai.

Unfortunately, when you roll the dice in this casino, you're up against each and every one of them, all looking at, and acting on, the same data you're looking at. It's just that you're in only one time zone, and they're spread across the twenty-three others, which means you're up against all of them, even when you're sleeping. Sound like fun?

And it's not just day traders in India and Rwanda, either. In this casino you're constantly matching wits with the cleverest card sharps of the major investment firms on Wall Street. And do not assume that because they work for big and often slow-to-react investment firms, they cannot get out of their own way. Far from it, these are highly trained, clever, and ruthless traders, and their bread is buttered by eating your lunch.

Yet even with all they've got going for them, the traders of Wall Street's big investment firms—known in the parlance as "market makers"—don't do as well as you might think. I know of no study that has quantified the performance of day traders as a group. But the big investment banks of the Street *do* report the results of their trading activity regularly to their shareholders and the Securities and Exchange Commission—and generally speaking, their performance is not all that great—mainly because they lack predictability and consistency. One year they're up, the next year they're a disaster. If the best in the business can't turn in consistently good results, how can an individual with limited experience, and even more limited capital, do any better?

Perhaps the best way to appreciate what all this means is to imagine a craps table at Las Vegas—the high-rollers table, complete with the scantily clad cocktail waitresses, the men in dinner jackets . . . the whole bit. In our little analogy, these people represent the major institutional traders of Wall Street—the big specialist firms on the floor of the New York Stock Exchange, the major market makers in the NASDAQ electronic market. In short, the heaviest hitters in the market. These days they are mainly momentum traders—Big Mo players in the local vernacular of Wall Street.

But let's add something else. Let's imagine that behind these Big Mo traders are hundreds of other players, all pressed up against them, each one frantically craning to place bets as well—all trying simultaneously to see not only what the heavy hitters are doing but what everyone else at the table is doing as well.

And know what? We haven't even gotten to the day trading part yet. All the back-and-forthing and nonstop second-guessing around the table is just what goes on among the pros. To see what day traders themselves are doing, you've got to go to another part of the casino—a whole separate gridiron-sized room that you normally find filled with people feeding coins into slot machines . . . only instead of slot machines the gamblers are all seated at little desks, munching pizza slices and swilling down Cokes while peering into computer monitors on which are displayed (are you ready for this?) graphically jazzed-up mathematical abstractions representing the current state of the chaos back at the high-rollers table—where, as you might have guessed by now, the high rollers are not only trying to fake out each other but are constantly sneaking sideways glances at a wall filled with computer monitors depicting, in a thousand flashing lights and flickering numbers, the current state of the chaos over in the day traders' room.

That is the game in which you'll be wagering your money, a sky's-the-limit craps game driven by the odd rule that anyone placing his bet can change it at any time—only you're not even in the room! You're down the hall in the slots room, along with thousands and maybe even millions of other people like you, trying to place bets on the outcome, one goal of which is for the high rollers to get all your money. Still want to play?

Now comes the best part of all: The computers that the pros in the high-rollers room use are the best and most reliable that money can buy—multimillion-dollar, double- and triple-backed-up systems that tie directly into the main databanks of the various exchanges where the trading actually occurs. By contrast, the computers that the bunch in the slot machine room get are crash-prone, unreliable PCs running software that was originally designed for games, graphics, and simple home office operations. As a result, the pros in the high-rollers room are constantly up to speed on everything that's going on in the slot machine room down the hall, whereas the crowd in the slot machine room are never really sure when (not "if") their computers are going to crash, plunging them into complete darkness as to what is taking place in the room where the craps game itself is occurring.

In short, day traders are constantly at the mercy of the rigged-up and crash-prone technology of the Internet. In a game in which minutes and even seconds can make the difference between a profit and a loss, the day trader in his paneled basement home office never knows when the Windows operating system on his desktop PC will freeze up—perhaps at the very instant he tries to place (or cancel) a trade. And just outside the walls of the house lurks the whole colossal, crash-prone Internet itself—a vast network of workarounds and make-do quick-fixes . . . all of them patched together to keep the old AT&T telephone system, built with copper wire for voice transmission only, functioning in the digital age. And if all that isn't bad enough, at the opposite end of this rigged-up arrangement is the day trader's online brokerage firm, besieged with its own ever multiplying computer problems and crashes.

Now given all that, if you *still* want to play, here are three approaches that seem to be working at the moment:

Playing stock split announcements: When a stock gets to, say, $200 per share, a standard 100-share purchase order costs $20,000. That's a bit rich for lots of people. But if a company simply announces that as of some specified future date a month or so down the road, the stock will be split two for one, then each current holder of a share at $200 will wind up being issued a second share, driving the market value of each down by 50 percent. That means a 100-share purchase order (known as a "round lot") will now cost only $10,000, presumably making it affordable to more people. If more people then begin to buy the shares, the mere fact of issuing a split will have caused the post-split price to rise. A number of Web sites now provide constantly updated lists of such stock split announcements. You can find them at

http://marketwatch.com/news/newsroom.htx,

www.moneycentral.msn.com, www.dailystocks.com,

and a number of other sites as well.

Playing earnings upgrades and downgrades: When analysts upgrade or downgrade their investment recommendations on a stock, many investors automatically buy (or sell) the shares, even if they don't know the first thing about the company. Whether or not the recommendations have much (or even any) intrinsic merit is an interesting question, but for now it is enough to know that they do have the power to move stocks. For $9.95 per month, you can thus get a reasonably good premarket summary of what the investment firms are recommending to their favored clients, by visiting

www.jagnotes.com.

You can also see lists of upgrades and downgrades, for free, on a number of different Web sites. The most up-to-date list is on the www.yahoo.com financial site. The ones to be found at

www.moneycentral.msn.com

are often so out of date as to be useless, since the whole point of the information, from the perspective of someone wanting to capitalize on momentum trading, is to get the information as soon as it comes out.

Playing sector leaders: When an entire sector of the market starts to pull ahead of the broad averages, momentum money starts to flow into it simply because it's said to be "hot." You can find up-to-date lists of the best performing and worst performing sectors for given time frames at www.moneycentral.msn.com, at

www.dailystocks.com, and at www.yahoo.com.

A more sophisticated—and potentially more rewarding (but riskier) —technique is to look for ultra-volatile stocks in volatile market periods, and then trade them at their inflection points, that is, when they stop going up and start doing down, and when they reverse course and go back up again.

Finding these sorts of stocks isn't difficult. In fact, the stock market is all but drowning in them these days—the result of what, at this writing, is an eighteen-year (and continuing) super–bull market. I know of no serious student of the stock market who thinks this boom—which has lifted prices by an average of 18 percent annually, versus roughly 5 percent annually between the end of World War II and the start of the super–bull market in August of 1982—will continue indefinitely. Rather, the most informed thinking on the matter seems to feel that the boom at some point in the 1990s changed into a speculative bubble fueled by excessive growth in the money supply.

Whether or not that is in fact what happened need not concern us here, for whatever the cause of the stock market surge, it has undeniably produced hundreds of stocks that are trading at valuation multiples far, far beyond all known historical experience, to say nothing of the averages for the market as of this writing (the spring of the year 2000). More important, whether the market continues on its present upward course or collapses tomorrow doesn't matter; either way, these stocks can be expected to behave with greater volatility, both up and down, than the market as a whole—for no other reason than that is how they have behaved from the start.

Where do you find such stocks? Easy. Go to the Microsoft Money-Central Web site and use its "Finder" tool, which is located at

www.moneycentral.msn.com/investor/finder/customstocks.asp.

This is an incredibly versatile stock-sorting and research tool. With it you can locate individual stocks—or indeed whole industry sectors of stocks—using almost any sorting parameter you can think of. Since we are looking for the most volatile stocks we can find, go to the "Finder" tab, and click in the first "Field" box, then select "Company Basics." A pop-out window will open up. From it select "Exchange." Click in the next box to the right and select the equal sign (=). Then click in the third and final box to the right and select "NASDAQ." (We're going to select our menu of ultra-volatile stocks from NASDAQ only because NASDAQ is by far the most volatile of the major exchanges.)

Next, move back to the first box to the left and drop down to the second row in the display. Click on the box, and from the pop-out window select "Three-Month Relative Strength." Next, click in the box to the right, and from the pop-out window select "High As Possible" (if the trend of the market has been up in the last three months) or "Low As Possible" (if the trend of the market has been down). Finally, in the upper-right-hand corner of the entire "Finder" display you'll see a little box in which you can select the number of companies you want to view from your search. Type in 100. Then hit the "Run Search" button.

The Microsoft Investor search program will thereupon sort through all its data and return to you a list of the top 100 NASDAQ stocks that have outperformed the market by the greatest amounts in the last three months. Among these you will likely find companies that neither you nor almost anyone else has ever heard of before—companies that have nonetheless been rising (or falling) at two and three times the rate of the market as a whole—and often at rates much greater even than that.

Next, click on the hot-linked symbols of each company on the list and up will come a Microsoft Investor company report for each company, one after the next. A lot of the information in these reports concerns fundamental financial data, which we'll deal with later in the book. But one section of the report is useful for our purposes here. It's called "Recent News," and it lists all major press coverage about the company for the last sixty days. Check out the news. If there is none—or if all you see are endless "P.R. Newswire" press releases by the company itself—then you may safely assume that the company is rising or falling for basically no justified reason whatsoever—in short, that the stock has been captured by momentum players who have begun trading its shares because everyone else has been doing the same.

Under such circumstances, you may also assume something else: When the overall market reverses course, this stock will too—only much more dramatically, swinging back abruptly to where it was originally, as technical momentum traders either race out of—or jump back into—the shares.

This sort of thing happens constantly with NASDAQ stocks, and spotting these movements can amount to found money for the nimble trader.

If you want to quicken your heart rate a bit, forget the "Three-Month Relative Strength" search that is available via Microsoft Investor, and try capitalizing on the swings that can occur in a single day. This is what real day trading is, in fact, all about. The goal: to spot developing trends before the market opens for trading in the morning, then to capitalize on them, rolling in and out of stocks as they heat up and cool down throughout the day.

How do you find such stocks? Pre-opening commentary on CNBC television is one popular source of such tips. In recent years I have seen countless occasions in which a CNBC reporter has leaned into the camera and said something positive about a stock, causing trading volume in the shares to leap a hundred-fold within seconds as viewers all over the planet instantly placed orders for the shares.

Internet chat rooms and message boards have become another popular place to search for leads. Yahoo maintains the biggest collection of such message boards on the Web, but there are many others that are just as popular. A Web site operator known as Go2Net runs a collection of message boards at the address www.siliconinvestor.com. You can find yet more message boards at a Web site named

www.ragingbull.com.

There is yet another Web site—www.dailystocks.com—that functions as a kind of one-stop-shopping service for nearly *all* message boards. Go to the site, enter a stock's name, and up will come a list of all major message boards containing chatter of one sort or another about the company.

The interesting thing about all these message boards is that literally anyone on earth can place any message he or she wants on them—which makes them a fabulous venue for the spreading of rumors. Whether the rumors are rooted in truth or are out-and-out lies is pretty much beside the point. What matters is that people read them and react accordingly—causing momentum to begin building in the shares . . . at which point traders begin buying on the basis of the developing momentum, and before you know it a stock is soaring in value for no other reason than, well, it is soaring in value.

Arguably the most influential source of all for tips and leads are the Internet's proliferating number of day trading chat rooms. The most well known of them is located at www.trading-places.net, but from my experience the best advice comes from a rival outfit: www.undergroundtrader.com. The man who runs the site, a Mr. Jea Yu, has even published a useful book on day trading. It's called *The Undergroundtrader.com Guide to Electronic Daytrading* (McGraw-Hill, $39.95), and it discusses, in reasonably clear language, the difference between bid and ask, how to read a Level II NASDAQ computer screen, how to tell whether a stock is being moved up or down by the lead market maker in the shares—the "axe"—and other such arcane matters.

In any case, none of these services is free, and memberships can run as high as $300 per month or even more. But they amount to a kind of rumor central for day traders, featuring chat room moderators who try to talk stocks into orbit by predicting that they will rise. The most successful of these services are, naturally, the ones with the biggest followings.

The day trader's hunt for momentum information normally begins at around 8:30 A.M. each morning, which is to say an hour before the market itself opens. As of this writing, plans are already in the works at both the New York Stock Exchange and the NASDAQ electronic exchange to extend trading into the evening hours, and eventually to twenty-four hours a day—which means, I suppose, that the day may soon be upon us when the entire Internet-wired world is engaged in nothing but a round-the-clock hunt for momentum. For the moment, however, it seems there's still time to sleep.

Be that as it may, at 9:30 A.M. the day trader places his orders and waits for his momentum plays to go up. Then when they stop rising he sells them and rolls over into the next group of stocks. And what if they don't go up? (Then follow the advice of Will Rogers and don't buy them in the first place!) Day traders do this over and over again all day long, then sell whatever they're still holding at four o'clock and go home. Then at 9:30 the next morning they start the same thing all over again.

The name of the game is not to make a killing on one or two big stocks, but to scalp profits from one-eighth and one-quarter-point swings in the minute-by-minute intraday movements of *lots* of stocks. With a home computer and an online trading account, you can, for example, buy 1,000 shares of a $10 stock like Cyberian Outpost, hold it until the stock nudges up to $10.125, and then sell it. At an online brokerage firm that charges as little as $5 per trade, you'll walk off with $115 pretax. Do that all day long and, if you don't go crazy in the process, you can make a decent living . . . provided, of course, that your stocks actually go up the way you expect them to. If, on the other hand, they go down instead . . . well, do the same arithmetic as before, only put minus signs in front of everything.

Who exactly invented day trading is a matter of some dispute. There's a fellow in New Jersey named Harvey Houtkin who is widely cited in the press as the father of the industry—the proof of which seems to be that Mr. Houtkin is said to be the first person to have hit on the idea of setting up an actual school to teach the various skills involved in day trading. The course costs $5,000, which is a lot of money in my book, and to day-trade using the software program that you learned in the course you have to open up an account with Mr.

Houtkin's online trading company and maintain a minimum balance of $20,000, which is a lot of money in *anybody's* book.

But you can save all the trouble (and money) involved in becoming a day trader in that fashion by simply clicking to the following Web site every morning at about 8:00 A.M.

www.island.com

Doing so will take you to the Web site of the Island Electronic Communications Network and show you a list, constantly updated, second by second throughout the day, of the twenty hottest NASDAQ stocks traded on the Island Electronic Communications Network.

Why care about that? Because the Island Electronic Communications Network is affiliated with the Datek Online brokerage firm, which is the most widely used brokerage firm on the Web for active day traders. Thus, in true technical analysis tradition, you can click to this Web site at any time during the day and see, for free, exactly which stocks are attracting the most attention among other day traders, without having to pay some day trading chat room service $300 a month to learn the same thing.

With the resulting information, you can make a ton of money if the stars line up just right. For example, during the Wednesday before Thanksgiving back in November of 1999, I happened to notice that, for no aparrent reason whatsoever, a stock called Ariel Corp. suddenly popped up, at about 7:45 A.M., at the very bottom of the Island ECN's "Top 20" list. It was a name I'd never heard of before, and when I checked for any news about the company I found out why I'd never heard of the outfit: There was no news about it at all—just a series of press releases announcing that the company had received approval to manufacture a certain kind of computer insert card for local networks.

There were no follow-up stories in the trade press or anywhere else to suggest that this was important news, but by the time I looked again at the Island ECN's Top 20 list a few minutes later, Ariel had jumped halfway up the list and stood at the number ten spot. In other words, for no reason other than a basically meaningless press release, the company had popped up on the Island list as one of the top twenty stocks in premarket trading. Then, by the simple fact of being on the list at all, it had started to attract investors, pushing it higher and higher on the list as the minutes ticked by.

By the time the stock market opened for trading at 9:30 A.M., Ariel was the hottest stock on the Island list, and within minutes thereafter it was the hottest stock on all of Wall Street, rising within two frantic days of trading from $3.50 per share to an astounding $57 per share—and all on nothing but a single press release that unleashed a stampeding herd of momentum traders.

The trick with this kind of trading is, of course, to get in early—and then get out while there are still plenty of people willing to buy your shares. These people are known as Wall Street's "Greater Fools"—which is simply another way of describing why investors seem ever willing to buy overpriced stock: Because they're counting on the existence of a Greater Fool to bail them out by passing the hot potato along. The trouble is, you never know when the Greater Fool will turn out to be *you*—the investor who turns to his broker and says, Okay, let's sell the damned stuff, and the broker answers, Fine, but to whom?

In the case of Ariel, you could have bought the stock at almost any point on Wednesday, November 24, 1999, at prices between $5 and $13 per share, and still at least quadrupled your investment overnight. But by noon on the next trading day, if you hadn't sold out already you weren't going to. Reason: The stock abruptly dropped to $19, and thereafter fell apart altogether.

Every day trader dreams of making a killing in a stock like Ariel—especially after the fact when, with the perfect 20/20 vision of hindsight it's easy to see how much could have been made. Let's see: You buy 10,000 shares of Ariel at $3.50 per share on margin—which is to say, by borrowing half the money from your broker, so you really only have to come up with $17,500. Then you sit back for two days and wait, and watch your $17,500 investment magically blossom into $560,000. Ain't life grand when things work out that way?

The trouble is, of course, that timing such swings is almost impossible because you can never know—no matter how many three-minute Stochastics charts you look at—at what point the bottom will drop out from under you. The only thing you can know for sure is that at some point it will, and the more you linger around trying to grab that last dime, the greater grow the odds you'll wind up clutching nothing but thin air.

If you sense from the foregoing that I'm not a big fan of day trading, you're right. When it comes to timing swings in the market, you can never get enough information to know for certain whether the trend that you think you see in the data is *continuing* or whether it has already passed into history. A three-month momentum trend doesn't tell you what happened last week, and a one-week trend doesn't tell you what happened yesterday. Nor for that matter does a one-day trend tell you what happened ten minutes ago.

Technical analysis in general—and day trading in particular—is like history itself. No matter what stock you're watching, or what trend you're looking for, every bit of data you accumulate is already part of (and thereby changing) the history into which it is passing. It is a metaphysical truth that everything we know or can ever learn must be part of the past for us to know or learn it. Eugène Ionesco thus wasn't just mouthing off when he said, "It is impossible to predict something until it has happened."

Nonetheless, now you at least know what the basic elements in the game are, and can thus sound with-it at cocktail parties if someone should walk up and say, "Hey, do you think Yahoo's got support at $420, or is this sell-off going to continue down to $380?" You can answer, "I dunno . . . the on-balance volume doesn't look great, but I wouldn't rule out at least a technical bounce any day now. Did you check out the twenty-day moving average?"

Next, we'll turn to an area of investing that isn't nearly so complicated, is largely jargon-free, and is based ultimately on common sense. It is a field of investing that will bring you good, predictable, consistent, lifelong returns if you simply do your homework—which is, as we'll see, a whole lot easier than it ever was before thanks to the advent of the Internet. We speak, of course, of fundamental analysis—the art and science of figuring out what a company is really worth in its own right before investing in its stock.

chapter five

Some Basics About Fundamental Analysis

Stripped to its essentials, fundamental analysis amounts to nothing more mysterious than figuring out how much a stock is worth even if no one else in the world seems willing to buy it. Of course, the subject can be made a whole lot more complicated than that, and for an exhaustive, technical discussion of the entire matter, you can buy the definitive book on the subject—*Security Analysis* by Benjamin Graham and David Dodd. First published in 1934, and updated regularly ever since, this is the bible of many of the twentieth century's most successful investors, most notably Omaha super-investor Warren Buffett. But you don't need to know what Warren Buffett knows on the subject . . . unless, of course, you're planning to be a billionaire, in which case you might as well stop reading *this* book right now. Our purpose here is not to get you into the *Guinness Book of Records* but to help you use the Internet in order to manage a personal portfolio in a way that will let you sleep at night while still making money.

To understand how fundamental analysis works, you need to have at least a basic familiarity with three tables of financial information: the balance sheet statement, the income statement, and the cash flow statement. These statements are all filed by public companies, on a quarterly basis, with the Securities and Exchange Commission in Washington. And since May of 1996, the SEC has, in turn, made them available electronically over the Web, which means they're now available to you as well—and for no more trouble than the click of a mouse.

Why bother to obtain them at all? Because balance sheets, income statements, and cash flow information are the basic building blocks for all fundamental analysis on Wall Street—the stuff that investment firm clients routinely pay hundreds of thousands of dollars per year to obtain from the firms' analysts. In this chapter, I'll show you how to get precisely the same information off the Web, for free, and what to do with it once you've got it.

Fundamental analysis involves the search for value, not on Wall Street but rather in the financial details of the individual companies themselves. Now, granted, there are plenty of people who will tell you that this is a pointless exercise—that value is a relative thing, and that in the end something is worth only what someone will pay for it . . . so that rather than focus on the company, you should focus on the market.

The argument for the position is easily expressed: You might think that your home—the lovely builder Colonial with the Garrison front that you bought for $150,000 three years ago—is now worth $300,000 simply because you put a $1,200 Karastan carpet in the entrance hallway and made the place look like a million bucks. But in the end, what you *think* doesn't matter. In the end, what matters is how much someone will pay you for the place. So ask yourself this: What if a buyer came along and said, "Tell you what . . . I'll let you keep the rug if you give me the house for half off." Would you take up the offer and sell? Depending upon your circumstances—which is to say, how badly you needed the money—you just might . . . which is why technical analysts will tell you there's no such thing as absolute value in the world, and that in the end, everything depends on how much someone is willing to pay.

Here's the problem with that: What if gold is selling for $300 an ounce, and that Karastan carpet in the entrance foyer in fact has thirty pounds of the precious metal sewn into it—hidden perhaps on the underside in long, glittering threads in the jute backing? In that case, the house might be worth a whole lot more than someone is willing to pay for it, only the buyers don't happen to know it—so much more, in fact, that a buyer might be justified in saying (if he only knew the truth), "Tell you what, I'll give you 150 grand for the rug, and you can keep the house!" The task of fundamental analysis can thus be understood in very simple terms: to find the gold that's under the rug.

The aforementioned three tables of financial information will tell you if the gold is there or not. We will begin with the balance sheet because that is the logical place to start. The balance sheet won't tell you what the company's prospects are over time, but it will tell you whether the company is rich or poor at any given moment—and knowing that is as good a place to start as any.

Technically, the balance sheet represents a snapshot, at a specific moment in time, showing how much the company "owns" and how much it "owes" and what would be left if you sold off the former to pay off the latter.

What the company owns are its *assets*, what it owes are its *liabilities*, and the difference between the two is the company's *equity*—which is to say, what the shareholders would be left with if all the company's assets were sold off for cash in order to pay off all the company's liabilities.

All balance sheets of publicly traded companies in America are organized in essentially the same way: the assets on top, the liabilities on the bottom, then a bottom-line calculation showing the business's equity that belongs to the shareholders. Here is what a balance sheet for Amazon.com, the Internet retailer, looked like as of September 30, 1999:

AMAZON.COM, INC.
CONSOLIDATED BALANCE SHEETS
(in thousands, except per share data)

(UNAUDITED)

	September 30, 1999	December 31, 1998
	ASSETS	
Current assets:		
Cash	$ 43,149	$ 25,561
Marketable securities	862,536	347,884
Inventories	118,793	29,501
Prepaid expenses and other	55,590	21,308
Total current assets	1,080,068	424,254
Fixed assets, net	221,243	29,791
Other investments	196,317	7,740
Intangibles and other, net	705,932	179,263
Deferred charges	36,239	7,412
Total assets	$2,239,799	$648,460

LIABILITIES AND STOCKHOLDERS' EQUITY

Current liabilities:		
Accounts payable	$ 236,711	$113,273
Accrued advertising	24,567	13,071

nterest payable	10,045	10
Other liabilities and accrued expenses	73,572	34,413
Current portion of long-term debt and other	12,776	808
Total current liabilities	357,671	161,575
ng-term debt and other commitments and		
contingencies	1,462,203	348,140
ockholders' equity:		
Preferred stock, $0.01 par value:		
Authorized shares–150,000		
Issued and outstanding shares–none	–	–
mmon stock, $0.01 par value:		
Authorized shares–1,500,000		
ssued and outstanding shares–339,235 and 318,534		
shares at September 30, 1999, and		
December 31, 1998, respectively	3,393	3,186
Additional paid-in capital	1,027,655	298,537
Note receivable from officer for common stock	(1,171)	(1,099)
Stock-based compensation	(32,180)	(1,625)
Accumulated other comprehensive (loss) income	(18,957)	1,806
Accumulated deficit	(558,815)	(162,060)
Total stockholders' equity	419,925	138,745
Total liabilities and stockholders' equity	$2,239,799	$648,460

There are many, many places where you can download such a table from the Web. They are available from almost all the well-known personal investing sites, from the SEC's own Web site, and from various commercial services.

In my experience, the best one by far is a site known as FreeEDGAR. Just click on the following link and you'll be taken right to it: www.freedgar.com. One of the great virtues of this site—besides its ultra-reliable computers that never seem to crash or even run slowly—is that you don't need to know the ticker symbol, or even the full name of the company you're looking for. Just type in the first few letters of the name, and up will come a list of every company with those letters in its name. Then just read down the list until you find the one you're looking for, and click on it. In a few seconds you'll get a list of every financial filing the company has on record in the SEC's computer database. Just scroll down the list until you see the most recently filed 10-Q statement, which will contain the latest quarterly filing of the company's income, balance sheet, and cash flow statements. Click on the link for it, and up will come the entire filing, which you can then download onto your own hard drive.

Next, just open up the document with your word processor, and you'll see a list of tables. Look for the one called "Balance Sheet" and click on it, and you'll jump instantly to the part of the filing containing the balance sheet itself.

Now you've got something to work with. Look at the Amazon.com balance sheet on page 100. The column to the right shows what its balance sheet consisted of when the company filed its most recent full-year report to the SEC, known as a 10-K—in this case, December 31, 1998. The column to the left shows what the balance sheet looked like at the end of the period covered by the latest quarterly filing—that is, at September 30, 1999, nine months later.

You can get a very good idea of how a company has been doing by simply looking at the way these numbers have changed over time. In the case of Amazon.com, we can see that its total assets—that is, the sum value of all the stuff that the company owns—had roughly quadrupled during the period, and as of September 30, 1999, stood at aproximately $2.2 billion. That's a lot of assets for a company that didn't even exist at all five years earlier.

But look down the table further and we see that Amazon's debts (technically speaking, its current liabilities plus its long-term debt) had also roughly quadrupled, and as of September 30, 1999, stood at approximately $1.5 billion. In other words, the company's assets had been growing, in part at least, simply because its debts had also been growing. That sounds rather contradictory but it isn't. If you have $1,000 in a passbook account, and you're that lucky soul who doesn't owe a penny to anyone, we might properly say that your personal financial equity is $1,000 (your assets of $1,000 minus your liabilities of zero). But if you go to the bank and borrow $500 and stick it in your passbook, you've now increased your assets by 50 percent, but only because your liabilities have been increased in the process. Basically you're no richer than you were before you borrowed the $500, since your assets (which are now $1,500) need to be offset by your liability, which is that $500 loan. Net result? Your personal equity is still only $1,000.

The same thing happens when a company borrows money. The company's assets go up, but so do its liabilities, so its bottom-line equity will tend to remain about the same.

In the case of Amazon.com, however, not only are the assets and liabilities greater, but so too is the bottom-line equity. How is that possible? To find the answer, run your eye down the right-hand column of the balance sheet, row after row, and compare each number with the number in the column to the left, looking for big increases in each category between December 31, 1998, and September 30, 1999. What you'll notice is that the company's total assets increased by roughly $1.6 billion during the period, but its total liabilities rose by only $1.1 billion. In other words, the company increased its assets by $500 million more, during the nine months in question, than its borrowings increased during the same period. So, where did the $500 million come from?

The answer lies toward the bottom of the table, where you'll find a line item reading "Additional paid-in capital." This represents money that the company collected by selling aditional stock in itself to investors. How much more? Check the two columns. At the start of 1999 the company showed roughly $300 million in additional paid-in capital. By September 30, 1999, the total had jumped to approximately $1 billion. In other words, Amazon.com sold somewhere around $700 million of additional stock during the period. If that stock had not been sold, the shareholder equity number at the bottom of the table—approximately $420 million—representing total assets minus total liabilities, would in fact have been a negative number of somewhere around −$300 million. In other words, Amazon.com's debts would have exceeded its assets and, on a balance sheet basis, the company would have been insolvent, which is to say, bankrupt.

We can therefore conclude, by a simple two-minute eyeballing of Amazon.com's balance sheet, that as of September 30, 1999, the largest and most rapidly growing consumer retailing operation on the Web was not really as healthy as it appeared to be; its assets were growing sharply, but only because it had been borrowing money and selling stock. The funds were not being generated by the internal growth of the company's actual retailing business.

To see how Amazon.com's actual business has been faring over time, we need to turn next to the second of the Big Three financial documents, the income statement, which is sometimes referred to as a company's statement of operations. Here is what Amazon.com's income statement for the three-month and nine-month periods ended September 30, 1999, looks like, from the same 10-Q filing that contained the above-mentioned balance sheet:

AMAZON.COM, INC.
CONSOLIDATED STATEMENTS OF OPERATIONS
(in thousands, except per share data)

(UNAUDITED)

	Quarter ended September 30,		Nine months ended September 30,	
	1999	1998	1999	1998
et sales	$355,777	$153,648	$963,797	$356,992
ost of sales	285,300	118,823	760,998	276,680
ross profit	70,477	34,825	202,799	80,312
perating expenses:				
Marketing and sales	86,555	37,454	233,222	84,325
Product development	44,608	13,227	102,298	29,168
General and administrative	18,512	4,951	44,301	10,220
Merger, acquisition and investment related costs, including amortization of intangibles and equity in losses of affiliates	99,481	19,486	175,255	24,901
Stock-based compensation	11,789	1,214	16,570	1,591
Total operating expenses	260,945	76,332	571,646	150,205
ss from operations	(190,468)	(41,507)	(368,847)	(69,893)
terest income	12,699	4,755	36,479	9,790
terest expense	(21,470)	(8,419)	(66,424)	(18,017)
ther income, net	2,159	–	2,037	–
Net interest expense and other	(6,612)	(3,664)	(27,908)	(8,227)
et loss	$(197,080)	$(45,171)	$(396,755)	$ (78,120)
asic and diluted loss per share	$ (0.59)	$ (0.15)	$ (1.23)	$ (0.27)
nares used in computation of basic and diluted loss per share	332,488	301,405	323,064	292,206

Unlike balance sheets, which show a company's static financial condition at a given moment in time, income statements are designed to show *trends* in the business: Are sales increasing or declining? Are costs rising or falling? What are the trends in the subcomponents of each of those major two categories? Income statements are designed to help an investor answer two basic questions: (1) Is this a good business to be in, and (2) Is the company's management running the business well or not?

Unlike a balance sheet, which gives you only two columns of information, an income statement gives you four. The first two columns to the left compare the latest three-month period with the same period of the year before. This is done to help you account for possible seasonal fluctuations in the business. Sales of Christmas cards soar in the final quarter of the calendar year as the holiday approaches, then immediately collapse in January and only begin to recover the following autumn. So if you were to compare the revenue that a greeting card company collected in the October–December quarter with what it took in during the three following months of January through March, you might conclude that the company's business had collapsed. On the other hand, if you compared the "year-over-year" quarters, it might be the case that revenues are *increasing* and that the company is in fact healthy and growing.

The two columns to the right attempt to put the quarterly data to the left in some sort of perspective. To do this, the two columns to the right take the accumulated data from the start of the company's current fiscal year (for most companies, the fiscal year begins on January 1, though some companies begin their fiscal years in March, July, and even September—the same date that is used by the U.S. federal government for its own books and records). These aggregated quarters are then compared with the equivalent periods of the year before. Thus, in the first quarter of a company's fiscal year, the 10-Q income statement will have only two columns of information (for the current and year-before quarters). The second quarter's 10-Q will contain four columns—for the current quarter and the year-earlier period, and for the first six months of the year and the equivalent year-earlier period. The third-quarter 10-Q filing will do likewise except that the two columns on the right-hand side will cover nine-month periods. The fourth-quarter financials will come in the form of a full year's worth of data, presented in what is known as a 10-K report, or an annual report, as it is also known.

Now look at the Amazon.com income statement for the September 1999 quarter. It shows that revenues ("net sales") more than doubled over the year-earlier period, to nearly $356 million. But notice that during the full nine-month period, revenues actually nearly tripled from the year-earlier time frame. In other words, revenue growth for Amazon had actually slowed by almost 50 percent in the third quarter as compared to the two earlier periods.

Now look at the next line item below revenues—"Cost of sales." This represents the price that Amazon.com itself is paying for the stuff it sells on its Web site. There's something interesting hidden in these numbers. Do you see it?

Look at the difference between the cost of sales and the sales themselves. This is the company's gross profit, and is labeled as such on the statement. Generally speaking, you can't increase your profits very much by trying to lower your cost of sales because, unless the company is run by complete idiots, you can assume they're already buying their goods for the lowest prices possible. So, if it turns out that, over time, the company's gross profit margin begins to decline we may assume that either its cost of sales are rising, or it is cutting its own retail markups to stimulate sales.

In 1999, inflation at the consumer level in the U.S. economy was almost nonexistent, and with retail marketing competition on the Internet intense, we may assume that Amazon.com's cost of sales did not increase at all during the period; if anything it probably declined. But notice that in 1998, the company's gross profit (gross profit divided by net sales) was 22.7 percent, whereas by September of 1999 it had fallen to 19.8 percent. Why? The most obvious explanation is that the company was discounting its retail prices in order to stimulate sales.

Sometimes this sort of marketing tactic can make sense. But it's not that easy to justify when you're already losing money even before you begin the discounting. By doing so, you're simply guaranteeing that your losses will widen.

Now move your eye down to the next group of costs, labeled "Operating expenses." This covers just about every expense the company has except taxes and interest on its borrowings. Notice that even though quarterly sales have barely doubled between 1998 and 1999, total operating expenses have nearly quadrupled. Result: A more than four-fold increase in Amazon.com's operating loss, and at the bottom line, its net loss as well.

Obviously, this is not a healthy situation. To stimulate sales in the face of growing competition on the Internet, the company began discounting its prices even as it aggressively boosted spending on marketing, advertising, and sales promotion. The result? A loss of $197 million for the quarter.

How is the loss accounted for? Go back to the balance sheet and you'll find it right there, buried within the last liability item on the statement: "Accumulated deficit." The number on the balance sheet reads "($558,815)," * but that represents all the losses to date since the beginning of the business. To see that this is so, take the accumu-

---

* Numbers inside parenthesis on financial tables are always negative, which is to say, minus, numbers.

lated deficit from the balance sheet as of December 31, 1998—($162,060)—and add to it the total losses ("Net loss") from the income statement for the full nine months of 1999—($396,755). The result—($558,815)—will exactly match the accumulated deficit as shown on the balance sheet at September 30, 1999.

The more we look at the company's financials, the less healthy this Amazon.com operation is beginning to seem. After all, a half billion dollars in losses for a five-year-old Internet start-up company ain't chump change no matter how you look at it.

Now granted, some of those losses don't represent cold hard cash flying out the door. See that "operating expenses" item on the income statement called "Merger, acquisition and investment related costs . . ." of $99 million? As the statement says, much of that consists of "Amortization."

These expenses occur when a company acquires another company at some premium price over and above what the acquired company's assets are valued at on the balance sheet. The result is what is known in accounting as "goodwill," and accounting rules require the acquiring company to charge it off, a little bit every year, until it's all gone.

To see how much goodwill Amazon.com actually has on its balance sheet, go back to the balance sheet and look among the assets. You'll see roughly $700 million of it listed there as of September 1999, labeled "Intangibles and other, net." Most of that is nothing but goodwill, telling you that over time it will disappear from the balance sheet as the company charges it off, and that Amazon.com's assets will shrink accordingly. From the income statement you can see that perhaps as much as $99.5 million was charged off in the September 1999 quarter alone ("Merger, acquisition, and investment related costs . . .")

Goodwill and similar write-offs are real and important because they reduce a company's assets without simultaneously reducing its liabilities, meaning that the equity of shareholders in the business is reduced instead. But these write-offs don't immediately burn up cash—the very lifeblood of any business.

To see how fast cash money is flying out the door, we need to go to the third statement in Amazon.com's quarterly 10-Q—its statement of cash flows. Here is what it looks like, once again from the same 10-Q filing we obtained from the www.freedgar.com Web site:

AMAZON.COM, INC.
CONSOLIDATED STATEMENTS OF CASH FLOWS
(in thousands)

(UNAUDITED)

	Nine months ended September 30,	
	1999	1998
Operating activities:		
Net loss	$(396,755)	$(78,120)
Adjustments to reconcile net loss to net cash used in operating activities:		
Depreciation and amortization	22,935	6,182
Amortization of deferred compensation related to stock options	16,570	570
Noncash merger, acquisition and investment related costs, including amortization of intangibles and equity in losses of affiliates	175,255	24,082
Loss on sale of marketable securities	6,086	–
Noncash interest expense	26,116	15,455
Net cash used in operating activities before changes in operating assets and liabilities	(149,793)	(31,831)
Changes in operating assets and liabilities, net of effects of acquisitions:		
Inventories	(89,292)	(10,784)

Prepaid expenses and other	(32,685)	(12,528)
Accounts payable	121,771	25,447
Accrued advertising	11,057	8,403
Interest payable	10,035	(61)
Other liabilities and accrued expenses	6,526	13,691
Net cash provided by changes in operating assets and liabilities, net of effects from acquisitions	27,412	24,168
Net cash used in operating activities	(122,381)	(7,663)
esting activities:		
ales and maturities of marketable securities	3,460,139	117,669
urchases of marketable securities	(3,993,422)	(315,608)
urchases of fixed assets	(181,859)	(18,779)
cquisitions and investments in businesses	(222,853)	(14,374)
Net cash used in investing activities	(937,995)	(231,092)
ncing activities:		
roceeds from issuance of capital stock and exercise of stock options	36,930	11,325
roceeds from long-term debt	1,260,639	325,987
epayment of long-term debt	(184,710)	(77,383)
inancing costs	(35,151)	(7,783)
Net cash provided by financing activities	1,077,708	252,146
ffect of exchange rate changes	256	(411)
et increase in cash	17,588	12,980
ash at beginning of period	25,561	1,876
ash at end of period	$ 43,149	$ 14,856
plemental cash flow information:		
ixed assets acquired under capital leases	$ 25,850	$ —
ixed assets acquired under financing agreements	5,608	—
tock issued in connection with business acquisitions	635,343	217,241

Many analysts will tell you that a company's statement of cash flows is really the only thing you need to look at, period—it is *that* important. What the cash flow statement does is tell you whether the company is *generating* or *consuming* cash money. Cash flow statements are cumulative from the beginning of the year, which means that you're seeing a total of how much money came in, or went out, throughout the whole of the period, not just during the latest three months. (Don't ask me why it's done this way, but it is, so remember it.)

In any case, to derive an actual cash position for the company, the statement of cash flows takes the bottom line net income number from the income statement (in this case, that $397 million cumulative loss for Amazon.com during the first nine months of 1999), then adds back into it all the noncash expenses that went into the loss in the first place (nearly $250 million).

There's a lot of stuff on these statements that you don't need to know the first thing about—but there's also one thing that's critically important: whether the company generated or consumed cash from its operations.

To find out in Amazon.com's case, go to the top third of the cash flow statement, labeled, "Net cash used in operating activities" (also known as Cash Flows from Operations), and look at the net number at the bottom of the section. In Amazon.com's case, the number is very disturbing indeed. It shows that during the first nine months of 1999, the company burned through more than $122 million, which is a huge amount of money.

Just how big is that, really? Well, look at it this way: During the year-earlier nine-month period, the company burned up only $7.7 million (check the column to the right), so the cash burn rate has soared more than fifteen-fold in a year.

How much longer can something like that go on before all the company's money is gone? To find the answer, go back to the balance sheet (the first of our three financial reports) and see what kind of cash is available to fund the burn rate. As of September 30, 1999, Amazon.com's "Cash" and "Marketable securities" totaled roughly $900 million, which is a lot of money. But if you read the text section of the 10-Q labeled "Management, Discussion and Analysis" (not reproduced here) you'll see that Amazon.com plans to spend at least some of that money on building more warehouses to support its product delivery system to customers, so not all of the $900 million is available. Meanwhile, if spending, discounting, and promotion-driven growth continue as they have, the cash burn rate could perhaps double in the year ahead, to $400 million and maybe even more than that, suggesting that Amazon.com could be out of ready cash entirely inside of two years' time.

Trends like these take time to emerge in the financials of companies—though in the case of Amazon.com they appeared more rapidly than many people had expected. Nonetheless, once they become apparent, the market can exact a terrible toll on the stock.

Between the time Amazon.com went public in the spring of 1997 and when it finally peaked in December of 1999, Amazon.com soared an almost incomprehensible 6,000 percent in value, making millionaires of many members of the company's management, and showering lesser but still substantial wealth on many lucky individual investors. But once doubts began to set in regarding the company's fundamentals, the stock began coming right back down again, losing nearly half its value in barely a month's time. By the summer of the year 2000, Amazon's stock price had collapsed from a split-adjusted all-time high of more than $100 to barely $14 per share, wiping out 80 percent of its value in less that eighteen month's time.

Bottom line for investors? Whether Amazon.com ever recovers its glorious moment as the late 1990s superstock of momentum investing doesn't matter. What matters is that the run-up had nothing to do with the performance of the company itself, but rather with the fickle enthusiasms of momentum traders. This means, in turn, that holders of its stock were at risk of seeing their value plunge overnight should the market begin at last to focus on the real fundamentals of the company—which is inevitably what happens someday to all companies.

chapter six

Earnings: The Holy Grail of Fundamental Analysis

There is a scene at the beginning of the movie version of Tennessee Williams's classic play *A Streetcar Named Desire* in which Blanche DuBois tries to find her way to her sister's home in the French Quarter of New Orleans. Looking for the streetcar that will take her to a slum dwelling by the name of Elysian Fields, she stops a passing sailor and, in complete bewilderment, asks for directions. The sailor obligingly offers help to the stranger, and thereafter unfolds a great dramatic tragedy.

But only at the end do we learn the moral to the tale of Blanche DuBois, as we find her being escorted from Elysian Fields to a Louisiana state mental hospital. And, once again, she is offered the extended hand of a stranger willing to guide her way—this time in the person of a state psychiatrist leading her to her final, grim fate. As he extends his arm, she takes it and looks at him with desperate, confused eyes, then says in one of the great lines of the theater: "Why thank you, whoever you are, for I've always depended on the kindness of strangers."

I think of that play—and the refrain that marks its finale—every time I hear some bright young Wall Street investment banker declare that earnings aren't necessary, that the world has entered a "New Paradigm," and that the ticket to rising stock prices is revenue growth, or EBITDA growth, or some new and even more cutting edge concept on the frontiers of permanent prosperity.

You hear that a lot in connection with the dot.com stocks, which became a must-have obsession among momentum-driven investors during the latter half of the 1990s, then abruptly became must-sell pariahs as the year 2000 began. And it's easy to understand why the buying binge grew, for who can quarrel with the wealth that momentum investing had showered upon holders of shares ranging from such household names as Yahoo and eBay to obscure but high-flying shares like VerticalNet and E.piphany. In the same way that their very names seem to defy conventionality, so too do the rationales that support their ever-higher stock prices.

But the wealth of momentum investing lasts only as long as the willingness of investors to hold the shares simply because everyone else seems to do the same. Result? When fashion changes and the momentum traders move on, the shares come crashing back to earth since nothing held them aloft in the first place but the mass delusion of all at the party that no one would put on his coat and leave.

Consider the sad story of an imploding internet e-commerce stock called Value America. This company, headed by a man whose last previous achievement in business had been to preside over the Chapter 11 bankruptcy of an earlier public company he had led, was taken public in the spring of 1999 by the Wall Street investment firm of BancBoston Robertson Stephens, for the lofty sum of $23 per share.

Propelled by the hype surrounding almost any IPO in the

e-commerce game, the stock leaped to $69 per share on its very first trade in the aftermarket. But it was momentum investing—and that alone—that caused the price to triple in minutes. When the traders saw that the shares would go no higher, they began bailing out and the stock began a long, relentless slide that eventually carried it down to less than $6 per share.

Why did Value America prove such a disappointment? Because when the momentum traders left and value investors began picking through the rubble, it quickly became clear that there was nothing to salvage. The company's prospects clouded over the very instant investors took a look at the financials and discovered that it would be years, if ever, before Value America could generate a dime of earnings. And without earnings, Value America was like Blanche DuBois—dependent on the kindness of strangers to survive the day.

The red flags were there for any investor to see—but most just didn't bother to look, ignoring among other things the fact that, at the time the company went public, it had all of eighteen months of actual retail experience under its belt. But e-commerce was hot, and as a result, no one seemed to mind—or indeed even notice—that the founder's most recent previous experience at running a public company, a $90-million-a-year (revenues) lighting fixtures maker, had filed for Chapter 11 bankruptcy in 1993.

So good a salesman was founder Craig Winn, in fact, that, to get Value America off the ground, he secured more than $30 million in start-up capital from backers like Paul Allen, co-founder of Microsoft, and Frederick Smith, the chairman of FedEx (formerly Federal Express).

Winn's beguiling pitch was simple: Retailing on the Web may be a narrow-margin business, but you could nonetheless make a lot of money at it if your volume was big enough and you didn't stock any inventory on your own. When a customer ordered something from your site, you'd simply pass the order along to the manufacturer, and *that* company would ship it.

On that premise, and not much else, Value America went public in April of 1999 with a 5-million-share offering at $23 per share, putting a total market value of more than $900 million on the business. Within minutes, Wall Street was revaluing the company upward to more than $2.5 billion.

But the euphoria didn't last long, for it soon became clear that the company couldn't grow except by losing money—and that the more it grew, the deeper into the red the business sank. In the first nine months of its life as a publicly traded company, sales roughly doubled—but only because, in an effort to generate revenue growth, the company began discounting the price of its merchandise so fiercely that its gross margins vanished.

Gross margin—defined as sales minus the cost of goods sold—is what you're left with before you take out any other cost of running the business, from salaries to your operating expenses, your headquarters administration, and so on. Throw all *that* into the mix, and Value America's sales might have doubled, but its losses quadrupled. Before you knew it, the stock had fallen from $69 to $6 and the buzzards of looming bankruptcy were circling the company . . . all because the company had been unable to make a convincing case that it would ever be able to turn a profit—a problem that no one had bothered to focus on when momentum traders were in the driver's seat and Value America's stock was burning up the track. In January of 2000 I warned in print that Value America's finances were such a mess that the company's stock, then selling for $6 per share, might eventually fall all the way to zero. Eight months later, Value America filed for bankruptcy, and with its stock selling for 75 cents, closed down its business.

In fact, earnings are ultimately all that stands between *any* corporation and the fate of Blanche DuBois (over Value America)—the strangers in this case being the Wall Street investors who may or may not be there to pony up the money needed to keep a company going when it can't survive on its own.

As a result, fundamental analysts are forever devising new and more ingenious ways to measure the risk and put a price on it— namely, by calculating how much in the way of earnings a company had in the *past,* how much it's got *now,* and how much it is likely to have in the *future*—then to figure out what is called the net present value of that future earnings stream is . . . all to decide whether the company is over- or underpriced now, as against its peers, based on its future earnings potential.

The classic measurement in this regard is the price of the stock divided by earnings per share. It is calculated by taking the company's total earnings and dividing them by the total number of shares outstanding, then dividing *that* number into the price of a share of the stock.

Thus, if Yahoo earned $61,133,000—as was the case in 1999—and the company had roughly 516 million shares in existence at the time, we may say that the company had just under 12 cents of earnings per share. If we then divide that per-share earnings number into Yahoo's price in April of 2000 ($133 per share), we come up with a price/earnings (or P/E) ratio of 1,108. That is a stupefying ratio when you consider that a company like Microsoft was then selling for about 50 times earnings.

But there is more to the story than that. For starters, these are *trailing* price/earnings ratios, meaning the current price of the stock divided by the earnings of the previous twelve months. These are the numbers you most often see quoted in the newspapers and on TV, but they are *not* the numbers Wall Street goes by. Wall Street isn't interested in what happened yesterday, it is interested in what is going to happen tomorrow. And this in turn means that the only price/earnings ratio Wall Street cares about is the current price of the stock divided by what Wall Street's various analysts think the company will earn in the future. This helps explain why Yahoo might seem so over-priced on a *trailing* earnings basis. Reason? Wall Street's analysts think Yahoo's earnings will roughly quadruple in the next two years, meaning an earnings-per-share number of 51 cents by December of 2001. And when you divide *that* number into the current Yahoo price of $133, you get a price/earnings number that, while still enormous, is no longer in another solar system: roughly 261 times year-ahead earnings.

There is, of course, no guarantee that the analysts are right, and that Yahoo will earn anywhere near what they are forecasting. But because the company does in fact have earnings—and because the growth of those earnings can be projected into the future—it is possible to come up with a basis of valuing the company as a self-sustaining entity. When the stock price of such an entity rises, it almost always means that, in the end, the analysts expect the company's earnings will grow more than had been predicted. Conversely, when the price weakens it is because they think earnings growth is going to be disappointing.

You can find all this sort of thing calculated for you, for any stock you can think of, with a research tool bearing the name Value Wizard. It is located at

http://www.numeraire.com/value_wizard/index.htm

and is part of a Web site run by the Vanguard Software Corp. of Cary, North Carolina. The site is worth a visit just to play around with the software tool, which is free to anyone.

There are plenty of other earnings-related Web sites that are also worth visiting. There are even a group of sites devoted to nothing but Wall Street rumors about what the earnings of various companies are likely to be. These are known as "whisper numbers," referring to the Wall Street scuttlebutt having to do with whether a company will likely overshoot or undershoot the consensus forecast of Wall Street analysts. You can find the consensus numbers at www.dailystocks.com and a number of other places, and the whisper numbers at www.earningswhispers.com.

If you want to start comparing price/earnings ratios of individual companies within whole sectors of business—if for no other purpose than to unearth the most overpriced and underpriced companies within their peer groups—there is no better site for the task than Microsoft's www.moneycentral.msn.com. Click on the site's "Finder" tab, then select, under "Custom Search," the industry group in which you are interested; let's say "Drugs," and within drugs, "Biotechnology." Then, under "Analyst Projections," select "Forward Year p/e" and run the search. You'll get all ninety-six biotechnology stocks in the group, showing the consensus forecast of Wall Street's analysts about their year-ahead earnings per share for each stock, divided into the stock's current price.

There are literally dozens of different earnings-related yardsticks you can apply to stock prices via the MoneyCentral "Finder" tool. You can find the most over- and underpriced stocks based on six different types of trailing earnings, based on price to cash flow, based on average net, gross, and pretax income over the previous five years, and on and on and on.

You can compute price/earnings ratios for individual stocks, for groups and indexes of stocks, for sectors of the economy, and for the entire stock market—and then measure one against the other to see which, if any, might be over- or underpriced.

For example, you can find the annual high, low, and year-end price/earnings ratios for the Standard & Poor's 500 index and its predecessors, dating as far back as 1871, by clicking on the following link: http://www.globalfindata.com. The S&P 500 contains 500 of the largest publicly traded companies in America representing more than $1 trillion in market value.

The Web site, maintained by a research and data collection company called Global Financial Data in Los Angeles, will tell you that in 1998, for example, the price/earnings ratio of the index stood at 32, meaning that the average of all stocks in the index was selling for 32 times its current earnings. Yet only four years earlier, the same index was selling for a P/E of 16, meaning either that stock prices had stayed the same while earnings had fallen by 50 percent or that stock prices had risen twice as fast as earnings. In fact, earnings had risen during the period, but not nearly as much as stock prices, which had actually tripled.

When stock prices rise, year after year, at rates substantially in excess of the growth in earnings, you are looking at an investment bubble in the making. How inflated can that bubble get? Over the more than 120 years covered by the S&P data on the www.globalfindata.com Web site, the price/earnings ratio of the stocks in the S&P index averaged 15.5, meaning that the index sold, on average, for 15.5 times its current earnings in any given year.

Compare that number to the price/earnings ratio of the NASDAQ composite index on December 31, 1999: 281. This shows that speculation in NASDAQ stocks had grown so extreme as the 1990s progressed that, by the end of the decade, the NASDAQ index was selling on a price/earnings basis for an incredible 18 times the average price of the S&P index over the previous 127 years. In fact, even if we compare the December 31, 1999, NASDAQ P/E to the historically high December 31, 1999, S&P P/E (33), the NASDAQ stocks were *still* eight and one half times as more expensive, on a price/earnings basis, than the stocks in the S&P.

In December of 1996, when the S&P composite P/E stood at 20, and the NASDAQ P/E stood at "only" 37, U.S. Federal Reserve chairman Alan Greenspan addressed a dinner meeting of the American Enterprise Institute in Washington and warned of spreading "irrational exuberance" in the stock market. It was his first use of a phrase that has since become a commonplace description of the stock market of the late 1990s.

Yet few investors paid Greenspan's warnings any mind, and the market took off on a momentum-fueled rocket ride that carried the NASDAQ composite index from 1,300, which is where it stood when he spoke, to more than 5,000 by early 2000.

No one aboard such a rocket ride wants to imagine it ending badly, and all manner of explanations were soon being advanced to show how, this time, things would turn out differently—how, this time, trees really would grow to the sky. Wall Street analysts began speaking of a "New Paradigm" in business, of a world in which earnings no longer mattered and balance sheets had become obsolete.

Of course, nothing *ever* moves in one direction indefinitely—not in the cosmos, and not on Wall Street either, and scarcely had the NASDAQ index touched its peak of 5048 on March 10, 2000, than it keeled over and collapsed, losing 1,727 points, or fully a third of its value, in a mere twenty-four trading days, wiping out the investments of hundreds of thousands of individuals in less than a month and dooming hundreds of companies to almost certain extinction from their inability to sell more stock in order to stay in business.

The whole purpose of price/earnings-based research is, of course, to find companies that can avoid that fate when such market breaks come—companies that stand upright on their own and grow without external sources of financial support. Not every company that relies on external capital to grow is a bad investment; some, particularly in the biotechnology sector, have turned out to be great successes. But no one can know, at the start of the race, which are going to be the winners at the end and which will drop out along the way. And even the winners are likely to go through sickening price declines when the economy weakens, interest rates rise, and money becomes scarce.

Consider a company called Human Genome Sciences, which is involved in genetic research on the human body. Anyone who bought a share of the company's stock in January of 2000, when the price was $80 per share, must have thought himself a genius when the shares soared to nearly $220 within a month. Then, just as abruptly, they collapsed, and within four more weeks were at $80. Main reason for the decline? A precipitous slide in nearly all technology stocks as interest rates began to rise and investors started to worry that companies without earnings might not survive an economic downturn.

They were right.

Take, for example, Boston Chicken, which was collapsing into bankruptcy from earnings starvation at just about the moment when Value America was preparing to go public.

In the annals of twentieth-century American business, it is hard to find a better company than Boston Chicken to track the round-trip fate that awaits those who invest in an outfit whose operations generate no earnings: You begin with a combination of high hopes and maybe a bit of trepidation as you climb aboard that streetcar named Desire . . . and you end up a ward of the state.

For a time in the early 1990s, Boston Chicken was the darling of Wall Street. The company was sold to institutional investors in November of 1993 at slightly less than $20 per share, and the institutions thereupon turned around and resold their shares in frantic aftermarket trading that instantly drove the shares to more than $50. In the three years that followed, the shares nearly doubled yet again, and by 1996 they had reached the split-adjusted equivalent of more than $80.

What drove them skyward? Well, by the start of the 1990s, the postwar baby boom generation was beginning to spread out notice-ably in the middle, and America's obsession with health was reaching new heights. Result: Boston Chicken seemed the restaurant chain of the hour. Its aggressively cultivated image of healthful and nutritious home cooking seemed so gosh darned American you just had to like it. After all, if you didn't like meat loaf and chicken pot pie, well, maybe you didn't like your own mother—and who was going to ad-mit to *that?*

By the time Boston Chicken popped up on my personal radar screen—which is to say, more or less in the autumn of 1996—there were Boston Chicken outlets all over America . . . more than a thou-sand already with new ones opening every week. And I'll be the first to admit that I really did like the food (everything but the meat loaf, but that's another story). Just as the TV commercials said, your Boston Chicken eating experience was so yummy and complete—the turkey entrées, the corn bread, the green beans, and the apple pie dessert—why, it made you think of Thanksgiving every day of the year . . . and all for $6 per person.

There was just one problem: Every time I went into a Boston Chicken restaurant, I was usually the only customer there! At noon on a Saturday, in Fairfield County, Connecticut, I'd be the only per-son eating lunch in just about any Boston Chicken I wandered into. And it was no different on a Wednesday evening, or a Sunday night—or at almost any other time. Here was a company with 1,200 plus restaurants scattered all across America, and so far as I could tell, no one was eating in them except me.

So one day—more out of curiosity than anything else—I opened up my computer, logged on to www.freedgar.com, and downloaded the latest 10-K for Boston Chicken to see what the financials of this high-flying restaurant company actually looked like. Here is the in-come statement:

BOSTON CHICKEN, INC. AND SUBSIDIARIES
CONSOLIDATED INCOME STATEMENTS
(in thousands, except per share data)

	Fiscal Years Ended		
	December 25, 1994	December 31, 1995	December 29 1996
		(53 weeks)	
Revenue:			
Royalties and franchise related fees	$43,603	$74,662	$115,510
Company stores	40,916	51,566	83,950
Interest income	11,632	33,251	65,048
Total revenue	96,151	159,479	264,508
Costs and expenses:			
Cost of products sold	15,876	19,737	31,160
Salaries and benefits	22,637	31,137	42,172
General and administrative	27,930	41,367	99,847
Provision for relocation	5,097	–	–
Total costs and expenses	71,540	92,241	173,179
Income from operations	24,611	67,238	91,329
Other income (expense):			
Interest expense, net	(4,235)	(13,179)	(14,446
Gain on issuances of subsidiary's stock	–	–	38,163
Other income, net	74	314	137
Total other income (expense)	(4,161)	(12,865)	23,854
Income before income taxes and minority interest	20,450	54,373	115,183
Income taxes	4,277	20,814	42,990
Minority interest in (earnings) of subsidiary	–	–	(5,235)
Net income	$16,173	$33,559	$66,958
Net income per common and equivalent share	$ 0.38	$ 0.66	$ 1.01
Weighted average number of common and equivalent shares outstanding	42,861	50,972	66,501

On the face of it, the company looked to be doing well, to say the least. The company's net income—the money that was left over after all the annual bills were paid—had risen from $16.2 million in 1994 to nearly $67 million in 1996. That's a 319 percent increase in net income—which is another word for earnings—when revenues for the same period had risen only 175 percent. In other words, every year more and more money was dropping to Boston Chicken's bottom line as earnings—earnings that were growing twice as fast as the revenues they were supposedly coming from.

That's the kind of income statement that a company would kill for because it means not only that the business makes money, but that it makes so much money that the excess can be plowed back into the operation to make yet *more* money—and all without borrowing a dime or selling a single new share of stock to raise capital.

Well, that's what things looked like if you didn't look too closely. But do you see the top line on the income statement labeled "Revenue"? There are actually three parts to the revenues. Look at them.

The first thing you might notice is that a lot of Boston Chicken revenue wasn't coming from selling those yummy turkey dinners at all. Roughly 44% of the company's revenue was in fact coming from something vaguely described as "Royalties and franchise related fees." And another 25 percent was coming from "Interest income." In other words, nearly 70 cents of every dollar the company collected was coming from activities that didn't appear to involve selling food to customers at all—which was hardly surprising, since, based on what I'd been seeing with my own eyes, there weren't many customers in the stores to begin with.

What are "Royalties and franchise related fees"? One of the great things about computerized financial research is that questions like that are relatively easy to answer—usually by simply locating a discussion of the matter somewhere in the 10-K filing. And the best thing of all is that you don't have to read the whole document . . . just search the text for other appearances of the phrase, using the appropriate tool in your computer's word processing software—and in no time at all you'll find out what Boston Chicken means by the term.

In this case it turns out that the phrase refers to money that Boston Chicken collected from people who had started up separate, independent companies to run Boston Chicken restaurants as franchise licensees. A franchise licensee pays a yearly fee—known as a royalty—as well as a start-up fee, for the privilege of running a franchise restaurant.

That sort of arrangement is common in the fast food restaurant business. But what's not so common is the huge amounts of licenses and fees that Boston Chicken was charging its franchisees for the privilege of conducting business under the Boston Chicken name. In 1996, roughly 214 franchised stores opened for business, and the company took close to $32 million in initial, opening-for-business fees and assorted other one-time charges.

How did the company account for that $32 million? Well, common sense says it should have been treated as some sort of asset on the balance sheet because it represented an investment by the franchisees in setting up a business to sell Boston Chicken meals, which would naturally increase the value of the Boston Chicken brand name.

But rather than treat it as a capital investment by the franchisees in the Boston Chicken business, the company booked it as actual revenue on the income statement. So right off the bat, you could see that the "revenue" was at least $32 million higher than it should have been. Instead of 1996 revenues of $265 million, the company ought to have reported revenues of no more than $233 million at most for the year.

And that was just the start of the trouble. Every 10-K and 10-Q filed with the Securities and Exchange Commission contains a "Management's Discussion and Analysis" section (known in the Wall Street vernacular as an "MD&A") as well as several pages of footnotes to the financial data in the various tables. Reading through this part of the Boston Chicken 10-K, you could have seen that the company was raising money through stock sales on Wall Street, then lending the money to the company's franchisees to get them started in business, then booking the interest on the loans as yet another component of revenue on the income statement. That accounted for the third major subset of revenue on the income statement—"Interest income," which totaled roughly $65 million during 1996. This money also wasn't revenue from the restaurant business but simply the interest derived from investing the proceeds of stock sales on Wall Street. Take the $65 million out of revenue and you'd have been left with less than $200 million in revenue from the actual sale of meals in the stores, or barely enough to cover the company's operating costs, which came to $173 million for the year. On an operating basis, the company was in fact generating almost no profits at all—which, once again, wasn't very surprising since from all that I could see, the stores were not attracting the numbers of customers needed.

But there were still more revelations to be mined from the financials. When a company lends large amounts of money to borrowers, prudent banking practice would require the lender to set aside a portion of each periodic interest payment as a reserve in case one or more borrowers were to default. You would normally expect to find this on the company's balance sheet as an asset that would fluctuate in relation to the volume of loans outstanding at any given time. But here is what the company's balance sheet from the 1996 10-K looked like, and as you can see, there are no loan-loss reserves to be found on it anywhere. Why? Because the company was taking every dime of proceeds from interest payments and applying them directly to revenues on the income statement instead of reserving for the possibility that some of the borrowers might default.

BOSTON CHICKEN, INC. AND SUBSIDIARIES
CONSOLIDATED BALANCE SHEETS
(in thousands, except per share data)

	December 31, 1995	December 29, 1996
	ASSETS	
Current assets:		
Cash and cash equivalents	$ 310,436	$ 100,80
Accounts receivable, net	13,445	22,43
Due from affiliates	9,614	10,24
Notes receivable	5,462	
Prepaid expenses and other current assets	1,536	4,05
Deferred income taxes	3,322	8,92
Total current assets	343,815	146,46
Property and equipment, net	258,550	334,74
Notes receivable	450,572	800,51
Deferred financing costs, net	15,745	13,36
Goodwill, net	–	190,43
Other assets, net	5,195	58,08
Total assets	$1,073,877	$1,543,61

LIABILITIES AND STOCKHOLDERS' EQUITY

Current liabilities:		
Accounts payable	$ 12,292	$ 40,43
Accrued expenses	9,095	36,54
Deferred franchise revenue	8,945	10,65
Total current liabilities	30,332	87,63
Deferred franchise revenue	2,072	7,74
Convertible subordinated debt	129,872	129,84
Liquid yield option notes	177,306	182,61
Deferred income taxes	16,631	40,21

...er noncurrent liabilities	833	6,292
...ority interest	–	153,441
...mmitments and contingencies		
...ckholders' equity:		
Preferred stock–$.01 par value;		
authorized 20,000,000 shares;		
no shares issued and outstanding	–	–
Common stock–$.01 par value;		
authorized 480,000,000 shares;		
issued and outstanding: 59,129,301		
shares in 1995 and 64,245,868 in 1996	591	642
Additional paid-in capital	675,611	827,611
Retained earnings	40,629	107,587
Total stockolders' equity	716,831	935,840
Total liabilities and stockholders' equity	$1,073,877	$1,543,616

Yet the possibility of default was clear enough, for as one of the footnotes in the 10-K stated plainly, the company's franchisees themselves had been losing money, and in 1996 racked up aggregate net losses of more than $156 million for the year.

So, what would happen, one might have wondered, if the franchisees defaulted on their loans and the company had not set aside enough money to cover the resulting losses. Well, elsewhere in the 10-K could be found what eventually turned out to be the grimmest news of all.

To qualify for loans in the first place, a franchisee would have to have spent more than 75 percent of its own capital before getting any money from Boston Chicken—an arrangement that calls to mind the procedure by which families qualify for handouts under government welfare entitlement programs: First spend everything you've got, then we'll consider helping you.

Thereafter, if a borrower were to spend at least 80 percent of the

money lent it by Boston Chicken and *still* not be operating profitably, Boston Chicken would "convert the loan into equity"—which is
to say, simply take the operation over and begin running it as a
company-owned.

This meant that Boston Chicken would be able to avoid writing off
the defaulted loans as worthless only by taking the worthless, money-
losing restaurants they financed onto Boston Chicken's own balance
sheet while simultaneously transferring the losses onto Boston
Chicken's income statement. In other words, a guaranteed prescrip-
tion for bankruptcy for Boston Chicken itself.

And that is precisely what happened as one after the next, the failing restaurants began to default on their loans, at which point Boston
Chicken took them over as company-owned stores and the losses
soared out of sight. By the end of 1997 the company was running $36
million in the red, even on its peculiar accounting. On an operating
basis, the losses totaled $211 million—and more than $300 million if
all the twisted accounting were straightened out. In other words, the
company had made the complete round-trip on that Streetcar Named
Desire and now faced that grim moment when it could no longer
count on the kindness of strangers. For five full years the company had
been selling stock tranche after stock tranche to raise the money to
create the loans to book the interest and fees that it was calling "revenue," and now suddenly, when it needed to sell stock more desper-
ately than ever, the price had crashed to barely $3 per share and it
couldn't sell a 100-share lot to anyone. Next stop: bankruptcy.

In a bankruptcy proceeding, a company tries to reorganize its finances in a way that will permit it to pay its bills. Failing that, the
court presiding over the reorganization simply orders the liquidation
of the business. One good way to see how much trouble a company
might have in reorganizing itself is to look at what financial analysts
call the "current ratio." This is a simple math formula that you can

easily calculate in your head by looking at the balance sheet. As we saw in Chapter 5, the top part of the table consists of the company's assets, and the bottom part consists of its liabilities. But each of these parts is itself separated into two parts—assets that the company is likely to have for a year or less, and liabilities that will also be paid off in less than a year. These comprise the company's "current balance sheet"—current assets and current liabilities.

On the current assets side of the ledger you find things like cash and marketable securities—things that are in the form of cash already or can easily be converted into cash to pay bills as they come due. On the liabilities side you find things like bills that are owed already (accounts payable) and loan repayments that are coming up in short order.

To calculate the company's current ratio just do a quick eyeball of the current assets and current liabilities totals (every balance sheet adds them up for you) and see if the assets can be divided by the liabilities—that is, if the current assets are larger than the current liabilities. If they're not—if there are more current liabilities than current assets and, thus, if the assets cannot be divided by the liabilities even once—you're looking at a ratio of less than one, or a company that has bills coming due in the immediate future and no obvious way to pay them.

(By the way, you can get a continuously updated list, based on the latest quarterly filings of every company reporting to the SEC, of the companies with the best and worst current ratios on Wall Street by simply clicking over to the Microsoft Investor Web site and running one of the "Finder" searches we discussed in Chapter 4. Once again, go to http://moneycentral.msn.com/investor/finder/customstocks.asp and try it. Running a current ratio check on any company you're planning to invest in will give you a quick and easy glimpse into its current financial health.)

In the case of Boston Chicken the company's current ratio was positive according to the balance sheet as of December 31, 1996. But a year later it had swung massively into the red—the result of unpaid bills piling up, and unsold inventories accumulating in warehouses. The end was near.

The curtain finally fell the following October when, unable to sell any more stock to pay its bills, the company filed for bankruptcy protection under Chapter 11 of the federal bankruptcy code (it "went Chapter 11" as they say on Wall Street). But even that wasn't the end of it, because—as the current ratio so clearly foreshadowed—reorganizing the business to run profitably simply wasn't going to be possible. This meant that there was but one step left: liquidate the assets.

To see what would result from a liquidation, here's Boston Chicken's balance sheet as of October 4, 1998—the day the company filed for Chapter 11. Once again, it comes from simply downloading the quarterly 10-Q for the period from www.freedgar.com. Though the quarter in question technically ended September 30, 1998, the document wasn't filed until early November, and by that time the company had filed for Chapter 11, so the lawyers simply told them to include the balance sheet as of the date of the filing.

BOSTON CHICKEN, INC. AND SUBSIDIARIES
(DEBTOR-IN-POSSESSION EFFECTIVE OCTOBER 5, 1998)
CONSOLIDATED BALANCE SHEETS
(in thousands, except per share data)

(UNAUDITED)

	December 28, 1997	October 4, 1998
	ASSETS	
Current assets:		
Cash and cash equivalents	$ 90,559	$ 16,85
Accounts receivable, net	13,894	3,79

nventories	16,132	25,053
Prepaid expenses and other current assets	1,436	7,945
Total current assets	122,021	53,643
operty and equipment, net	530,582	648,247
tes receivable, net	609,175	33,622
ferred financing costs, net	24,570	19,706
odwill, net	639,364	894,757
her assets, net	77,062	59,384
Total assets	$2,002,774	$1,709,359

LIABILITIES AND STOCKHOLDERS' EQUITY

rrent liabilities:		
Accounts payable	$ 33,205	$ 23,326
Accrued expenses	85,207	163,352
Other current liabilities	14,119	11,266
Secured debt obligation	–	166,437
Senior Secured Revolver–Boston Chicken, Inc.	–	87,300
Total current liabilities	132,531	451,681
ferred franchise revenue	5,723	–
nvertible subordinated debt–Boston Chicken, Inc.	417,020	417,020
nvertible subordinated debt–Einstein/Noah Bagel Corp.	125,000	125,000
uid yield option notes	197,442	209,704
nior debt–Einstein/Noah Bagel Corp.	24,000	20,700
her noncurrent liabilities	44,753	57,607
ority interests	253,630	243,721
mmitments and contingencies (note 8)		
deemable preferred stock	–	83,373
ckholders' equity:		
Preferred stock–$.01 par value;		
20,000,000 shares authorized;		
no shares issued and outstanding	–	–
Common stock–$.01 par value;		
480,000,000 shares authorized;		
issued: 71,400,179 shares in December and		
77,130,853 shares in October	714	771

(continued on next page)

**BOSTON CHICKEN, INC. AND SUBSIDIARIES
(DEBTOR-IN-POSSESSION EFFECTIVE OCTOBER 5, 1998)
CONSOLIDATED BALANCE SHEETS (continued)**
(in thousands, except per share data)

(UNAUDITED)

	December 28, 1997	October 4, 1998
LIABILITIES AND STOCKHOLDERS' EQUITY (continued)		
Additional paid-in capital	918,266	941,117
Accumulated deficit	(116,305)	(841,335)
Total stockholders' equity	$ 802,675	$ 100,553
Total liabilities and stockholders' equity	$2,002,774	$1,709,359

Look at the current ratio by this time. At nearly $452 million of current liabilities and a little less than $54 million of current assets, the company had no hope at all of ever turning itself around. But more important, the balance sheet also made clear that in a liquidation, the shareholders would be wiped out. Although the shareholders stand first in line when it comes to benefiting from a company's earnings power, they're last in line when a liquidation occurs. Only after the bondholders and all other creditors are paid off from the proceeds of an asset sale do the shareholders get what's left.

What they're supposed to get can be found on the next-to-last line on the balance sheet, labeled "Total stockholders' equity." That's the residual amount when all liabilities on the balance sheet are subtracted from all the assets.

In Boston Chicken's case, the shareholder equity was supposed to equal roughly $100 million. With 77 million shares outstanding, that would have worked out to roughly $1.30 per share, which was obviously a calamity for anyone who bought into the company at even $5 per share, let alone its all-time high of $80. But $1.30 was at least something, and those who received it could have framed the check and hung it in the den as a reminder that on Wall Street, as elsewhere, it pays to read the fine print before handing over your money.

Unfortunately, that $100 million in balance sheet equity for Boston Chicken's shareholders was an illusion. In Chapter 5 we discussed goodwill, being the balance sheet asset item that is really nothing more than a bookkeeping device designed to account for the difference between the value of an acquired company's balance sheet assets and the purchase price paid for the business by an acquirer. If a beauty parlor has assets of $5,000 (some chairs, some blow-dyers, what-have-you) and somebody comes along and pays $100,000 for the business, the $95,000 has to be accounted for somewhere—and that somewhere is the goodwill entry on the acquiring company's balance sheet; the $5,000 of blow-dyers and hair lotions is added to "Property, plant and equipment," and the $95,000 becomes good-will—the theory being that what you've really acquired for your $100,000 is $5,000 worth of beauty parlor stuff and $95,000 worth of loyal customers . . . in other words an ongoing business.

But what happens if the business stops being ongoing and you're forced to liquidate the assets to pay the creditors? What happens is, the goodwill instantly becomes worthless because, well, who is going to buy it? In the case of a liquidation, nobody.

That's what happened to Boston Chicken. Along the way, the company got into the bagel restaurant business, and wound up with 51 percent of a company called Einstein/Noah Bagel Corp., which was overflowing with balance sheet goodwill. When Einstein/Noah Bagel's assets filtered through to Boston Chicken's balance sheet, millions of dollars in goodwill resulted on the asset side of the ledger. But Einstein/Noah Bagel Corp.'s financials were essentially no different from Boston Chicken's, meaning that by the time Boston Chicken went into liquidation, Einstein/Noah itself wasn't worth much of anything. Moreover, every time Boston Chicken acquired a failing franchisee and converted it into a company-owned operation, yet more goodwill wound up on the balance sheet.

As a result, by the time the company liquidated its operations, Boston Chicken's balance sheet brimmed with nearly $900 million of goodwill that was essentially worthless. Take the goodwill out of the picture, and, on the day the company filed for bankruptcy, its actual, salable assets totaled only about $800 million, whereas its liabilities equaled more than $1.7 billion. Bottom line? Not a penny left for the shareholders, who discovered as much when McDonald's bought the restaurant sites for $173 million. That money was divided among various creditors, and Boston Chicken itself, so far as its shareholders were concerned, simply ceased to exist.

It was a 100 percent wipeout of a business that, at its heyday, had been valued on Wall Street at more than $2.6 billion and wound up, in the end, being worth nothing at all.

There were many points along the way when investors could have glimpsed the future and escaped (relatively) unscathed. Yet most chose to buy the stock simply because it was going up (momentum investing) or sit with it on the way back down because Wall Street analysts insisted the company's future was bright.

By simply checking the company's regular quarterly reports, any investor could have seen that sooner or later Boston Chicken was destined, like Blanche DuBois, to end up a ward of the state. In the end, its entire business was based on the kindness of strangers. Its earnings were an illusion based on the company's ability to sell stock in a rising stock market, then filter the proceeds through its own income statement as "revenue." When the harsh glare of daylight shattered the illusion, the stock crashed, the business imploded, and in less than a year it was out of business—as clear a lesson as one could ask that, in the end, earnings really do matter.

chapter seven

Cash Flow: The Bottom Line of Business

There are many seasoned and successful investors who will tell you that, when it comes to a company's finances, what *really* counts is the business's cash flow. They say this because a company's ability to generate actual cash money is ultimately why it is in business. They have a point.

You can talk all you want about a company's earnings, or its assets, or the shareholder equity on its balance sheet, but in the end it's the money in the cash drawer that really decides whether the company has a future or not. In this chapter we'll look at the various sources available to you on the Web to unearth a company's true and undistorted cash flow picture, then apply that knowledge to two celebrity stocks that went public in the latter half of the 1990s, then crashed and burned as a result of cash flow starvation. But first, a bit of background on what cash flow is all about.

There are few topics that are more confusing than cash flow analysis, though in reality the subject is quite simple. The whole purpose of cash flow analysis is, of course, to determine how much actual folding stuff—that is, cold hard cash money—the business actually generates during any given period. Simple? Of course.

The problems arise when you discover that "cash" means different things to different people. For example, if you go to the popular Motley Fool Web site (www.fool.com), which is much visited by new investors on the Internet, and search for a definition of cash flow, this is what you'll get:

> *The most common measurement for valuing public and private companies used by investment bankers. Cash flow is literally the cash that flows through a company during the course of a quarter or the year after taking out all fixed expenses. Cash flow is normally defined as* earnings before interest, taxes, depreciation, and amortization (EBITDA).

But is cash flow *really* the same as EBITDA? If so, then why do dozens of major companies such as Seagram, owner of Universal Studios and much else, include a qualifying statement in their financial filings when informing shareholders and the SEC of their "EBITDA results"? The statement reads, "Financial analysts generally consider EBITDA to be an important measure of comparative operating performance. However, EBITDA should not be considered in addition to, or as a substitute for, operating income, net income, cash flows, and other measures of financial performance in accordance with generally accepted accounting principles."

That qualifier is in there because the Financial Accounting Standards Board, which oversees accounting rules for publicly traded companies, makes the companies put it there. They do that because EBITDA doesn't really measure cash flow at all; rather, it measures a company's earnings *before* the enumerated nonoperating EBITDA costs—interest on the company's debt, taxes, depreciation, and amortization—are deducted from revenue. In other words, EBITDA is really nothing more than, in most cases, plain old "operating income"—your revenues minus your cost of goods sold and your administrative and marketing expenses. In effect, EBITDA measures earnings you're left with *if* you don't count a lot of what you owe.

Analysts like this number because it shows what income the business is capable of producing if viewed in isolation, without any debt on the balance sheet, or the depreciation write-off of any equipment, or the writing down of any goodwill, or the payment of any taxes.

But what does this figure really tell you about the company? In fact, it tells you next to nothing. A company's taxes are real and unavoidable and have to be paid. Depreciation and amortization are also real expenses. And as for the interest on the company's debt, well, if you don't pay that you'll be headed for court.

In reality, EBITDA has mainly been used by companies with heavy debt loads—typically in the media, and typically having been taken on as a result of leveraged buyouts or takeovers. These companies use EBITDA as a way to say, in effect, "Look how much money we'd be making if we just didn't owe so much to our bankers and bondholders . . ."—a rather disingenuous statement for management to make, since, in most cases, management put the debts there to begin with (and often for no other purpose than to enable it to gain control of the company).

When investment analysts speak of cash flow, they're not talking about EBITDA at all—at least the knowledgeable ones aren't. In reality, they're talking about the statements of cash flows that are contained in every 10-K and 10-Q filing by a public company.

These statements didn't even appear in quarterly and annual reports until the 1980s, when the Financial Accounting Standards Board, which oversees such things, began requiring companies to include them. The accounting folks issued that rule because cash flow statements give a much better picture of the company's health than do income statements, which are subject to all sorts of trickery and manipulation. Says Howard Schilit, an accounting professor at American University and a recognized authority on accounting shenanigans by business, "Cash flow information is king. If I had to make a forced choice between having earnings information and having cash flow information, I would take the latter."

That is because the statement of cash flows puts the honesty back into the income statement. The statements track, quarter by quarter throughout the year, the cumulative net income (or loss) from the beginning of the year through the end of the current quarter. Then, quarter by quarter, the cash flow statements add back into that net income or loss number every *noncash* charge that was deducted from it in the income statement along the way. These noncash charges include such things as amortization and depreciation, but they also include decreases in inventories and prepaid expenses, and so on.

What you end up with is the actual *cash* money generated by the company during the period. You can get a good, though somewhat abbreviated, summary of a company's cash flow by going to the Microsoft MoneyCentral site and pulling up a report on almost any company you can think of. Go to www.moneycentral.msn.com, and call up a "Company Report" on Harley-Davidson, the motorcycle company. Then scroll down to the section labeled "Annual Cash Flow."

In the subsection entitled "Cash Flow from Operations," you might notice that the actual cash being generated by the business has risen every year since at least 1995 and, what's more, that as of September 30, 1999 (the latest data period available at the time of writing), cash flow already exceeded the total for all of 1998. In other words, with three months still to go the company was on its way to yet another record year.

Cash flow from operations is important—in the end, it's indispensable—to a company's long-term growth prospects and, indeed, to its very survival. That is because cash from operations is ultimately the only genuinely reliable source of funds any company has available to it if it wants to invest in its own business and grow. Sure, it can always borrow money, or sell more stock, when interest rates are low and the stock market is booming. But when interest rates rise and money grows scarce, lenders start to worry about getting repaid, and eventually they become so persnickety that they tend to lend only to borrowers who don't actually need the money. Meanwhile, with stock prices weakening, it becomes impossible to sell more shares to the public because investors simply shrug and say, "Why should I buy from you today when I can get the same thing cheaper in the market tomorrow?"

How much cash flow is enough? One way to get at least a ballpark sense of the matter is to look at the second subsection in the statement of cash flows report: "Cash flows from investing activities." Below is an example, from the 1999 10-K annual financial statement of Revlon, the cosmetic giant.

REVLON, INC. AND SUBSIDIARIES
CONSOLIDATED STATEMENTS OF CASH FLOWS
(dollars in millions)

	Year Ended December 31,		
	1999	1998	1997
sh flows from operating activities:			
Net (loss) income	$(371.5)	$(143.2)	$ 43.6
Adjustments to reconcile net (loss) income to net cash (used for) provided by operating activities:			
Depreciation and amortization	126.1	111.3	99.7
Loss (income) from discontinued operations	–	64.2	(0.7)
Extraordinary items	–	51.7	14.9

(continued on next page)

REVLON, INC. AND SUBSIDIARIES
CONSOLIDATED STATEMENTS OF CASH FLOWS (continued)
(dollars in millions)

	Year Ended December 31,		
	1999	1998	1997
Loss (gain) on sale of certain assets, net	1.6	(8.4)	(4.4)
Change in assets and liabilities:			
Decrease (increase) in trade receivables	187.1	(43.0)	(70.0)
Increase in inventories	(22.5)	(4.6)	(16.9)
Decrease (increase) in prepaid expenses			
and other current assets	12.6	(11.4)	0.4
Increase (decrease) in accounts payable	10.8	(49.2)	17.9
Increase (decrease) in accrued expenses			
and other current liabilities	20.5	52.5	(2.8)
Other, net	(47.5)	(71.4)	(73.0)
Net cash (used for) provided by			
operating activities	(82.8)	(51.5)	8.7
Cash flows from investing activities:			
Capital expenditures	(42.3)	(60.8)	(52.3)
Acquisition of businesses, net of cash acquired	–	(57.6)	(40.5)
Proceeds from the sale of certain assets	1.6	27.4	8.5
Net cash used for investing activities	(40.7)	(91.0)	(84.3)
Cash flows from financing activities:			
Net increase (decrease) in short-term			
borrowings–third parties	12.3	(16.3)	18.0
Proceeds from the issuance of long-term			
debt–third parties	574.5	1,469.1	760.2
Repayment of long-term debt–third parties	(464.9)	(1,270.9)	(690.2)
Net proceeds from issuance of common stock	0.1	1.1	0.2
Net contribution from parent	–	–	0.3
Proceeds from the issuance of debt–affiliates	67.1	105.9	120.7

Repayment of debt–affiliates	(67.1)	(105.9)	(120.2)
Payment of debt issuance costs	(3.5)	(23.9)	(4.1)
Net cash provided by financing activities	118.5	159.1	84.9
ffect of exchange rate changes on cash			
and cash equivalents	4.3	(2.0)	(3.6)
et cash used by discontinued operations	–	(17.3)	(3.4)
Net (decrease) increase in cash and			
cash equivalents	(9.3)	(2.7)	2.3
Cash and cash equivalents at			
beginning of period	34.7	37.4	35.1
Cash and cash equivalents at end of period	$ 25.4	$ 34.7	$ 37.4
upplemental schedule of cash flow information:			
Cash paid during the period for:			
Interest	$146.1	$133.4	$139.6
Income taxes, net of refunds	8.2	10.9	10.5
upplemental schedule of noncash investing activities:			
In connection with business acquisitions,			
liabilities were assumed (including minority			
interest and discontinued operations) as follows:			
Fair value of assets acquired	$ –	$ 74.5	$132.7
Cash paid	–	(57.6)	(64.5)
Liabilities assumed	$ –	$ 16.9	$ 68.2

Look at the "cash flows from investing" subsection, which spells out, among other things, how much money is being plowed back into the business by the company by investing in new property, plant, and equipment. *If the company is investing more in this way than it is generating in cash from its operations, then it must be making up the difference from external sources.*

And that is exactly what Revlon did in 1999. During the year it invested $42.3 million in new property, plant, and equipment. But, by looking at the first section in the statement—"cash flows from oper-ating activities"—you can see that once it got through paying its bills, the company had no cash flow from its operations at all and in fact came up $82.8 million short on the year. So, how did it cover the shortfall? Check the third subsection in the statement—"cash flows from financing activities"—and you'll see that Revlon issued $574.5 million in long-term debt obligations, then used the proceeds to re-pay $464.9 million in existing obligations. Bottom line from the pa-per shuffle, which included some debt sales to a Revlon affiliate? The company wound up with cash of $118.5 million.

That cash was the money Revlon used to pay for its capital invest-ments and to cover its operating losses—a process that, in some re-spects, reminds one of the person who takes out a mortgage on his house and uses the proceeds to buy the family groceries.

You can find the problems of cash starvation in lots of companies, but one of the best places to look is among what are known as celebrity stocks. On one level these are stocks that don't need to be judged by technical analysis or fundamental research either, just plain old common sense. Like the street hustlers who seem to materialize out of nowhere, umbrellas-for-sale at the ready, whenever the first raindrops fall downtown, celebrity stocks almost always multiply late in bull markets. Reason? As bull markets progress, the store shelves of the investment firms become depleted of worthwhile merchandise, and underwriters and promoters start scratching around to drum up business with whatever is left—the stuff that wouldn't sell earlier in the cycle when investors were more discriminating and cautious about what they'd buy.

Simply put, celebrity stocks are investment world trash that gets dressed up in the finery of some high-recognition Hollywood star or sports personality, in hopes of blinding naive investors to the truth of their grim prospects, which almost always result in cash flow starvation. In the bullfight for investment dollars on Wall Street, celebrity endorsements are thus very often nothing more than the matador's cape—and you know what happens to the bull in those contests.

Celebrity stocks are, in a sense, the reductio ad absurdum of a venerable Madison Avenue marketing gimmick known as the celebrity endorsement. For example, back in the 1940s, a young Hollywood heartthrob named Ronald Reagan appeared in countless magazine ads with the pitch that Chesterfield cigarettes were somehow "smooth" to the taste. The *real* message, of course, wasn't that Chesterfields were smooth (whatever that means) but that it was suave to smoke them.

Celebrity endorsements have since become so commonplace they've by now become the white noise of commercial TV. Remember Michael Jackson for Pepsi? Or Michael Jordan for MCI WorldCom, or James Earl Jones for Bell Atlantic, or Lily Tomlin for Fidelity Mutual Funds, or Susan Lucci for Ford, or Jerry Seinfeld for American Express, or James Brolin for AAMCO, or Fergie for Weight Watchers?

The idea behind such ads is never to convince you that you can play in the NBA by switching to MCI. No, the idea is simply to get you to look up from whatever it is you're doing when Michael Jordan comes on the screen and starts talking to that Elmer Fudd or Daffy Duck cartoon character about five-cents-on-Sundays phone calls from MCI. Brand recognition, they call it on Mad. Ave., and when done right, with the right high-recognition celebrity as the centerpiece, the ads can be very effective. Examples include the long-running Candice ("the dime lady") Bergen series for Sprint, and the clever Paul Reiser ads for AT&T.

On Wall Street, however, the goal of celebrity ads is different. Instead of building brand awareness, celebrity involvement with a stock is designed to transform the celeb's fame into an implicit—if unartic-ulated—endorsement of the investment potential of the stock itself. "You can trust me," goes the message. "So do yourself a favor and go out and buy this stock."

In fact, of course, just because a person is a celebrity is no guaran-tee that he or she knows the first thing about the business he or she is endorsing—or, indeed, about any business at all. What's more, at-tempting to rub off one's fame on the stock is a pretty good tip-off that there's nothing much worth promoting about the company it-self, so the underwriters have decided to promote the celebrity in-stead. On Mad. Ave. this is called selling the sizzle instead of the steak. With the birth of the Internet, selling sizzle has become easier than ever, as online investing has flung open Wall Street to millions upon millions of inexperienced and naive investors who are easy prey for promoters. Then, as the "newbie" investors pile in, momentum traders follow and the vicious cycle of an upwardly spiraling worth-less stock begins.

Consider Iran-contra minute-of-famer Oliver North's body armor company, Guardian Technologies, which went public to much hoopla back in the late spring of 1996—in the process becoming one of the very first companies with its complete financial history available over the Internet for investors to scrutinize before handing over their money. Sadly, most seemed to pay no attention to the opportunity at all, with dire consequences.

By the spring of 1996, the stock market had already gotten frothy enough that even the right-wing *Semper Fi* wacko behind the Iran contra scandal was able to create a business and take it public. His game? To cash in on the notoriety created by his international skul-duggery on behalf of the Reagan administration nearly a decade earlier.

Back in the late 1980s, you could scarcely pick up a newspaper without reading of Ollie's exploits. He eventually beat a perjury conviction, which was overturned on a technicality on appeal. Then, with that out of the way, he hooked up with direct mail biggie Richard Viguerie and started flooding the country with fund-raising pleas to help him beat the commies—an effort that eventually led to his failed effort to win a U.S. Senate seat from Virginia.

After that he flipped the old left-turn signal and moved into the ultimate passing lane of American life—Wall Street. All he needed was some money, as well as something to be the boss of—which was where the IPO came in.

Back in 1989, Ollie had started a company (if we may call it that) called Guardian Technologies International. The name conjured some sort of high-tech security operation, but Guardian Technologies was actually just Ollie and one of his Iran contra buddies—an ex-cop turned CIA agent named Joe Fernandez—who figured they could make a few bucks by selling bulletproof vests.

When a company goes public in an IPO, the Securities and Exchange Commission makes it file an S1 registration statement, or, if it's a small-beer operation with not much to say for itself, an SB2. Either way, the company must explain why it wants money from the public and disclose the more important risks that investors undertake by investing in the business. In this case, the deal was ridiculous. The company had been living hand-to-mouth for years, often right down to the level of Ollie and Joe having to go scrounging around for loans and side-deal stock sales to anyone they could talk some money out of. The SB2 showed loans as big as $100,000 and as small as $1,200 on its books. Many of the company's bills had been paid with stock instead of money. The list of stockholders included a man in Brooklyn, some people in Jericho, Westbury, and Middle Village, Long Island—even a shell company in the Channel Islands, an offshore tax haven.

What would you have gotten if you'd joined the list and bought shares in the IPO? In a word, raped! For starters, much of the proceeds were destined never to reach the company at all. Guardian's underwriters, Landmark International Equities, expected to raise $4.9 million in the offering. But about $1.3 million of the total was intended to go either to Landmark as its underwriting fee, or to pay for various "consulting" services and what-not—which mainly meant payments to stock promoters to flog the shares to the gullible. In the end, Guardian wound up with only $3.6 million of actual folding stuff to stick in the bank.

The resulting equity dilution for investors in the offering was astounding—like pouring Lake Erie into your bathtub. At its latest accounting prior to the IPO, the company reported 17 cents per share in net tangible book value, which would rise to $1.24 per share once the cash from the IPO was added to the balance sheet and then divided by the total shares outstanding (roughly 3.2 million). That was great for Ollie and his gang. But the outside investors were paying an asking price of $5 per share in the IPO and winding up with stock having tangible net worth of $1.24.

Yet none of this deterred investors in any way, and when the shares came public at $5 each, they leaped instantly in aftermarket trading to $9, or nearly twice what even the underwriter itself had figured they were worth. Then, as anyone might have guessed, the shares started to slide as the business turned out to be a mirage. Four years later they're selling for 80 cents per share.

At any point during the slide, investors could have logged on to the Internet, called up the company's financials from www.freedgar.com, and seen Guardian Technologies' deepening troubles. Here's what the company's balance sheet looked like at the time of the IPO, downloaded from www.freedgar.com:

GUARDIAN TECHNOLOGIES INTERNATIONAL, INC.
BALANCE SHEETS
JUNE 30, 1996 AND 1995

(UNAUDITED)

	June 30, 1996	June 30, 1995
ASSETS		
current assets:		
Cash and cash equivalents	$3,080,644	$ 11,615
Accounts receivable	155,500	38,222
Inventories		
Raw materials	189,699	45,950
Work in process	88,330	1,635
Finished goods	31,389	60,908
Prepaid expenses	21,167	42,291
Total current assets	$3,566,729	$200,621
property and equipment:		
Leasehold improvements	$ 114,494	$114,494
Manufacturing equipment	63,477	44,235
Office furniture and equipment	61,150	38,416
Land	255,224	—
Construction in process	253,010	—
Less accumulated depreciation	(177,304)	(156,962)
Total property and equipment	$ 570,051	$ 40,183
other Assets:		
Certifications and patents	$ 119,749	$110,205
Less accumulated amortization	(115,781)	(89,813)
	$ 3,968	$ 20,392
Deposits	16,625	5,326
Total other assets	$ 20,593	$ 25,718
Total assets	$ 4,157,373	$266,522

(continued on next page)

GUARDIAN TECHNOLOGIES INTERNATIONAL, INC.
BALANCE SHEETS (continued)
JUNE 30, 1996 AND 1995

(UNAUDITED)

	June 30, 1996	June 30, 1995
LIABILITIES AND STOCKHOLDERS' EQUITY (DEFICIT)		
Current liabilities:		
Notes payable	$ –	$ 67,800
Notes payable—related parties	1,200	110,610
Accounts payable	523,764	368,512
Customer deposits	3,212	–
Accrued expenses	57,597	51,581
Total current liabilities	$ 585,773	$598,503
Stockholders' equity (deficit):		
Common stock, par value $0.001, authorized 15,000,000 shares, issued and outstanding 3,342,483 shares in 1996; par value $1.00, authorized 5,000,000 shares, issued and outstanding 357,900 shares in 1995	$ 3,342	$ 358
Additional paid-in capital, including contributed services of $37,500 in 1996 and $50,000 in 1995	4,121,932	1,798,548
Less notes receivable for the purchase of common stock	(33,080)	–
Preferred stock, $.20 par value, authorized 1,000,000 shares; no shares issued and outstanding in 1996 and 1995	–	–
Accumulated deficit since December 7, 1995 (termination of S corporation status in which a deficit of $2,320,227 was applied against additional paid-in capital)	(520,594)	–
Accumulated deficit	–	(2,130,888)
Total stockholders' equity (deficit)	$3,571,600	$(331,982)
Total liabilities and stockholders' equity (deficit)	$4,157,373	$266,521

See that big $3 million cash item on the asset side of the balance sheet in 1996? That's the net proceeds the company took in from the IPO. Now here's the statement of cash flows from the same period:

GUARDIAN TECHNOLOGIES INTERNATIONAL, INC.
STATEMENT OF CASH FLOWS
FOR THE SIX MONTHS ENDED JUNE 30, 1996, AND 1995

(UNAUDITED)

	June 30, 1996	June 30, 1995
Cash flows from operating activities:		
Net loss	$(505,638)	$(308,421)
Adjustments to reconcile net loss to cash		
used by operating activities:		
Depreciation	5,156	15,187
Amortization	14,462	11,507
Contributed services	50,000	50,000
Change in assets and liabilities:		
(Increase) decrease in accounts receivable	(55,256)	21,523
(Increase) decrease in inventories	(72,395)	43,313
Increase in prepaid expenses and deposits	(3,505)	(15,374)
Increase in accounts payable and accrued expenses	409,951	127,897
Decrease in customer deposits	(54,859)	–
Net cash used in operating activities	$(212,084)	$ (54,368)
Cash flow from investing activities:		
Purchase of property and equipment	$(550,210)	$ –
Acquisition of patent rights	(9,544)	–
Net cash used in investing activities:	$(559,754)	$ –
Cash flows from financing activities:		
Proceeds from short-term borrowings	$ –	$ 185,910
Principal payments on short-term borrowings	(222,292)	(137,943)
Proceeds from public offering	4,985,250	–
Public offering costs	(1,286,783)	–

(continued on next page)

GUARDIAN TECHNOLOGIES INTERNATIONAL, INC.
STATEMENT OF CASH FLOWS (continued)
FOR THE SIX MONTHS ENDED JUNE 30, 1996, AND 1995

(UNAUDITED)

	June 30, 1996	June 30, 1995
Proceeds from issuance of common stock (prior to public offering)	–	15,000
Net cash provided by financing activities	$3,476,175	$62,967
Net increase in cash and cash equivalents	$ 2,704,337	$ 8,599
Cash and cash equivalents at beginning of period	376,307	3,016
Cash and cash equivalents at end of period	$3,080,644	$11,615
Supplemental disclosure of cash flow information		
Cash paid during the period for:		
Interest	$ 18,300	$ 2,362
Income taxes	$ –	$ –

See that −$212,084 number under "Net cash used in operating activities" as of June 30, 1996? That's the sum total of the actual cash money consumed in running the business for six months.

Now here's what the balance sheet looked like three and a half years later, in the autumn of 1999—the latest data available as I write:

GUARDIAN TECHNOLOGIES INTERNATIONAL, INC.
BALANCE SHEET
SEPTEMBER 30,1999

(UNAUDITED)

ASSETS

rrent assets:	
Cash and cash equivalents	$ 330,318
Accounts receivable	131,246
nventory	143,886
Notes receivable	285,000
Prepaid expenses and other	287,986
Total current assets	1,178,436
perty and equipment, net	55,087
estment carried at cost, plus equity	
n undistributed earnings	1,150,000
posits and other	117,019
Total assets	2,500,542

LIABILITIES AND STOCKHOLDERS' EQUITY

rrent liabilities:	
Accounts payable	103,565
Accrued expenses and other	37,264
Notes payable	91,978
Total current liabilities	232,807
areholders' equity	
Preferred stock, $.20 par value, 1,000,000 shares	
authorized; no shares issued and outstanding	–
Common stock, $.001 par value, 15,000,000 shares	
authorized; 1,310,498 issued and outstanding	1,311
Additional paid-in capital	4,507,227
Accumulated deficit	(2,240,803)
Total shareholders' equity	2,267,735
al liabilities and shareholders' equity	$2,500,542

Not only is most of the cash from the IPO gone, but so are most of the company's assets. Indeed, the whole balance sheet seems to be shrinking to oblivion.

Now look at the cash flow statement for the nine months also ending September 30, 1999:

GUARDIAN TECHNOLOGIES INTERNATIONAL, INC.
STATEMENTS OF CASH FLOWS
FOR THE NINE MONTHS ENDED SEPTEMBER 30

(UNAUDITED)

	1999	1998
Cash flows from operating activities:		
Net income (loss)	$ 36,202	$(280,051)
Adjustments to reconcile net income (loss) to cash		
provided by (used in) operating activities		
Depreciation	31,035	66,443
Amortization	6,885	6,149
Gain on sale of property and equipment	(109,759)	–
Compensation expense	–	36,500
Equity in net earnings of affiliated entity	(300,000)	–
Change in operating assets and liabilities:		
(Increase) decrease in:		
Accounts receivable	62,472	174,614
Inventories	36,900	238,510
Prepaid expenses and other	(117,793)	(100,199)
Increase (decrease) in:		
Accounts payable	(90,161)	(85,065)
Accrued expenses and other	25,057	(105,019)
Net cash provided by (used in) operating activities	(419,162)	(48,118)
Cash flow from investing activities:		
Purchase of property and equipment	(648)	(6,429)
Sale of property and equipment	877,941	–

cquisition of patent rights and certification	–	(1,300)
Payments on notes receivable	620,000	–
ssuance of notes receivable	(505,000)	(500,000)
vestment in Structural Holdings, Inc.	(850,000)	–
Jet cash provided by (used in) investing activities	142,293	(507,729)
sh flows from financing activities:		
Proceeds from short-term borrowings	91,978	–
Proceeds from long-term borrowings	–	1,900,000
Principal payments on long-term debt	(170,728)	(992,304)
Proceeds from issuance of common stock	100,000	–
Jet cash provided by (used in) financing activities	21,250	907,696
ease (decrease) in cash and cash equivalents	(255,619)	351,849
sh and cash equivalents, beginning of period	585,937	109,461
sh and cash equivalents, end of period	330,318	461,310
plemental disclosure of cash flow information:		
Cash paid for interest	37,609	$110,405
Debt assumed by sale of building	$1,857,379	$ –

While the balance sheet's assets have shrunk by close to 40 percent, the company is burning more cash in its operations. See that −$419,162 in "Net cash provided by (used in) operating activities"? Multiply it by four-thirds and you've got an annualized number (−$557,485.50). That is the sum burned up to run the company for a year—a company that is 40 percent smaller, in terms of assets under management, than it was three years earlier.

So add it all up and what investors got for investing their money with a celebrity and never checking the numbers that actually under-pinned the business was soaring cash flow losses, disappearing assets, dwindling shareholder equity, and a stock price that fell by 80 percent since its very first trade in the public market.

And the Guardian Technologies story is hardly unique. There are golfing great Jack Nicklaus's chain of golf instruction emporiums,

Golden Bear Golf; Donald Trump's gambling business, Trump Hotels and Casino Resorts; and the Olympic-class champ of them all, Planet Hollywood International, starring Demi Moore, Sylvester Stallone, and numerous other Hollywood figures.

Each of these companies was promoted to investors by brokers and investment bankers as a good place to put one's money precisely *because* of their association with some celebrity or other—and in each case the stocks in question turned out to be huge disappointments that in the end contained little or no cash to run the business.

Consider the sad fate of investors in Donald Trump's company, Trump Hotels and Casino Resorts. This is a Wall Street horror tale of what happens to investors when they ignore a company's cash flow situation and get distracted instead by such measures as EBITDA and earnings growth. They end up with a company having plenty of what doesn't matter, and not enough of what does—cold hard cash. In bull markets and booms, cash on hand often doesn't matter because rising stock prices allow companies to sell their shares to the public on the "invest in a celebrity" gimmick, and selling stock brings in some temporary cash. But once a particular company, or sector of the market, falls out of favor—or indeed, the whole market starts to weaken—these companies inevitably get flattened.

From start to finish, that has been the story of Mr. Donald Trump and his New Jersey–based casino business. His ability to conjure the appearance of great wealth out of very little actual net worth—both in his personal life and in the financial affairs of his company—has made him the poster boy for the American Dream. But behind the drawn curtains of his finances one finds very little real substance—which is why his stock was selling for more than $35 per share in the spring of 1996, and four years later, for barely $2.75.

As the world learned long ago, no one is a better source of information on the business world heroics of Donald Trump than Trump himself—all of which information has been set forth in fulsome detail in three separate volumes of his self-congratulatory autobiography, the high points of which get trotted out repeatedly in his habitually coitus interruptus campaigns for the presidency.

So let us move instead to the less-well-trodden ground of Trump the Business Legend, specifically his attempt to transfer the secret of his personal success (borrowing more money than he could ever hope to repay in a thousand lifetimes) to the company bearing his name. Sadly, the effort resulted in a debt load of such fabulous dimensions as to engulf and devour the whole of the cash flow thrown off by his company—a major operator in a business legendary for its production of cash . . . suggesting that the day may not be far off when Trump Hotels and Casino Resorts follows its namesake down the path into bankruptcy court that he himself trudged for certain of his businesses a decade earlier.

By industry standards, the Trump casino business is indeed a major player: a $1.4 billion-a-year (1999 revenues) business, with 9,000 employees. The trouble is, the entire business was assembled out of the business bankruptcy rubble of Trump's corporate financial collapse at the start of the 1990s (he never went bankrupt personally), and it was knitted together using borrowed money and financial engineering deals that enabled Trump to rebuild his fortune while impoverishing his shareholders in the process. For more than a decade, several Wall Street investment banks busied themselves force-feeding debt-driven financings into the company on Trump's behalf. In June 1995, the Wall Street investment bank Donaldson, Lufkin & Jenrette, unable to sell more debt, but needing to infuse Trump's business with cash from somewhere, took the stub end of the business—the ill-fated Trump Plaza casino—and bundled it together with some blue-sky plans for a riverboat casino in the Chicago area, then fobbed the whole thing off on the public at $14 per share in a $140 million stock offering.

This created a new company burdened with the same problem of excessive indebtedness as had plagued the previous ones. The offering statement was filled with happy-face talk about the "brand recognition" value of the Trump name, and of management's plans to "capitalize" on same. But the company was operating in the red already, and under a section labeled "Risk Factors" could be found a grim confession about the future: "Management does not currently anticipate being able to generate sufficient cash flow from its operations to repay a substantial portion of the [company's] mortgage notes, and cannot predict repayment prospects for the senior secured notes."

Yet for all the fine talk about restructuring and deleveraging, Trump's company has remained stuck with what—after a couple of additional clever gimmicks—has ballooned into a staggering $1.8 billion in long-term debt on its balance sheet, making it, relative to its size, one of the most heavily indebted operations in American business.

Because of that indebtedness, the company has been losing money from day one of the income statement. But the real problem is that the company's actual flow of cold hard cash simply hasn't been enough to pay the bills and still keep the facilities spiffed up and inviting-looking. So, behind the overwrought edifice of Mr. Trump's onion-spired architectural egregium (aka "the Taj") and the associated other colossi of his gambling spectacularia, lurked the Potemkin Village squalor of a deferred maintenance nightmare, with huge and ever-growing capital costs that have gone unmet because there just wasn't enough money for the job.

Meanwhile, the stock has endured a three-year-long swan dive that has carried it from more than $30 per share to less than $2 these days, as if the word has gotten around that when you hit the jackpot at one of Trump's slots, the machines spray you with *E. coli* germs instead of money. In fact, the reason for the slide was visible to anyone who took the trouble to look at almost any quarterly or annual report filed by Trump's company with the SEC.

Here is the Trump Hotels and Casino Resorts statement of cash flows for the years ended December 31, 1996, 1997, and 1998—the latest full-year reporting periods available for the company at the time of this writing. The filing was plucked in barely thirty seconds' time from the www.freedgar.com Web site, but could as easily have been retrieved from any of a dozen different sites.

TRUMP HOTELS AND CASINO RESORTS, INC.
CONSOLIDATED STATEMENTS OF CASH FLOWS
FOR THE YEARS ENDED DECEMBER 31, 1996, 1997, AND 1998
(in thousands)

	1996	1997	1998
Cash flows from operating activities:			
Net loss	$(65,677)	$(42,128)	$(39,718)
Adjustments to reconcile net loss to net			
cash flows provided by operating activities:			
Noncash charges:			
Issuance of stock grant awards and			
accretion of phantom stock units	467	194	–
Issuance of debt in exchange for			
accrued interest	4,589	10,156	11,614
Extraordinary loss	60,732	–	–
Depreciation and amortization	69,035	89,094	84,123
Minority interest in net loss	(26,022)	(24,186)	(22,878)
Accretion of discount on mortgage			
notes and amortization of loan costs	7,475	11,062	12,331

(continued on next page)

TRUMP HOTELS AND CASINO RESORTS, INC.
CONSOLIDATED STATEMENTS OF CASH FLOWS (continued)
FOR THE YEARS ENDED DECEMBER 31, 1996, 1997, AND 1998
(in thousands)

	1996	1997	199
Provisions for losses on receivables	9,140	9,160	15,535
Equity in loss from Buffington Harbor L.L.C.	925	3,478	2,969
Interest income Castle-PIK notes	(5,491)	(9,190)	(10,591
Valuation allowance of CRDA investments and amortization of Indiana gaming costs	3,371	8,944	7,155
Increase in receivables	(19,661)	(25,138)	(17,550
Decrease (increase) in inventories	175	(2,301)	207
Increase in due from affiliates	(1,230)	(14,769)	(11,953
Decrease (increase) in prepaid expenses and other current assets	1,129	(3,454)	(4,101
Increase in other assets	(15,992)	(538)	(5,507
Increase (decrease) in accounts payable, other accrued expenses, and other current liabilities	16,866	(7,110)	8,246
(Decrease) increase in accrued interest payable	(33,499)	645	1,341
Decrease in other long-term liabilities	(1,872)	(2,864)	(2,738
Net cash provided by operating activities	4,460	1,055	28,488
Cash flows from investing activities:			
Purchase of property and equipment, net	(245,424)	(79,246)	(38,294
Restricted cash	52,043	(13,000)	10,477
Purchase of CRDA investments, net	(7,122)	(11,996)	(10,848
Investment in Buffington Harbor L.L.C.	(24,884)	(1,231)	(199
Investment in Trump's Castle PIK notes	(38,700)	–	–
Purchase of Taj Holding, net of cash received	46,714	–	–
Purchase of Trump's Castle, net of cash received	17,604	–	–
Net cash used in investing activities	(199,769)	(105,473)	(38,86

sh flows from financing activities:			
Purchase of Treasury stock	–	(17,276)	(2,259)
ssuance of common stock, net	386,062	–	–
ssuance of Trump AC notes	1,200,000	95,605	–
Retirement of long-term debt	(1,156,836)	–	–
Retirement of NatWest loan	(36,500)	–	–
Debt issuance costs	(41,405)	(4,254)	(2,021)
Debt payments–other	(39,187)	(21,518)	(77,918)
Proceeds from borrowings	39,716	16,440	67,000
Net cash provided by (used in) financing activities	351,850	68,997	(15,198)
increase (decrease) in cash and ash equivalents	156,541	(35,421)	(25,571)
sh and cash equivalents at beginning of period	19,208	175,749	140,328
sh and cash equivalents at end of period	$175,749	$140,328	$144,757

See that $28.5 million total for "Net cash provided by operating activities" in 1998? It's certainly better than the 1997 or 1996 numbers, right? But if you look down to the section entitled "Cash flows from investing activities" you'll see a 1998 item entitled "Purchase of property and equipment, net" in the amount of $38.3 million. That's the amount of money the company spent during the year on new equipment and maintenance of what it already owned. Should it have spent more, simply to keep even with the inevitable deterioration of what was already there? Well, look back up to the "Cash flows from operating activities" section and you'll see by how much money the company wrote down its existing property and equipment ("Depreciation and amortization") during the year: $84.1 million.

In other words, the company wrote off $84.1 million worth of its assets during the year as functionally worthless, and reduced its balance sheet asset base accordingly. But it reinvested only $38.3 million back into the business—and even that lowly amount was nearly $10 million more than its total cash flow from operations during the year. This was no òne-time fluke but a pattern that had been repeating itself year after year.

The main reason for the crunch was the more than $200 million per year in interest costs on the debt—a burden taken on by the company's stockholders for the privilege of having the Trump name hang over the door of their company's casino entrances. With a fifth of a billion dollars coming right off the top every year, there's simply not enough left to run the company in a way that makes it worth something as a long-term investment. That would require reinvesting surplus cash back into the operation.

Thanks to Donald's mountain of debt, there simply is no surplus cash; the actual, tangible assets of the business—the slot machines and roulette tables, the hotel rooms and lobbies, and roofs on the buildings—are wearing out and being depreciated on the income statement faster than they're being replenished, rebuilt, and improved via the cash flow statement. In the process, the equity on the balance sheet is disappearing. (When I visited the Trump Castle Hotel in Atlantic City in the summer of 1998 I found myself marveling not at the busloads of bankrupted and ruined day-trippers heading homeward from their recreational adventure to the Jersey Shore, but at the threadbare feel of the place. Trump's overflowing ego had inspired him to place a neon sign spelling out "Trump Castle" in twenty-foot-high letters atop the building. Unfortunately, the scrimping on maintenance extended all the way to the roof, where two of the letters had burned out on the sign and not been replaced, leading to the hilarious result that the sign lit up the night sky proclaiming the building beneath it to be the "rump astle" hotel.)

Simple arithmetic now tells us that the gambling colossus over which Mr. Trump presides and holds a controlling 38 percent stake may be purchased and driven off the lot for just a few farthings north of $60 million. Which in turn means that Mr. Trump's own stake in the matter reduces down to a clarified gruel of less than $23 million.

As a contrast, take a look at Bill Gates, who dresses in attire that would have made Sam Walton look spiffy, owns a company with $14 billion worth of tens and twenties on tap (cash and cash equivalents as we say in the game), and don't owe nuttin' to no one. Meanwhile, here we still find the Sun King, alone on stage in his shiny suit finery, reading from his *I'm Donald Trump!* script to the emptied seats of an audience that has long since left the theater. Of course, no longer can he command face time in prime time, so we now tend to encounter him rattling up and down the back stairs of the media like mother's nutty brother. Flip on the tube some rainy Sunday afternoon and there's the Donster, doing weekend cable TV. What's left after that—playing straight man for Don Imus on AM radio? The wealth and power of Trump remains what it always has been—a financial hologram conjuring the Oz-like image of all that he's got while handily leaving out all that he owes, even as he boasts of his controlling interest in a casino operation that, so far as his shareholders are concerned, has all the financial sex appeal of an open sore on one's personal parts.

At $2.75 per share, Wall Street is now valuing Trump Hotels and Casino Resorts at more or less $60 million—which seems like a pittance until you realize that, on a balance sheet basis, $60 million may in fact be about all the company is worth.

True, the balance sheet shows working capital (current assets minus current liabilities) alone of somewhere around $76 million. But that only tells you what would be left if you paid off all the short-term debts with the company's short-term assets. As for the rest of the balance sheet, well, here's where it gets interesting because at least $140 million of the company's long-term assets appear to depend one way or another on the viability of the company's long-term debt in order to remain viable themselves. That's because, at some point along the way, Trump had the company go into the market and actually buy back some of the bonds it had previously sold to the public—the purpose of the buyback apparently being to prop up the price of the bonds in the market. In any case, those bonds thereafter began appearing as roughly $140 million worth of assets on the balance sheet even though, if the company defaults on repaying them, they'll basically be worth nothing in spite of the fact that the company will continue to owe the money on the liability side of the balance sheet.

Get all that stuff out of the picture and Trump Hotels and Casino Resorts' actual honest-to-God, take-'em-to-the-bank long-term assets amount to not much more than $2 billion—against which rest more than $1.8 billion worth of long-term debts. And therein lies the dark cloud of uncertainty hovering over the whole operation, for how much of that asset base consists of leaky roofs, threadbare carpets, paint-peeling walls, and God knows what else?

One of the best, most time- and labor-saving tools I know of to spot cash flow problems in the making—for celebrity stocks or indeed any company—is a software program called Spredgar. This nifty little program runs in conjunction with Microsoft Excel spreadsheets (more about them in a minute) to make fabulously enlightening charts out of any 10-K or 10-Q filing in the EDGAR database. Hence the name "Spredgar"—as in, spreadsheets and EDGAR, get it?

A spreadsheet refers to a class of mathematical computer programs that can perform an almost incomprehensible range of calculations, from the extremely simple to the room-emptyingly complex. Ten years ago there were a number of different spreadsheet programs available for desktop computers, but most are no longer on the market. The race has pretty much come down to the Excel program from Microsoft and the Lotus 1-2-3 program from IBM. Since the folks at

Spredgar never bothered to write a program that can run with Lotus you can get a pretty good sense of which way things are moving in the field.

In any case, to learn more about spreadsheets and how to use the Excel package from Microsoft, go to the Web site for Barnes & Noble (www.barnesandnoble.com) or Amazon.com (www.amazon.com) or Borders (www.borders.com) and order a copy of the *10 Minute Guide to Excel 97* by Jennifer Fulton, which is by far the easiest, clearest, and most useful introduction you'll find anywhere for using spreadsheets. The book is available for $11.99 and is worth every penny. (Forget about the user's guide that comes with Excel itself; the thing stinks.)

Next, if you don't already own an Excel program, buy one. All in all, you'll get the best price by buying it as part of Microsoft's Office 2000 "suite," which includes Excel, Microsoft's Word 2000 word processing program, and a calendaring, e-mail, and personal contacts package known as Outlook 2000. Whatever you may think of Microsoft or Bill Gates, the whole world is using his products. If you don't use Excel, you'll miss out not only on Spredgar, but lots of other programming on the Web that's been written specifically for Microsoft products.

Anyway, once you've got Excel installed on your computer, go to the Web site for Spredgar—www.spredgar.com—and order a copy of the Spredgar program. It sells for $250, but is 50% for students and it will save you hundreds of hours of drudge work yearly. All you do is click on the link that says "Download Now," and the package will install itself on your machine, embedding itself in your Excel program in about twenty minutes. You can try it out free for a day and see if you like it, and my bet is you'll be amazed at what it does.

For example, just open up your Excel program and click on the top of the page, on a button labeled "Spredgar." Up will pop an up-to-the-minute list of every company filing in the EDGAR database. Then just scroll through until you find the company you want to Spredgarize and click on it. The program will then dial into the Securities and Exchange Commission's database in Washington and pull into your computer a complete list of all the filings in the EDGAR database for that company.

Next, select the latest quarterly or annual report (10-Q or 10-K) from the list and click on it. In a flash, the Spredgar program will extract all the data from the filing and assemble it into just about every financial ratio, chart, graph, and table you can think of. Ten years ago, teams of investment bank analysts would spend days preparing such charts and tables for their firm's clients, and the clients would pay tens of thousands of dollars to get them. Thanks to the EDGAR database, the Internet, the Spredgar package, and your home computer, you can get exactly the same thing in a few seconds, for a modest investment.

On the other hand, if you don't want to purchase Spredgar and an Excel program, or commit the time to learning to use them (it can take a couple of hours), just go to a site like

www.moneycentral.msn.com,

click on "Investor," then use the "Custom Search" feature on the "Finder" tab to run a screen that searches for companies in any given industry that are selling for a lower "stock price to cash flow per share" ratio than the average for the industry as a whole. Then you can examine the individual cash flow statements of the companies that interest you to see if they are worth your money.

Had you done that in the spring of 1998 you might have come up with a precision instrument maker named Newport Corp. It was selling for 18 times cash flow at the time, when its rivals were all selling at higher multiples, which is why I recommended it in *Playboy* that June as a good long-term investment. Two years later, Newport was selling for nearly $190 per share, or more than 100 times earnings, before eventually collapsing in the dot.com meltdown. You would have had the same luck with Harley-Davidson, the motorcycle folks, if you'd bought that company at the end of 1994 when I recommended doing so in the pages of *Esquire*. At the time, Harley-Davidson was selling for roughly 13 times cash flow when the rest of its peer group were all selling for higher P/Es. Since then cash flow has doubled and the share price has quintupled.

Most important of all, you'd have seen that at its high of more than $35 per share in June of 1996, Trump Hotels and Casino Resorts was selling for an absurd 200 times cash flow when a rival like Mirage Resorts, which was bigger and healthier in every way, was selling at the same time for barely 14 times cash flow. Enough said.

chapter eight

Over the Counter Bulletin Board Stocks: The Ultimate Minefield for Investors

This much I know: On Wall Street, there is no riskier place to put your money than the Over the Counter, or OTC, Bulletin Board market, as it is known these days. Swindlers abound, law enforcement is lax, and if you toy with it long enough, you're bound to get scammed. And I also know something else: With the rise of the Internet, all of the above goes twice over, as the Bulletin Board has developed into a global bunco emporium in which the unwary are as likely to be fleeced by scamsters operating out of a shell company hideout in the Isle of Man as by a gang of Mafia wiseguys in Brooklyn—both of which are such commonplace occurrences you just wouldn't believe it.

Through the 1990s, the Bulletin Board—which mainly lists prices of "penny stock" (the polite word is "microcap") companies—was easily the most volatile, crime-infested securities market in America . . . mainly because stocks could be traded on it without the issuing companies having to file financial reports of any sort, to anyone. This opened up the possibility of abuses beyond reckoning.

A financial filing requirement was enacted at the start of 1999, and a phase-in period followed, with the result that by the time this book went to press, all Bulletin Board companies were either filing periodic financial reports to the SEC or had been ejected from the system and were trading in the "pink sheets" (more about these shortly). In practical terms, though, nothing much has changed since the crime and larceny has simply moved from the Bulletin Board to the pink sheets, where the thievery and swindling continue unabated.

Think of this whole world as Wall Street's answer to Manhattan in *Escape from New York* and you'll have the basic idea of what's going on here—a market that abounds with charlatans, con artists, liars, thieves, Mafia torpedoes, drug dealers, and on and on. You can make a lot of money in such a place, but you can also ruin your life. Beware.

In this chapter we'll look at how suckers are fleeced in this ultimate sub-basement of Wall Street, and how the game is played by "pump-and-dump" promoters who use press releases and Internet message boards as their bait to reel in the gullible and the greedy. And if, after all that, you still want to try your hand, I'll give you some tips for how to turn the odds in your favor, at least momentarily. You'll learn about the Bulletin Board Web site maintained by the National Association of Securities Dealers (www.otcbb.com), about sites maintained by Bulletin Board stock promoters like Charles Arnold

(www.stockmaker.com),

and Edward Williamson, a convicted murderer who served time in federal prison for killing a taxi driver back in the 1960s and up until recently ran a penny stock promotion site under the name

www.stocksfifthavenue.com.

We'll also take a tour of various message boards and chat rooms like those of Raging Bull (www.ragingbull.com) and Silicon Investor (www.siliconinvestor.com) to see how promoters spread their fertilizer.

But before getting into any of that, first a bit of background about the Over the Counter market and the pink sheets—and how they came to be the stalking grounds for Wall Street's most larcenous rogues. Both are, embarrassingly enough, the direct outgrowth of the exclusionary, monopolistic practices that have governed the behavior of the New York Stock Exchange for most of its 200-plus years of existence.

From the moment some twenty-four New York merchants met in Corre's Hotel in lower Manhattan on March 21, 1792, and agreed to begin trading post–Revolutionary War government bank stocks and bonds based on prices quoted only among themselves—that meeting being said by historians to mark the birth of the NYSE—the Exchange has viewed itself as the organizational embodiment of Wall Street itself. Yet the price that investors have paid for such arrogance has been the proliferation of rogue venues like the Over the Counter market, and more recently, the Bulletin Board.

For several months following that long ago meeting at Corre's Hotel, the cartel met under a buttonwood tree at No. 68 Wall Street. But business was picking up (and also it would rain from time to time) so the group moved inside and began meeting at a coffeehouse at the corner of William and Wall streets. In 1817 the boys drew up a constitution and began selling "seats"—in effect, lifetime memberships—to what they were now calling their "Exchange," for $400 each. Finally, in 1863 the Exchange took up residence at its present address down the street.

All this growth took place against the backdrop of the most phenomenal accumulation of financial capital in human history, as the American continent was opened to exploration and development and the wealth of the world poured in to harvest the bounty while the fruits of that investment flowed back out. The New York Stock Exchange was the eye of the needle through which nearly all of it moved, from the British capital that financed America's railroads, to the homegrown capital of financiers like J. P. Morgan that accumulated as a result.

By century's end there were railroad stocks, sugar stocks, telegraph stocks, electric stocks, coal and iron stocks, gas stocks, rubber stocks, and more. There was even a daily newspaper—the *Wall Street Journal*—to follow their daily prices on the only place an investor could buy or sell any of them: the New York Stock Exchange. With the twentieth century came the Rockefellers and Standard Oil, the du Ponts, and General Motors. Stocks bearing names like U.S. Steel and Sears, Roebuck materialized. There was Westinghouse, Anaconda Copper, Woolworth Co., and American Can Co.—the entire parade of blue-chip American business . . . and once again the only place you could invest in any of it was on the New York Stock Exchange.

When the stock market crashed in 1929—at the end of a speculative bubble not unlike the one that began developing in the latter half of the 1990s in technology stocks—and the Roosevelt administration later passed legislation creating the Securities and Exchange Commission to protect individual investors from the sort of price rigging and market manipulation that had flourished in the 1920s, the New York Stock Exchange was given special treatment and allowed to police its members and activities on its own. It was a move that further cemented its self-perception as an organization that existed by some sort of divine right as a monopoly enterprise in the heart of free enterprise capitalism.

But monopolies are dictatorships of the marketplace, and by the start of the 1920s a rebellion was already under way. The revolt began on June 27, 1921, when a group of sidewalk brokers who had been excluded from the NYSE and had taken to conducting their business daily on the sidewalk at the corner of William and Beaver streets, marched up Wall Street singing the Star-Spangled Banner and took up residence in a newly completed exchange of their own across Broadway, behind Trinity Church. They called their new home the New York Curb Exchange, and kept that name for the next thirty-two years, until changing it in 1953 to the American Stock Exchange.

Meanwhile, still other brokers had begun trading in stocks that were considered so wildly speculative that neither the NYSE nor the Curb Exchange wanted to touch them. This came to be known as the Over the Counter market, and with the arrival of computers on Wall Street at the start of the 1970s, the trade association representing these brokers—the National Association of Securities Dealers (NASD)—instantly saw an opportunity.

For the National Association of Securities Dealers, the arrival of the computer on Wall Street was the rough equivalent of the discovery of fire: Nothing afterward was ever the same again.

Officials at NASDAQ don't like to be reminded of the fact, but it was not so many years ago when the whole of NASDAQ was known as simply the Over the Counter market—the place where you'd go to find a quote on a stock so obscure and unloved that no bona fide exchange would even list it for trading. Back when I first began covering Wall Street at the end of the go-go 1960s, there were men on the Street whose only business in life (at least the only business about which they'd talk to a reporter) was answering the phone in dingy offices and quoting Over the Counter stock prices to customers.

It was a business filled with men who chewed on White Owl cigars and lived in Scarsdale and other such places. Some of them made you want to rush right home and take a good long bath. I knew one such man, named Richard. He was a big, roly-poly fellow who came to work in a chauffeured limo each morning from his home in Greenwich. And the thing I remember most about him—except for his manner of quoting stock prices (which I'll get to in a minute)—was the remarkable instability that seemed to infect his finances. One day he was bidding on Kennedy's yacht, the next day the sheriff was showing up with an attachment order and hauling off the living room furniture.

I think the instability must have derived from the uncertain cash flow that came with the business of quoting prices in OTC stocks. Here's how Richard would try to improve that situation if you called up for a "bid" on, say, Technitronics, Inc. (companies that ended with "tronics" being big in those days): He'd try to chisel you a couple of bucks on the price—something that could not happen on the NYSE because the specialist would never get involved in the first place.

Richard would say, "Techie...? Wayduhminit..." and begin scratching through various piles of papers on his desk.

If he couldn't find what he was looking for in, say, ten seconds, he'd bellow in the general direction of the hallway, "Marion! Bring me them damned quote sheets...!" and by and by this woman would come in with a lipstick-stained Chesterfield in one hand, and a sheaf of papers in the other. She'd toss them indifferently on his desk, then depart in a cloud of exhaled cigarette smoke.

Through all this, Richard's customer would be waiting on the other end of the phone for Richard to give him the bid on "Techie," which he'd find (if he was lucky) on one of the pieces of paper that Marion had tossed onto his desk. The particular piece of paper in question—which (presumably) would have arrived that morning in the mail—would be a list of the latest (and presumably best) quoted bids and asks on not just Techie but all actively traded Over the Counter stocks. All broker-dealers in OTC stocks were expected to report their transactions daily to the clearinghouse that published the list, but mostly Richard never bothered—and when he did, he usually marked up the price (which is what everyone else did also).

Now if it turned out—to Richard's great good fortune (and your bad luck)—that Richard himself actually owned some shares in Techie, and he were to see from the papers that Marion had given him that the stock had traded only a day earlier at $3 on the bid, he would turn back to the phone and say something designed to improve his cash flow at his customer's expense.

He'd say, "Yeah . . . Techie . . . it's five and an eighth, ya want some . . . ?" and proceed to sell you, at a roughly 66 percent markup from the going price, a fistful of Techie from his very own personal account. Nice arrangement, no? Somebody would call up asking to buy a $3 stock, and his broker would get to sell it to him for $5-plus— and no one would be the wiser.

That would be Richard with his "dealer" hat on—selling you shares from his own personal inventory at the outrageous "spreads" for which the OTC market was famous.

On the other hand, let's say Richard wasn't "long" Techie after all. Were that the case, and you wanted some, he'd have to go out and actually find some. Richard hated doing that because it amounted to real work. So he'd turn back to the phone and say (possibly just plucking a number out of the blue), "It's five dollars on the bid but I gotta phone around if you want some." Then he'd go out for lunch, inhale a plate of oysters Rockefeller and the end cut of a standing rib roast over at Fraunces Tavern or maybe Michael's Pub, then waddle back to the office by way of one or two of his buddies' places, looking for anyone who might be long some Techie and be willing to let it go for $4. This would be Richard with his "broker's" hat on—same outrageous markup, with Richard himself once again stepping into the transaction as a dealer before the shares ever reached his customer.

The Richards of Wall Street disappeared in the 1970s with the arrival of the computer, which enabled the National Association of Securities Dealers to institute a system for electronically posting all

OTC stock transactions on computer screens. But their legacy—and the essentially corrupt system of multiple broker-dealers all scamming each other and the public while quoting competing prices on stocks—remains the basis of what is now known as the NASDAQ (for National Association of Securities Dealers Automatic Quotations system) stock exchange.

There are three submarkets within NASDAQ: the NASDAQ National Market, which consists of roughly 3,000 companies that can show at least 400 shareholders and a minimum $5 per share stock price; the NASDAQ Small Cap market, which consists of some 1,400 smaller and cheesier companies; and finally, the OTC Bulletin Board, which consists of 6,500 securities that are basically not worth much of anything at all but nonetheless have more than 400 broker-dealers willing and even eager to quote prices in their shares.

These dealers are attracted to the Bulletin Board for the same reason you find seagulls over landfills: Just beneath the surface lies a mountain of buried garbage. In the case of the Bulletin Board, the garbage came, up until the end of the 1990s, in the form of what were known as "nonfiling" companies—referring to businesses that were so small and cruddy as to be exempt, under one rule or another, from having to file audited financial statements with either the SEC or their shareholders. In other words, they were companies that could make public statements about their financials without actually having to back up anything they say. They could issue press releases full of the most outrageous malarkey imaginable, and there'd be no way to check the accuracy of the claims contained in it.

Why it is that the SEC allows brokerage companies to publish buy-and-sell quotes for the stocks of companies that cannot supply audited financial statements even to their own shareholders, let alone anyone else, is one of life's enduring mysteries. Nonetheless, it appears that the regulators thought they were somehow serving the public interest when, back in 1997, they implemented a permanent system of electronically publishing quotes from broker-dealers in Bulletin Board stocks.

The basic idea seems to have been to increase "transparency" (a fancy way of saying "to discourage price-rigging") in the Over the Counter market by requiring broker-dealers to publish their latest reported transactions in Bulletin Board stocks for all other broker-dealers to see and act on instantly.

In fact, the implementation of the OTC Bulletin Board rule, in April of 1997, simply multiplied the opportunities for abuse almost infinitely, since, with the rule's enactment, quoted prices for essentially worthless companies became suddenly available, on a second-to-second basis via the Internet, to investors all over the world.

This was all supposed to change with the enactment, beginning in 1999, of an NASD rule requiring all Bulletin Board stocks to file regular financial statements with the SEC or be delisted from the NASDAQ system altogether and thrown into the pink sheets—the hard copy system of printed weekly quotes that was used as far back as the days of our Richard, the cigar-chomping broker-dealer from forty years ago. But the pink sheets, published by a New Jersey–based company named the National Quotation Service, are themselves now being automated, and by the time you read these words, the quotes will almost certainly be available worldwide on the Web, meaning that, for all practical purposes, nothing will have changed at all.

The best way to understand how Bulletin Board stock swindles work on the Web is to look at a couple of case studies. Consider in that regard the $1.2 billion hot-air balloon created out of nothing but a series of misleading press releases distributed over the Internet in the winter of 1998–99 by a delicensed and disgraced former stockbroker named Peter Tosto. Five stocks in all were involved in Tosto's scam—all secretly linked together, promoted, and controlled by Tosto from an office over a five-and-dime store in rural Georgia.

Nearly a decade earlier, Tosto had been expelled from the securities industry for swindling his own clients as a stockbroker. Having lost his license as a broker in the process, he simply set up a "public relations" firm named Investor Relations and started swindling investors all over again. And every time the SEC shut him down he started right up again.

Also mixed up in the affair was a Los Angeles–based brokerage firm named J. Alexander Securities. In September of 1998, J. Alexander was sued by a Wall Street investment firm, National Financial Services Corp., for promoting trading in a Bulletin Board stock—H&R Enterprises—that quickly became the focus of what the plaintiffs termed a "massive international securities market manipulation" in the summer of 1997.

J. Alexander Securities surfaced thereafter in connection with three companies—Citron, Electronic Transfer Associates, and Polus Corp.—that Tosto acquired as defunct penny stock shell companies. Using J. Alexander as their sponsor, Tosto got them listed for trading on the Bulletin Board, and they began changing hands at pennies per share in the summer and autumn of 1998.

When trading in the shares of the three companies exploded in the winter of 1998–99, I contacted the J. Alexander company to ask for copies of whatever financial statements were available on the three companies. But an official at the firm said to contact the companies directly—which proved impossible since all either had no phone numbers or had phones that were answered by voice mail recordings. Two of the companies turned out to have no addresses at all.

These three companies—together with two other Bulletin Board stocks in the ring—had nothing in common beyond the fact that all began issuing press releases in late 1998, talking up their futures as Internet companies.

As is typical in such hustles, the press releases were distributed by two competing organizations: New York–based PR News Wire, and the Business Wire of San Francisco. Both organizations serve the financial public relations community, and have policies of accepting press releases only from "member" organizations that fill out questionnaires indicating who they are. But beyond that, the organizations make no attempt to determine the accuracy of what's in the releases they distribute. The releases could claim that the issuing companies discovered gold in downtown Newark, New Jersey, and neither organization would ask them to prove it before sending out the release.

The releases go everywhere. They are distributed electronically to the main news wire services (Associated Press and Reuters), to newspapers, television, and radio newsrooms, to magazines, and to countless Web site operators. As a result, there is not a major investment site on the Web that doesn't wind up posting these releases on their sites as soon as they become available, linking them, as "news," to the stocks of whatever companies are mentioned in the releases. Thus, if you were to go, for example, to the Yahoo financial Web site

http://finance.yahoo.com

—and type in the quote symbol EDV for Envision Development Corp., an Internet outfit, you'll be presented with a quote and links for additional information about the company. One of those links will be labeled "news." Click on it and you'll get a list of headlines from Business Wire–distributed releases, issued by Envision Development going back several months. Of course these aren't news at all, just self-serving promotional items, issued by the company under the guise of being news, to bolster the company's stock price.

There is nothing illegal in this practice, just rather slimy—and the fact is, anyone who wants to invest in Envision Development can click on another "Additional Information" link on the Yahoo page and actually look at Envision's latest available financials, provided free of charge, though in abbreviated form, by Zacks Investment Research, a popular research service on the Web. Since Envision is a fully reporting operation on the NASDAQ exchange, it routinely files financial reports to the SEC. Research outfits like Zacks obtain them, boil them down, and sell them to the public—or, in this case, to Yahoo, which gives them away as a premium item to get people to use the Yahoo site.

But when a company issues a press release without actual backup financial data on file with the SEC, there's nothing for investors to go on except what's claimed in the release itself—and therein lay the opportunity that bunco artist Peter Tosto exploited in his swindle. Not only did his releases offer no supporting documentation for his claims, the releases came without even identifying Tosto as the author. Instead, the releases listed only a "contact" name and a telephone number in the rural town of Madison, Georgia. When I called the number, it was invariably answered by someone saying, "Corporate offices" or "Marketing consultants" and refusing to give his actual name. It was Tosto, in disguise.

Yet those releases were enough to stimulate interest in the stock of Tosto's five companies among traders, and as the prices rose, more traders piled in, sending the prices higher and higher, creating, in the end, a combined market value of more than $1.2 billion for the group.

Many of the shares of these companies reached investors, amazingly enough, by way of the white-shoe Wall Street brokerage firm of Morgan Stanley Dean Witter. One broker, in the firm's Austin, Texas, office, said he had been approached in a cold call roughly a year and a half earlier by a man identifying himself as Peter Lybrant. According to the broker, Lybrant claimed to be involved in financial consulting, and began passing along tips about hot Bulletin Board stocks, and the broker began loading up, both for himself and his clients. "I was talking to Lybrant five times a day," said the broker. "The stocks were flying." Meanwhile, the broker had passed along Lybrant's name to a Morgan Stanley colleague in the firm's Pikesville, Kentucky, office, and that broker too began loading up.

Both brokers said they had no idea that the man they were talking to—ostensibly Peter Lybrant—was actually Peter Tosto. But at least one individual who soon became involved in the operation said it wasn't long before he grew suspicious of Lybrant/Tosto's bona fides.

That person was a Beverly Hills stock promoter named Michael Ager, who was introduced to Tosto (who called himself Lybrant) through the Morgan Stanley broker in Austin. As a result of that introduction, Ager and a colleague met with Lybrant/Tosto over the Thanksgiving 1998 weekend at an Orlando hotel, listening as the man invited them to take on several companies and pump up their market values.

"He had five or six companies," said Ager. "He said, 'You can work one of them or all of them, I don't care. We just need to get volume.' He wanted us to get started immediately."

According to Ager, the man thereupon opened up a briefcase and showed him a valiseful of stock certificates, saying the shares represented essentially the entire public float of one of the companies.

"He said 50,000 shares of buying in the company would put the stock [then selling at $3] to $10 to $12 immediately."

Ager says he grew suspicious when he asked the man for a business card and he said he didn't have one. But that suspicion was apparently not enough to discourage him from becoming involved in the promotion of the stocks.

"We promoted one of the companies on our Web site [www.topstock.com]," says Ager. "And we did a dog-and-pony show with a lot of brokers, and the stock started to take off."

Behind this $1.2 billion microcap illusion of real business was, of course, the conjurer who concocted it in the first place: Peter Tosto. Officials in the Madison, Georgia, police department said he had blown into town about a year earlier, and was mostly known for his

Rolex watches and flashy cars. Another thing the locals noted was that he married a woman from out of town and immediately took *her* last name—Lybrant—while dropping his own. Only afterward, when news of his scam broke and the media descended on Madison did it become clear what Tosto had been up to: Having been permanently enjoined from scams on the Bulletin Board, he had simply moved from Los Angeles to Georgia, taken his wife's name as his own, then set himself right back up in business all over again—this time using the Internet to promote his billion-dollar swindle.

I published a story on MSNBC.com about all this and thereafter received lots of e-mail from people who had pumped a collective fortune into the stocks of Tosto's companies, only to see it all go up in smoke when federal authorities shut him down. And don't think the people who invested in these stocks were ignorant, foolish investors who knew nothing of Wall Street and finance. In the main, the thousands who got duped were either day traders looking for a quick killing but were unable to get out quickly enough to avoid getting fleeced themselves, or people who believed the claims of Tosto's bogus press releases and wound up simply throwing their money away.

Here's a letter from one such individual, a senior consultant for Exxon:

> *I have been caught in what I am fast learning was a scam from the word go. I learned of the company and stock, Citron, on a Web site and followed it for a couple of days. I then placed an order to buy thirty shares. I wound up buying at the peak—$40 per share—only to watch the stock fall to half that value by the end of the day. To add to my frustration, I learned a couple of days later, as did many others, that the SEC had suspended trading.*

The letter writer went on to agonize over having made the investment, and to ask if there were anything he could now do.

The answer, unfortunately, was that there was nothing to do—nothing because the investors had all walked into the situation without bothering to ask any questions about the bona fides of the companies in which they were preparing to invest. Now they were upset because the trap into which they had walked had snapped shut on their money.

A year later the jaws of justice finally snapped shut on Tosto himself. Following publication of my story, the U.S. Department of Justice and the Securities and Exchange Commission opened investigations into Tosto's activities, and wound up filing both criminal and civil charges against him. In Washington, the SEC charged Tosto and three cohorts with rigging the market in the three worthless penny stocks named in the MSNBC story: Polus, Citron, and Electronic Transfer Associates. In New York, federal agents arrested Tosto and charged him with securities fraud, perjury, obstruction of justice, and making false statements to federal prosecutors.

In their complaint, federal prosecutors charged Tosto with masterminding a scheme to manipulate the share prices of three dormant shell companies from pennies to as much as $40 per share, by market-rigging. Then, say the feds, Tosto reaped upward of $6 million of illegal profits by selling shares he secretly held in the companies, and depositing the proceeds in offshore bank accounts in the Isle of Man, Mauritius, and elsewhere.

As of this writing Tosto faces a total of fifty-five years in federal prison, and $12 million in fines, plus restitution of any illegal profits, on the criminal charges. That may be some sort of moral victory for his fleeced shareholders, but they shouldn't count on recovering much of their losses from him. That's because, although he personally appears to have profited to the tune of $6 million in the hustle, his investors lost a total of nearly $1.2 billion on the worthless shares.

• • •

Sadly, in the penny stock market such prosecutions are rare, and for every Tosto the feds catch, ten get away. That's because the SEC's Enforcement Division, which has the frontline jurisdiction in policing the market, is grossly understaffed for the job, and the bunco artists know it. Simply reading all the bogus and misleading "news" releases that pour forth from the Business Wire and PR News Wire every day would overwhelm the regulators—and reading them is just one step of dozens in developing cases that can stand up in court. "We've got limited manpower, so we have to focus our resources on cases that will do the most good," says SEC chairman Arthur Levitt. In other words, if you only steal a little—and thereby manage to scoot beneath the SEC's radar—you're not likely to get rousted by the cops at all.

Consider the instructive case of an indefatigable penny stock promoter named Edward Williamson. Williamson, fifty-two, runs—or at least is closely associated with—a successful stock promotion firm with headquarters in an elegant address on New York's Fifth Avenue, with another office in Wichita, Kansas, his boyhood home.

The firm in question, Fifth Avenue Communications, has helped a number of Over the Counter Bulletin Board stocks—several with fashionable dot.coms in their names—catch fire with investors, even as Williamson himself has participated in a mergers and acquisitions program for midcareer business and finance executives at the Wharton School of Business at the University of Pennsylvania.

But the folks at Wharton would have been astonished had they looked into the history of the man they chose to let into their program: a two-time federal felon with a rap sheet far beyond the ordinary for even a typical Wall Street sharpie.

Our story begins in 1967 when Williamson, then in the U.S. Marine Corps on Okinawa, killed a taxi driver during a robbery attempt. He was convicted of murder by a general court-martial and was sentenced to eleven years' confinement, which he served at a medium-security federal prison in El Reno, Oklahoma.

He became eligible for parole in June 1971 after serving a little under four years and was released a month later. He headed for Denver, setting himself up in the penny stock racket. By 1974 he sported the title of president of several Denver-area start-ups, all bearing impressive-sounding names in medical technology.

One of them—CEA Lab—thereafter went through a twenty-five-year series of name changes and permutations to emerge in the 1990s as the fountainhead of a slew of Williamson-linked stock promotions. By contrast, another of his early start-ups—Cancer Diagnostics—was popular for a time among penny stock gamblers back in the 1980s but has since been all but forgotten.

Throughout the 1980s, Williamson managed to stay out of trouble, but by the start of the 1990s his luck had run out. He had used his stock promotion company, Williamson & Associates, to buy an Englewood, Colorado, penny stock firm, Securities USA. Almost immediately, the National Association of Securities Dealers brought a disciplinary action against the firm, charging it with submitting inaccurate reports to the NASD, failing to maintain minimum net capital requirements, and funding a loan with a bad check. In the end, Securities USA was expelled from the industry, and Williamson had to agree never again to take an ownership interest, either directly or indirectly, in an NASD member firm.

But Williamson was hardly about to quit Wall Street altogether. By the mid-1990s he was busy in New York promoting the fortunes of a Queens, New York, company called OMAP Holdings that manufactured vending machines, electrical heaters, and some kind of patented device to make french fries.

In the process, he got swept up in an undercover FBI sting operation against penny stock promoters and was one of forty-four individuals arrested in October 1996. Williamson's special bad luck was to have attempted to bribe an undercover FBI agent to promote the OMAP shares—and to have advised the agent to help him cover his own tracks by issuing him a phony invoice for the bribe payment. In the spring of 1997, Williamson pleaded guilty to a criminal charge and was sentenced to two years of federal probation.

After his arrest, in an apparent effort to make the best of a bad situation, Williamson changed his company's name from Williamson & Associates to Fifth Avenue Communications. In January 1997, prior to pleading guilty, he had Fifth Avenue issue a press release saying that the business was being sold by its otherwise unidentified owner, CEA Lab (that, of course, being Williamson's own company from as far back as 1974), to a penny stock outfit going by the name of Auburn Equities.

Whether the Auburn transaction ever went through—or if it did, whether it meant that Williamson was no longer calling the shots at Fifth Avenue—is open to question. For one thing, a June 1998 membership profile supplied by Williamson about himself on the Silicon Investor Web site (www.siliconinvestor.com) lists his company affiliations as "Williamson & Associates" and "Fifth Avenue Communications"—indicating that eighteen months after having ostensibly sold the firm, he was claiming still to be involved with it. What's more, records on file at Network Solutions, a Web site registration service, show that as recently as March 28, 1999, Edward Williamson was listed as the billing contact for Fifth Avenue Communications' Web site (www.stocksfifthavenue.com), and his brother, Randy, was listed as the site's administrative and technical contact.

Meanwhile, Fifth Avenue has continued to pump out promotional materials in support of companies in which Williamson and/or his associates have apparent interests. There's been Stockup.com, which soared from pennies to more than $15 on a Williamson promotion. Thereafter, I wrote about the company, exposing its links to Williamson, and the company changed its name to Preference Technologies. These days it is selling for 75 cents per share. Another company,

AutoAuction.com, which claims to be in the business of auctioning automobiles over the Internet, rose from 50 cents to $9.50, then collapsed and is now, like Preference Technologies, selling for 75 cents.

At one point, Williamson's Web site said of this outfit, "The company projects revenue of $44 million, earnings of $1.4 million, or about 25 cents per share. . . . Solid business. Good growth rate. Great little acorn." Why the effusive praise? Because at the time it was promoting AutoAuction.com, the company's Web site was being run by Fast Eddie's brother, Randy.

Is it any wonder the regulators look at situations like that and just throw up their hands? Unraveling the entanglements and undisclosed interests in Fast Eddie's affairs would exhaust dozens of SEC investigators. And besides, as soon as they shut down one operation he'd simply open up a new one.

The Bulletin Board abounds with hustlers like Fast Eddie, many of them operating Web sites similar to his Fifth Avenue Communications site (www.stocksfifthavenue.com). The one thing they all have in common? An inexhaustible capacity for promoting essentially worthless stocks to the public as the next hot new thing. In addition to distributing "news" releases via the PR News Wire and the Business Wire, the promoters also like to publish "research reports" and "investment recommendations" on their sites—typically in return for stock in the companies themselves.

SEC rules require the promoters to disclose any compensation they've received for their promotional efforts, and since 1999 additional rules have banned promoters from being compensated in stock for their services. But most promoters either ignore the rules or publish fine-print disclosures that are almost impossible to locate on their Web sites. You can find a reasonably up-to-date list of penny stock promoters at a Web site bearing the name FinancialWeb.com. Located at www.financialweb.com, the company is itself publicly traded on the Bulletin Board, and is run by a fellow who set up a kind of whistleblower's Web site under the name Stock Detective, and subsequently changed the name to FinancialWeb.com. Go to the site, click on the tab called "Stock Detective," and you'll find a list of "Stinky Stocks" from the Bulletin Board as well as a list of Web sites that promote the dreck.

On the OTC Bulletin Board, all such promotional artifices and gimmicks lead ultimately to the "pump-and-dump" payoff—which is how the hustlers take their profits. In a pump-and-dump, manipulators like Peter Tosto load up on huge amounts of Bulletin Board stock at prices as low as 1 and 2 cents per share—and sometimes a lot lower even than that. Then, when the promoters begin to stir up interest in the company by way of phony and misleading press releases and worthless investment opinions, and the stock starts to rise, the manipulators slowly begin selling their shares into the rising market—all the way up until they've bailed out completely and move on to new prey . . . at which point the stock collapses with a thud.

For an example of how the game is being played, let us drop by for a premarket visit to the Web site maintained and operated by the Island Electronic Communications Network. This Web site, which we discussed in Chapter 4, is reached by the URL www.island.com. It is a favorite of day traders using the Datek Online investing service, providing visitors with free, minute-to-minute, trade-by-trade quotes of the twenty hottest NASDAQ stocks on the Island system during the ninety premarket minutes before the NASDAQ system opens officially for business at 9:30 A.M. Eastern Time each morning.

Go there, click on the link for the "Top 20" list, and by simply glancing at it for a few seconds and watching the relative positions of the stocks as they change in the rankings, you can quickly see which stocks are hot, and getting hotter, and which are not—even before the market itself opens. In effect, the Island Top 20 list amounts to a continuously updated popularity poll—a poll that will wind up, as 9:30 A.M. approaches, showing which stocks are likely to open with big up or down "gaps" from their previous day's closing prices when trading officially begins.

Armed with that intelligence, day traders instantly lock in positions in stocks that are marching up the list, then reach for their mouse buttons and click over to message boards maintained by financial Web sites run by Yahoo, Silicon Investor, Raging Bull, and others, to see what all the excitement is about concerning the stocks in question. There they encounter the promoters, suitably hidden behind pseudonyms and aliases, posting breathless messages about "upcoming news," "pending announcements," and "bombshell new products" that are due out any minute. Often, this is all it takes to cause newbie investors to the Web to get excited and place "buy-at-the-market" orders with their brokers in hopes of getting in on the action when the trading day officially begins at 9:30 A.M. Meanwhile, of course, the promoters, having already locked in their positions, stand ready to begin bailing out for big profits once the stocks begin to move.

In one case, a completely defunct Bulletin Board stock—Channel America Broadcasting—traded to astronomical levels for no other reason than momentum trading that was stirred up by frenzied minute-to-minute action among day traders. Though the company had in fact gone out of business and no longer existed, its stock soared during three wild days in February of 1999, by more than 1,200 percent, to 6 cents per share, then abruptly crashed back to earth and was soon selling again for barely a penny per share.

OTC Bulletin Board records maintained by the National Association of Securities Dealers listed Channel America Broadcasting in February of 1999 as being headquartered in an office in Lakeland,

Florida. But the phone number for the company was nonworking, and various government officials in the Federal Communications Commission said the company had in fact gone out of business years earlier.

Nonetheless, on February 23, 1999, an Internet message board sprouted a message from someone identifying himself as P. E. Allen, predicting a big run-up in Channel America's stock price the next day. On that and nothing more, investors began gobbling up shares at roughly one-half cent per share, until more than 40 million shares had changed hands and the price had soared tenfold in value to 5 cents per share. But what were they buying? No one knew, other than a penny stock that was going up.

However, a clue might have been found in a March 1997 press release that declared that Channel America—described as a "holding company for . . . [a] network of television broadcast affiliates"—had agreed to merge with a privately held production company headed by television back-talk personality Morton Downey Jr., who would become chairman of the combined entity. The release stated that the deal had been arranged by Select Capital Advisors, a Miami-based "international financial services holding company . . . with offices and affiliates worldwide," and headed by one Ronald G. Williams. Though Select Capital Advisors was not listed in any Miami area telephone directory, it did maintain a Web site at

www.selectcapitaladvisors.com,

which revealed that the Williams operation had previously raised money for Channel America.

As for Williams's contact with Downey, it turns out that Downey had been introduced to Williams via a Los Angeles–based penny stock promoter named Richard Langley, who was helping Downey raise money to launch a new television talk show. Langley had himself been only recently nabbed by the FBI in a Wall Street penny stock sting operation, and was awaiting trial on various charges. Downey said Williams asked him if he would produce and star in a series of shows promoting penny stocks on cable TV, to be distributed by Channel America Broadcasting. Downey professed an "uneasy feeling" about Williams, and declined, going on thereafter to host a short-lived series of penny stock promotional TV shows for Langley instead. (At latest report, Downey had licensed his name to yet another penny stock promotional operation—Discover Wall Street—that promotes penny stocks via the Web at

www.discoverwallstreet.com.

The man behind *that* site turns out to be a Chicago penny stock promoter named Jeffrey Bruss, who has lately been charged by the SEC with taking undisclosed fees for promoting penny stocks.)

As for Select Capital Advisors and Mr. Williams, it turned out that in 1992 Select Capital (then known as Onyx Financial Corp., with Williams at the helm) had had its books and records seized by investigators from the Dade County sheriff's department in connection with a fraud probe. Thereafter, Williams's legal woes deepened until, by the spring of 1997—when he met with Downey on behalf of Channel America—he was already facing fraud and racketeering charges in connection with swindling small businesses out of front money on promised financings that never materialized. In 1998, Williams was sentenced to a year in Florida state prison following a guilty plea on the charges and was granted work-release status to begin paying back various moneys that had been swindled. But when Williams violated his probation terms, his probation was revoked and he was sentenced to nine years, beginning last October.

As for Channel America Broadcasting, the company itself had evaporated into thin air. A New York–based television producer named Katlean de Monchy said she had done some work for the firm "five or six years ago," but believed they had thereafter gone out of business. Records at the NASD and SEC proved to be out of date and worthless. An official at the Federal Communications Commission said, "We don't know what happened to them. We think they went bankrupt." The National Association of Television Production Executives could find no record of the company in its database. No TV station had carried its programming in years. Telephone directory searches in Tampa, Ocala, and Lakeland, New York City, Los Angeles, and Darien, Connecticut—all locations where the company had once maintained offices—proved fruitless.

Yet for three wild days during the week of February 22, more shares of this mystery stock changed hands than those of almost any other stock in America—more than 70 million shares in all. In the frenzy, the stock climbed from a half-cent per share on Friday, February 19, to 5 cents per share three trading days later. Then, like a soap bubble, the price popped, and the shares were suddenly selling for 2 cents again. And through it all, no one at either the SEC or the NASD gave the slightest indication of being aware that anything was amiss.

The only sure way to avoid getting stuck in such pump-and-dump fleecings is never to dabble in Bulletin Board stocks in the first place. But if you really can't resist, here are some steps you can take to protect yourself at least a little:

> Never invest in any stock—Bulletin Board, pink sheet, or otherwise—if the company does not publish audited financial statements that are available to you on the Web via the EDGAR system. You may not actually even bother to read them, but if they're there at least you'll know the company's promoters won't be so ready to lie about their company's prospects.

> Be wary of investing in a penny stock that has at least doubled its price in the previous trading day, and *never* invest in *any*

penny stock that has more than quadrupled in price, from its previous low, in the last trading day. These stocks are almost certainly pump-and-dump operations, and though they may have a lot further to rise, you'll never know if they're about to pop the very second you buy them.

> Any company that issues a steady flow of PR News Wire and Business Wire press releases is potentially a risky investment. The mere fact that they keep churning out the releases should tell you the company's management is probably more interested in the stock than the underlying business. In the end, neither will probably wind up being worth much of anything.

> Before you invest in any company whose bona fides don't seem to pass the smell test, make a list of every name of every company and individual you know who has had anything to do with the company. Then go to the Web site for the Securities and Exchange Commission (www.sec.gov) and research each name through the site's search tool. If any names turn up disciplinary proceedings against it by the SEC, go no further: Just walk away—there are too many *good* stocks to invest in, so why become knowingly entangled with companies or individuals that are, as we say, "known to the authorities"?

Follow this advice and you may miss out on some high-fliers, but over time you'll come out ahead—and in the meantime you'll get to sleep at night.

chapter nine

Short-Selling: How to Turn Lemons into Lemonade

If you have noticed that a large amount of this book has been devoted to advice on how to avoid overpriced, overhyped stocks of one sort or another, you're right. As in medicine, the first rule for someone presuming to dispense investment advice is (or at least should be): First, do no harm.

On the other hand, for those with the stomach to capitalize on such situations, overpriced stocks can offer you some of the most rewarding opportunities in all of investing. The trick is not to go broke in the process of trying to exploit them.

In this chapter we're going to look at the arcane and much maligned art of short-selling, which is potentially one of the most lucrative activities available to any Internet investor. Unfortunately, it also happens to be one of the riskiest if you don't know what you're doing. Luckily, the research tools of the Internet tell you what you need to know to pick attractive candidates for short-selling—as well as what you need to know regarding when to place your bets.

You can get a good overview of short-selling at the following URL: www.geocities.com/WallStreet/Exchange/1371/SELLING.S.S..htm. It will link you to an introduction to investing site run by the GeoCities portal service. The text is easy to understand and basic, and definitely worth a few minutes of your time. You can also explore the concept of short-selling at www.prudentbear.com. The site is run by a well-known Texas short-selling firm, David W. Tice & Associates, and offers a wide array of facts about short-selling and past market manias, as well as an informative running commentary on the markets. There is also an interactive short-selling game you can play on the site to develop your skills. The game is free to anyone. Finally, you can find a useful introduction to the subject in, of all places, the *Encarta* encyclopedia, which is available online from Microsoft at

http://encarta.msn.com

Take a look at these sites and then dig into this chapter. You'll be doing so with the background necessary to peel away a lot of the confusion that many investors experience when confronting short-selling for the first time.

In a sense, short-selling is the only area of investing in which both fundamental and technical analysis properly belong together—fundamental analysis to identify the stocks that are overpriced, and technical analysis to tell you when momentum in the stock has shifted to the downside and the company is ready for shorting.

Simply put, short-selling is the practice of selling a stock before you even own it—in the belief that it will fall a lot in price by the time you actually have to buy it. The whole idea is very confusing—even fishy-sounding, to say the least. After all, selling something before you own it sounds like finding something before it's lost—which is just a fancy-pants way of describing theft.

But short-selling is both legal and widely practiced by some of the biggest and most conservative fund managers on Wall Street—as well as by every broker-dealer in the business. What's more, the concept is fundamentally very simple: You "short" a stock when you think it is overpriced and is bound to fall in value—just as you go "long" a stock when you think the opposite . . . that it is undervalued and bound to rise.

If you decide not to go Christmas shopping the week before Christmas because you know that everything you're planning to buy will be on sale the day *after* Christmas, we may rightly say that during the week in question you are, in effect, "short" the gifts on your Christmas list. If you've told the kids and relatives they'll be getting their presents as usual—only just a couple of days late—you've got at least a moral obligation to deliver something you don't yet own (the gifts). The reason you don't yet own them is that you're hoping they'll be selling for less than they currently are when you actually have to go and buy them.

If you don't own something, but you've got an obligation to acquire it and deliver it at some point in the future, you're "short" that thing. Conversely, if you decide to fill up your home heating oil tank in July because you figure that fuel oil prices will be higher in November when you have to start heating the house, we may say you're "long" heating oil: You've bought something you don't yet need because you know you'll need it eventually and you figure it will never be cheaper than it is today.

Short means you've sold what you don't yet own; long means you own what you don't yet need.

Applying this to stock market investing can yield very attractive profits if done properly, but you can also lose potentially limitless amounts of money. To that end, let me tell you the sad story of a Chinese-American woman named Ningh Li, who thought she understood all there was to know about short-selling and wound up all but ruined. After thirty-two years as a financial writer, I thought I'd heard just about every horror tale there was—then Ningh Li told me hers. It adds a whole new meaning to the cliché that you don't have to be a rocket scientist to make money on Wall Street. In Ningh Li's case, it turned out that being a rocket scientist proved an actual *obstacle* to making money on Wall Street.

Ningh Li is a charming woman in her mid-fifties who emigrated to the United States from China in the 1980s. She knew nothing about the ways of Wall Street or the stock market, and after arriving in the United States she had more to concern herself with than learning about it anyway.

As it happened, Ningh Li was—and is—an utterly brilliant mathematician, and as such had received full scholarship and fellowship offers to attend almost any university of her choice. There were offers from MIT, Rice, Brown, and Rensselaer Polytechnic Institute. She settled on RPI, earned a bachelor's degree in solid-state physics, a joint master's degree in electrical engineering and plasma physics (arguably the hardest and most confusing topic of applied math in the world), and a Ph.D. in space and fusion-plasma physics.

I'd have to say that those topics sound, on the face of them, a bit more daunting than, say, whether Amazon.com will turn a profit someday or not. On the other hand, Albert Einstein is said to have observed, when he wasn't working on his theories of relativity, that he found the U.S. federal income tax code to be the most complicated and confusing subject on earth. Go figure.

In any event, one thing led to the next and Ningh Li wound up as a top research scientist on NASA's deep-space travel and gravity control project at the Marshall Space Flight Center at Huntsville, Alabama. In that role she developed, among other things, a complete theoretical framework for the control of gravity, published treatises on same at scientific conferences around the world, and in the process was mentioned as a contender for the Nobel Prize in physics.

By the spring of 1998 the stock market had boiled up to historically unimagined heights, and Ningh Li began to wonder whether, with all her attention on gravity control and deep-space travel, she might have been missing the boat on what capitalism in the West was apparently all about: getting rich quick in the stock market.

So she took her entire life savings—roughly $250,000—and not knowing the first thing about what she was doing, logged on to the Internet on her home computer, found an online brokerage firm, filled out a new-account form that asked absolutely nothing regarding her experience as an investor or her knowledge of the stock market, and opened an account with her money.

Then, determined to get up to speed fast on investing, she started reading books and magazine articles on the topic. And when she came upon some advice that said she could make a lot of money by short-selling overpriced stocks that have no earnings, Ningh Li figured her ship had come in. So she went to her computer, clicked on to her online trading firm's Web site, and placed short-sale orders for a half dozen or so Internet stocks. And almost immediately thereafter, 1998's wild speculative frenzy in Internet stocks erupted—a frenzy that wiped her out before she even realized what was happening.

Ningh Li got totally, completely, 100 percent obliterated. She put $250,000 into short-selling Internet stocks and between the fourth of July and Thanksgiving of 1998 she lost every penny of it.

By not knowing what she was doing, one of the leading research scientists for the American space program—that is, a rocket scientist if there ever was one—had bet exactly the way every standard text on investing would have advised her to bet: To make money in an overpriced bull market, all you needed to do was short overpriced stocks with no earnings, and the more they went down, the more her own net worth would go up. But the overpriced stocks didn't go down, they kept going up higher and higher until there was no value left in her account at all.

Why stocks go up when the textbooks say they should go down is a question we'll turn to in a minute. And it's a point worth focusing on too, because when stock prices rise for reasons other than their underlying value, you may be sure that eventually they will return to earth. With such stocks, the market is telling you, in effect: Watch these prices because you will one day be able to sell the stocks in question for a lot of money—even if you don't yet own them. I know professional short-sellers who make 50 percent and higher returns on their short-side portfolios, year after year, in just this way. After all, when you short an overpriced stock, you've removed one major ambiguity about the future already: The market is telling you, with absolute certainty, that sooner or later the stock's price will go down; the only question is when. By contrast, an underpriced stock could, in theory at least, remain underpriced forever—at least if no one ever notices it, whereas an *over*priced stock has already gotten noticed: All eyes are upon it, and sooner or later its real value will be recognized.

Yet before getting into the details of how to spot such stocks, let's examine the process by which short-selling actually occurs. It is really quite simple: You ask your broker to borrow some stock for you in an overpriced company that you want to short, then sell the shares and place the proceeds in your account. If a stock that you're planning to short costs, say, $40, market regulations require that you put up a minimum of $20 (that is, 50 percent of the value of the shorted shares) as additional money in the account, which amounts to collateral for the transaction. The account will thus show a cash balance of $60.

What you do next, in a perfect world, is to sit back and wait for the stock that you've sold to fall to something approaching zero. When the stock falls to, say, $20, you still have to leave 50 percent of the stock's value (that is, $10) in the account as collateral plus another $20 (the value of the short position). This means you can withdraw $30 in cash. In other words, you've invested $20 to start the ball rolling, and now you're getting to draw out $30, meaning you've made 50 percent on your money. Every time the stock falls further, you can withdraw more or, alternatively, increase your short position.

That's what savvy traders did when Boston Chicken—our troubled retailer from Chapter 6—climbed to $40 per share in the autumn of 1996. Realizing the company had serious flaws in its business plan, and that the numbers in its financial statements just weren't adding up, short-sellers began aggressively borrowing shares via their brokers, then selling them in the belief that the price was destined to fall.

Of course, if Boston Chicken had gone *up* from $40 instead of down, well, you could have suffered the fate of Ningh Li. The problem is, if the price of the stock rises by more than the cash money you've put up to buy it ($20 in our example), you'll have to put up more cash or your broker will buy the shares on the open market whether you like it or not, close out your position, and deduct the loss from your account. Thus, had Boston Chicken risen to $60 instead of fallen to $20, you'd have been facing a "margin call" of $20 from your broker—and if you couldn't come up with the money he'd be closing out your position at $60 and coming after you—in court if necessary—for $40.

In the worst of all possible outcomes, you can get caught in something known as a short-squeeze, which is just about the worst thing that can happen to an investor except perhaps to borrow money from the Colombo family and not be able to pay it back. A short-squeeze occurs when large numbers of short-sellers create short positions in a security in expectations of a price decline yet the price actually rises—quickly and sharply enough that all of them are forced to rush into the market to buy back shares in order to close out their positions and avoid margin calls. If there's not very much stock available in the market to begin with, and if lots of desperate short-sellers suddenly want it, the price can go through the roof.

That is what happened to short-sellers who thought they'd spotted some easy money in late 1998 in the shares of an Internet start-up company called Shopping.com. The company had only recently gone public at $9 per share, with a mere $23,000 of shareholder equity on its balance sheet and barely $376,000 in revenues on its income statement. Yet within two months the stock had soared to nearly $30—not because business was great or the company's prospects were so promising, but because short-sellers had gotten caught off base when they bet that the stock would go down from $9 and it went up instead. Eventually the Securities and Exchange Commission halted trading in the shares when evidence surfaced that the underwriter of the company had *intentionally* rigged the market to prevent its own clients, who owned most of the shares, from selling out immediately after the IPO. This created the scarcity that forced the stock's price to take off for the moon and short-sellers to lose millions.

There is another—and somewhat technical—complication all short-sellers face: You can't short a stock when the last trade was down. This rule was adopted by market regulators back in the 1980s to prevent short-sellers from ganging up on stocks that are falling already. To prevent what would otherwise amount to a rabbit punch to a prizefighter who is heading for the canvas already, the "uptick rule" requires that the last previous trade be either at the same price as or higher than the trade before. This means that you'll be betting the stock price is going to fall when, in reality, the price is rising right before your eyes. You need a lot of self-confidence—and titanium nerves—to place such a bet.

How to avoid getting caught in such traps? The Internet offers plenty of tools. To begin with, anytime you short a stock you want to make sure of two things right off the bat: first, that there's a lot of stock freely trading in the market—that is, that the company has a hefty "float", and second, that a lot of the float isn't borrowed by short-sellers already. Here's how to do that:

The float: There are several research firms that publish reasonably accurate float numbers for stocks, but the best by far—and the one that the Wall Street pros rely on—is New York–based Market Guide. Go to the following Web site—www.marketguide.com—and type any stock symbol you'd like into the "Search" window. In a flash, up will come a financial summary of the company's performance in eight different categories of information. In the group entitled "Share Related Items" you'll find an entry for "Float." This will refer to the numbers of shares that are held by everybody other than officers, directors, and 5 percent or more owners—in other words, the number of shares that are available for trading day to day even if they don't actually trade. If the float is under one million shares, don't even think about shorting the stock; just remember what happened to Ningh Li. When you sell short, your losses are potentially limitless.

Is the stock unborrowable: Just because a company has a hefty float doesn't mean much if a lot of the stock is borrowed by short-sellers already. How do you find out if that is the case? The *Wall Street Journal,* *Barron's,* the *New York Times,* and many other newspapers publish monthly "short interest" tables provided by NASDAQ and the New York Stock Exchange. But you can get the same thing from the Web, the instant it is available. For NASDAQ stocks, go to the following Web site: http://www.nasdaqtrader.com and type in any NASDAQ-traded stock symbol you want, and select the latest, most current month from the nearby drop-down window. Up will come the number of borrowed shares in the stock at the latest tally (the "short interest"), the average daily trading volume in the stock, and how many days it would take for borrowed shares to be bought back based on the daily trading volume (the "days to cover"). The greater the number of days to cover, the greater the risk of getting caught in a squeeze. If more than, say, 20 percent of the float is already borrowed (the float divided by the short interest) or if it would take more than a week to cover all borrowed short positions and if the number has lately been rising, then forget about shorting the stock; the risk of getting caught in a squeeze is just too high.

So let's say you've now zeroed in on exactly the overpriced company you'd like to short. The company has doubtful earnings at best, the balance sheet is shaky, the business is hemorrhaging cash out of every pore, and the stock price has been driven to extreme—seemingly indefensible—heights.

Unlikely though such a situation may sound to you, in fact you can find stocks like that every day of the week on Wall Street. Here's one from the spring of 1997—a Florida-based company named Republic Industries. The company caught my eye for a simple reason: As a business it simply made no sense, being simultaneously in three completely separate and unrelated activities—automobile marketing, home security services, and the garbage business. How was one man going to run all that?

The man at the top turned out to be an aging Wall Street wunderkind named H. Wayne Huizenga. Huizenga had started out in 1971, at the tender age of thirty-three, co-founding Waste Management, a fancied-up sort of garbage collector that eventually became WMX Technologies, the "world's largest integrated environmental services company," as it described itself.

But after founding it, Huizenga grew bored with garbage, bailed out, and took over a nineteen-store video rental operation that he built into Blockbuster, "the world's largest video and music retailer." In 1994 he dumped Blockbuster on Viacom, a New York–based media company, for $8.4 billion, and set out to build "the world's largest chain of automobile dealerships." The result: Republic Industries.

The resulting growth was astounding. During the whole of 1995, Republic Industries actually took in gross revenues of only $260 million. But in just the next year, 1996, acquisitions ballooned the company's revenues nearly tenfold, to $2.36 billion. There was no other publicly traded company in America that reported even a fraction so rapid a growth rate that year.

Nor was the growth expected to slow. Quite the contrary, by the spring of 1997, Huizenga was predicting overall revenues for the year to top $10 billion—this for a company that showed only $95 million in revenues three years earlier.

But just because a company gets five or even ten times bigger in a single year doesn't mean it automatically becomes ten times more profitable. In 1994 and 1995—both being profitable years for Republic Industries—the company reported a total of nearly $34 million in net income. But then came 1996 and the start of Huizenga's wild takeover binge, and two thirds of the profits of the previous two years were wiped out in a $27.8 million tide of red ink. In fact, if you didn't count some $20.6 million in interest income earned on the cash proceeds of two secondary stock sales in 1996, the company would have booked nearly $50 million in net losses. Worse still, Republic's 10-K SEC filing for the year warned that on an operating basis the company was expected to go on losing money for "the foreseeable future," and moreover, would need "substantial additional capital" to keep growing in the meantime.

By the start of 1997, the stock had nonetheless topped $42 per share, as Wall Street continued to trust in "Wayne's Magic"—meaning that investors believed that, given enough time, he'd produce another Blockbuster Entertainment–type super-success story. In other words, investors were handing over their money on blind faith and nothing else.

A short-seller's retirement dream? Hold on. How could you have known that instead of plunging from $42 to $4.20 the very second you "laid on your short" (as we say in the game), Republic's stock wouldn't have soared from $42 to $420 and sent you into bankruptcy court instead?

The answer is, you couldn't possibly have known, which is why you want to be careful with these things, just as you want to be careful with a loaded gun. This is where the concepts of momentum trading come in. The mistake that Ningh Li made back in 1998 when she shorted every Internet stock she could get her hands on was just this: The stocks were grossly overvalued, to be sure, but not because investors were buying them based on any view of their business fundamentals and long-term growth prospects.

No, Ningh Li's stocks had been driven to nosebleed heights because momentum traders had chased them there. In other words, these stocks were rising not on their fundamentals but on the herd mentality of momentum traders, yet Ningh Li had sold them short on their fundamentals anyway. She had mistakenly believed that not even the herd mentality of momentum traders can keep an overpriced stock aloft, not realizing that, given the right circumstances, a rising stock price in a buoyant market will fall back to earth only when momentum traders lose interest in it and move elsewhere.

Thus, before shorting any stock—no matter how overpriced it is already relative to fundamentals—you want to make sure that momentum investors have begun to leave the shares. To do that, go to Microsoft Investor (www.moneycentral.msn.com), select a three-

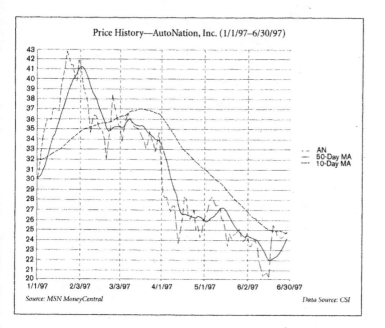

Price History—AutoNation, Inc. (1/1/97–6/30/97)

Source: MSN MoneyCentral   Data Source: CSI

month chart for the stock you want to examine, then add an "On Bal-ance Volume" line to the chart. This line will often indicate a "top" to the stock by beginning to decline when the stock is still rising. The di-vergence shows that the price is moving up even though fewer in-vestors are buying, suggesting in effect that the price will very soon decline.

Once a stock begins to decline, add a "10-Day" and a "50-Day Moving Average" to the chart. When the 10-day average falls below the 50-day average, it is time to sell the stock. Remember, you've got to wait for an uptick to sell, but you'll get one; no stock goes straight down forever.

To see what a chart of Republic Industries looked like in the spring of 1997, when it had already fallen by 30 percent from its highs, and I began publicly commenting that the stock clearly had further to fall, click on the following link:

http://moneycentral.msn.com/investor/charts/
charting.asp?Symbol=an#Big.

See how the 10-day moving average fell below the 50-day moving average in late February? At the time, the stock was selling in the high $30s. By May, it was down to the high $20s. Three years later, in the spring of 2000, Republic is selling for barely $6. As I said, properly done, short-selling can make you a lot of money.

So, pick a portfolio of a dozen stocks that meet all these criteria, and place your bets. Thus hedged against the possibility that you've made a couple of wrong choices, you'll make some decent money.

chapter ten

The Seductive Lure of IPOs: Looking for Love in All the Wrong Places

Ask any gambler to tell you when the promise of life shines brightest, and each and every one of them will tell you the same thing: It's when tomorrow becomes today and it is given to mere mortals to behold the future. It is how and why we fall in love—with each other, with Saratoga trotters at the starting gate, and with the turn of a one-eyed Jack at the Mirage.

It also happens to be why people invest in stock market IPOs. On Wall Street as anywhere else, the possibilities of life are grandest when its potential is least limited—in that eternal moment when the outstretched hand reaches to turn, face-up on the table, the card that fate dealt . . . in that moment of desperate hope when the man at the bar turns to the woman seated next to him and says, "You come here often . . . ?" and in that moment when the click of the mouse button still echoes in your ear as you place the online order to buy 100 shares at the open, no matter where the open might be.

In this chapter we'll take a cautionary look at where and how to buy IPOs over the Internet, and most important, we'll look at why the process of doing so is full of risk: for the simple reason that, as has been stressed so often in these pages, the rewards are so great when you pick a winner. The point to remember with IPOs—as with any kind of investment—is that over time the risks and rewards tend to balance themselves out, meaning that, over time, your 500-percent-in-a-day killings will be offset by losses elsewhere and you'll wind up, eventually, doing not much better than the market as a whole.

In almost no area of investing are the rewards—and thus the risks—greater than in the new issues market . . . or at least that corner of it known as the IPO market. The new issues market covers everything from stocks and bonds that are being sold to the public for the first time by 100-year-old industrial companies in the Midwest, to the small portions of equity in privately held Internet start-ups from Palo Alto and Mountain View, California.

It is the latter category—initial public offerings (IPOs) of stock in privately held companies—that has been generating all the excitement among investors in recent years. And that, in turn, is because the payoff for some of them has been so spectacular. Anyone having bought 100 shares of, say, Yahoo at its initial offering price of $13 per share back in April of 1996 would have nearly tripled his money in the first six and a half hours of trading, and as of this writing four years later would be sitting on a profit of 6,400 percent on the initial investment. In other words, anyone buying 100 shares of Yahoo at $13 per share back in 1996, would have seen his $1,300 investment grow, by the start of 2000, to more than $160,000.

Numbers like that have helped make the IPO market the hottest thing Wall Street has seen in decades, and the hotter it has gotten, the more investors it has attracted . . . which has made it even hotter, which has . . . well, you get the idea. And, once again, it is the growth of the Internet and online investing that has fueled the boom, as tens of thousands of new investors have streamed into the market, chasing the instant riches promised in the chat rooms—which riches have seemed miraculously enough to materialize simply as a result of being chased.

On the other hand, every reward brings an offsetting risk, and it is in the nature of risk not to recognize your exposure to it until it's too late—otherwise we'd all live in a world of perfect foresight, in which the winner of every race is known beforehand, and where there'd be no need for seatbelts because we'd all be able to see the accidents coming and take the necessary action to avoid them.

But life isn't like that, so no one could know when Yahoo went public in April of 1996 at $13 that the shares would almost instantly collapse after that opening day surge and by the start of summer would be selling for barely a third of their opening day high, making every investor who'd bought and held the shares a loser on the deal. Nor could anyone know that when Yahoo and the other dot.com darlings of the 1990s caught fire in the autumn of 1998 that it wouldn't be long before the investment bankers of the IPO market would be figuring out how to game the system so as to capitalize on the hunger of new investors who had begun pouring into the market in search of the next Yahoo.

In this chapter we'll look at the hot-potato-like ploy the underwriters came up with to sell their wares, and offer some suggestions about how you can get in on the action without becoming someone's dinner in the process. First, however, a brief historical background will help you understand the game itself, as well as appreciate how the growth of the Internet has changed all the rules in IPO investing.

There are dozens of different Web sites that provide information of one sort or another on IPOs, but for my money the best by far is located at www.hoovers.com/ipo/0,1334,23,00.html. This data-rich site is a service of Hoover's, a Web-based financial research service out of Austin, Texas. A lot of what Hoover's provides is available only for a monthly fee, but most of what they offer concerning IPOs is free, and, simply put, it is by far the best and most accurate to be found anywhere online. You can, for example, pay as much as $1,000 per year for an IPO alert service from a New Jersey company called the IPO Financial Network. But nearly everything you'll get is available for free either through Hoover's or competing services.

Here are some of the other services that I've found valuable from time to time: For up-to-the-minute information on IPOs that have been "priced" and are about to begin trading publicly in the aftermarket (we'll get into what all that means in a minute), use the Web site provided by Yahoo at http://biz.yahoo.com/ipo. As with almost everything provided by Yahoo, the information on the site is timely and reliably accurate, and because Yahoo's service is backed up by an enormous infrastructure of Internet servers and related computer equipment, you can download pages very rapidly—even with a pokey-slow dial-up connection from your local phone company.

You can find yet more information about IPOs—for example, when "lockup periods" and "quiet periods" expire, and various "bull and bear" forecast ranking for IPOs that have just come to market—at the Web site maintained by EDGAR Online. Those are the folks who pioneered the delivery of SEC EDGAR filings over the Web, and as the IPO market has boiled up, they've added IPO-related information to their site to get in on the action. Go to

www.edgar-online.com/ipoexpress

and you'll find it all there. Similarly, you can find reasonably up-to-date headline news items on various upcoming IPOs at a site called www.ipodata.com, and some useful research-related material on IPOs, such as offerings grouped by underwriters, at www.ipo.com.

But the simple fact is, you can find all this stuff, and a lot more, at

Hoover's, so save yourself some time and just click on over to that site and snoop around. Among the many types of IPO-related information you can find with a mouse click on the site are the following:

> A roundup of the previous week's IPOs, showing their offering price, opening price in the aftermarket, and their closing price on the first day of trading.

> A listing of all companies that filed IPO registration statements with the Securities and Exchange Commission during the previous seven days.

> A listing of all companies that are expected to set their offering prices, week by week, for the month ahead.

> A listing of how every IPO has performed in the aftermarket, month by month and quarter by quarter, as far back as June of 1996. The data is searchable alphabetically by the companies, and chronologically by month and quarter.

> A listing of IPOs by industry, showing, by percentages, which industries are attracting the most (and least) new IPOs.

> A listing of all IPOs, grouped by their underwriters—an extremely valuable tool since it is the ability of the underwriter to sell the shares that typically determines the success of the offering, and this data grouping allows you to see how the individual underwriters have fared in the past.

> A listing, in the latest quarter, of the best and worst quarterly performance, the biggest opening day gain, and other similar data.

In particular, check out the IPO "Beginner's Guide" on the Hoover's Web site, which is located at

www.hoovers.com/ipo/guide/0,1334,59,00.html,

and pay special attention to the process by which a company goes public. Generally speaking, the process falls into three parts, each of which is handled by the investment banker that is underwriting the offering.

First, a registration statement—typically known as an S1—is prepared and filed with the SEC. This is your first indication that stock in some company or other will eventually be sold to the public. You can set up an "alert" account with EDGAR Online or any number of other SEC-linked sites to be notified by e-mail whenever an S1 EDGAR filing hits the system. Granted, a lot of the information that you, as an investor, will be interested in—such as how many shares are being sold, and at what price—will not yet be included in the filing because the underwriters haven't yet figured out how many shares they can sell of the offering, to whom, and for how much per share. But there's a gold mine of other information in these preliminary filings, such as what the company's balance sheet, cash flow, and income statements look like.

You'll also be able to see, for example, whether the company is paying the top brass Midas-sized salaries, as well as perhaps rewarding them with excessive perks, and, indeed, whether management is conducting business transactions with the company itself. For example, does the CEO own the building that the company is renting as its corporate headquarters? Checking out the original S1 for Trump Hotels and Casino Resorts, you'd have found an absolute spaghetti plate of entanglements between Trump personally and his company. None of them are illegal, but they do underscore the sorts of conflicts that arise when management commingles its personal financials with the affairs of its company.

You can find such things disclosed in S1s under sections called "Certain Transactions" or "Certain Relationships," and they are typically a harbinger of trouble to come. After all, if the brass is dipping into the cookie jar before the company has even gone public, imagine what will likely be going on once the company gets capitalized with $50 million or more in fresh funds?

When the registration statement is filed with the SEC, the underwriter will organize what's called a "road show." In this stage, which can last from a few days to several weeks or more, the underwriter will schlepp the company's brass around to make presentations to various institutional clients of the firm, in cities across the country and even in Europe and possibly the Far East. The idea is for the underwriter to see how many shares can be sold to favored clients, and at what price.

Oftentimes you'll hear talk to the effect that some company or another is in a "quiet period" and can't speak to the press because it has filed a registration statement to go public and that the SEC bans it from making public utterances about the offering during such periods. But this is out-and-out crapola. There is no SEC rule, written or otherwise, about quiet periods or anything like them. This is nothing more than an invention of the underwriters to block the prying eyes of the press from peeking behind the curtain during road shows. In a minute we'll see why this has been important for the underwriters to do as the IPO market has boiled up, but for now it is enough to know that quiet periods don't exist in law or regulation and are simply a phony ploy designed to prevent the public from seeing and hearing what is said to favored clients during road show presentations.

Once the road show is completed, the offering gets "priced." The price—known formally as the "offering price"—usually turns out to be the average, or thereabouts, of what the institutional investors that attended the road show presentations had been willing to pay for their blocks of shares. This price usually reflects an extremely close and careful scrutiny of the company's financials by the investing firms, and generally speaking represents a pretty good benchmark for what the shares are worth, at that time, on a fundamental valuation basis. In any case, a day or two later, the offering will be "declared effective" and begin trading publicly—at whatever price is dictated by the forces of supply and demand—in the public aftermarket.

• • •

That is pretty much how IPOs have been brought to market for generations on end. But with the birth of the Internet and online trading, one thing has changed, and changed dramatically: The price paid by the institutions who participate in the road shows has stopped bearing any relationship whatsoever to the aftermarket price paid by individual investors once the shares begin trading publicly.

Historically, the institutions would pay, let us say, $20 per share for shares in an offering. Then when the deal began trading publicly in the aftermarket, the price might spurt to $21 or $22—the whole art of the pricing game by the underwriter being to hit that 10 percent markup "sweet spot" . . . to get as much as possible for the corporate client that is issuing the shares, without making it impossible for the institutions to turn around and unload a little bit of it in the aftermarket.

It was an ironclad formula that underwriters had adhered to for at least as far back as the IPO of Ford Motor Co. in 1956: The underwriter would sell the shares to its institutional clients for about a 10 percent discount from what they'd be expected to trade for in the aftermarket. This discount was, in effect, what the issuing company "left on the table" to induce the underwriter's clients to buy the stock, and it kept everyone happy. That was certainly so in the case of the Ford IPO, when the company went public at $64.50, giving investors an instant 10 percent profit when the shares jumped immediately to $70.50 in aftermarket trading.

That seductive promise of a quick 10 percent profit for the investor in an IPO became a standard of sorts for deals over the next forty years. But then came the bull market of the 1990s—the longest and strongest in the modern era—and with it, the 10 percent discount formula went right out the window.

One clear sign of the changing situation came in 1993 when the biggest retail brokerage firm in the world at the time—Merrill Lynch & Co.—underwrote a $20 per share stock offering for our old friends at Boston Chicken, only to see the stock's price more than double in the first hours of trading. So astonishing was this run-up—which echoed an earlier and even more explosive IPO by Home Shopping Network—that many on Wall Street wondered openly whether Boston Chicken would refuse to pay its underwriting fee to Merrill since the firm had so obviously—and grossly—underestimated market demand for the shares.

It was this run-up that changed Wall Street's whole view of IPOs: If a deal were *substantially* and *intentionally* underpriced, then investment firms might be able to float shares in companies far less financially attractive than the mighty Ford Motor Co. and still get gilt-edged investors to take some of the offering. Since risk is the flip side of reward, you could sell more risk by simply tossing in more reward—the exact same marketing strategy that junk bond wizard Michael Milken had used a decade earlier to sell high-yield debt to his firm's investors. Now, instead of peddling junk debt, Wall Street was about to begin selling junk equity.

The opportunity fell first to the white-shoe firm of Morgan Stanley, which teamed up with a smaller West Coast rival that had a background in computer and biotechnology deals—San Francisco–based Hambrecht & Quist—to sell shares in an Internet start-up company called Netscape Communications. The Netscape offering, which went to market in August of 1995 at $28 per share, proved a huge—indeed, an utterly unprecedented—success, soaring to $71 on its very first trade in the public market, before closing the day at $58. Result: a gain of more than 100 percent in value in a mere six and one half hours of trading.

No one could believe it. Here was a company that most people had never heard of on the morning of August 9, 1995. But by the next morning the story of Netscape's amazing debut on Wall Street was on the front page of the *New York Times* and people everywhere were asking each other, What's Netscape . . . ? What's a browser . . . ? What's the Internet . . . ?

On Wall Street, investment bankers were asking each other something else. Everyone wanted to know, What's the next Netscape?

And thus they began parading forth an unending stream of Netscape-like deals: Search engine companies (Yahoo, Lycos, Infoseek, Excite) and content providers (Go2Net, NewsEdge Corp.). There were Internet service providers (EarthLink Network and At Home Corp.). There were digital advertising agencies (24/7 Media, and DoubleClick) and Internet retailers (Amazon.com, Shopping. com, Egghead.com).

More and more they came, typically priced for only $10 or $15 per share—and all angled toward making a huge, reverberating splash in the aftermarket . . . the sort of splash to induce buyers to clamor for an opportunity to get in on the next Big New Deal . . . the sort of aftermarket demand needed to persuade the underwriters' clients to buy in at the premarket offering price, sit with the shares for a few hours, then flip them for a stupefying profit into the beckoning, outstretched hands of investors in the aftermarket.

Ecstasy is, of course, a relative thing. But on a day in mid-November of 1998, the joy of money reached a climax of sorts, as thousands of otherwise sensible people poured close to $500 million of their money into the IPO of an obscure Web site operator known as theglobe.com.

What exactly theglobe.com did as a business few could say—and fewer still even cared to learn. About all that anyone needed to know was that the company featured that odd shirttail of a name— ".com"—which identified it as a business enterprise (or location, or site, or some such) on the Internet.

There was, in fact, only one other thing besides the name's clumsy-sounding suffix that made theglobe.com of interest to investors: Namely, that on November 13, roughly 3.1 million shares of its stock were due to be sold to the public in an IPO—in this instance by the well-known New York investment banking firm of Bear, Stearns & Co.

Thanks to those two facts, investors had been lining up by the thousands for days and even weeks to get in on the action. Though no crowds could be seen surging along city sidewalks and spilling into the streets, their virtual presence could be felt as if the attraction that had drawn them were free tickets to a Garth Brooks concert. These investors had no interest whatsoever in the business track record of theglobe.com—which is just as well since the company basically had no track record to show for itself. All they knew was that word of theglobe.com's pending offering had been spreading through Internet chat rooms for weeks, as if the jungle drums of the digisphere were heralding the arrival of some colossal Kong of common stocks—a deal so majestic and awesome that no one dared miss bearing witness to its arrival.

Result? The first in a lengthening list of the kind of IPO sucker deals that have since become commonplace in the sector. Simply put, so many investors had phoned up their brokers and told them to buy TGLO, no matter what its price—in the jargon of the Street, they had placed "buy at the market" orders, which basically means they'd given their brokers blank checks—that when the shares began to trade in the aftermarket, there were no further buyers left to whom the first crop of buyers could sell. As a result, the company's stock, which had been priced by Bear, Stearns & Co. to its institutional clients at $9 per share, began trading in the aftermarket at an utterly unheard of $97 per share . . . a nearly 1,000 percent price surge in a matter of mere seconds.

This explosive opening trade "pop" gave the institutions that had bought in at the premarket offering price of $9 the opportunity to make the killing of all time and they instantly began bailing out in droves, sending the stock dawn from $97 to a closing price of $63.50, turning nearly every aftermarket investor in the deal into a spectacular loser.

Fed by breathless—but completely misleading—media stories of instant IPO millionaires minted by the dramatic opening trade pops from the offering price to institutions and the first trades in the aftermarket, thousands upon thousands of eager new investors have been drawn to the IPO game in hopes of buying low, selling high, and quintupling their money in twenty minutes of not terribly demanding effort. What they haven't realized is that only when they lose—by overpaying in the aftermarket—has it been possible for the institutional sellers in the premarket to win.

Thus, when VA Linux Systems, a computer company in a suddenly trendy sector of the market known as the Linux operating system sector, went public at $30 per share in December 1999, it leaped instantly to $299 on its first trade in the aftermarket, spurted thereafter to $320, then collapsed under an avalanche of institutional selling from holders that had bought in at the $30 offering price and now wanted out. Today the shares are selling for barely $40, a loss of 87 percent in value for every initial aftermarket investor in the deal. Or what about an Internet service provider named Crayfish Co., which went public three months later at $24.50, soared instantly on its first trade to $96, then climbed as high as $166 before collapsing at day's end to $126. Next day it fell another $42 per share, and at latest look was selling for $3.25. Loss to opening day investors in the aftermarket: as much as 98 percent of their money. It is this very fleecing of investors in the aftermarket that keeps the game going.

A few Web sites have attempted to put the aftermarket individual investors in control of the game—in effect, by turning the individuals into institutions in their own right—but generally speaking, the efforts have not been terribly successful. Consider a New York–based outfit called Wit Capital Corp. The company's Web site is located at www.witcapital.com.

What Wit Capital is attempting to do is offer aftermarket investors a way to become premarket investors instead—in other words, to become a fleecor instead of a fleecee. You begin the transformation by opening a brokerage account at Wit (minimum deposit $2,000). Then, when Wit manages to get itself included as a member of an underwriting syndicate for an IPO and gets allocated some shares for its customers, you can bid to purchase some of the shares at the same premarket price that major institutions are offered.

Taking their cue from Wit Capital, other online brokerage firms have also begun marketing IPO offerings to the public at "premarket" prices. Open an account at E*Trade Securities, the oldest and largest of the Internet-based brokerage firms, and you can get access to various IPO share offerings in much the same manner as you can get them through Wit Capital. You can get IPO stock as well through an account at Fidelity or Charles Schwab, though at Schwab you have to have a personal worth of at least half a million dollars, and at Fidelity your assets have to be in a Fidelity account.

The problem these outfits all have is that they're only able to get tiny allocations of truly hot IPOs. The major Wall Street underwriters like Goldman Sachs and Morgan Stanley Dean Witter discover the best deals first, and they naturally keep the most promising ones for themselves, tossing Wit a few crumbs now and then for appearances' sake.

This means that Wit only gets small allocations of hot deals, which the firm then has to parcel out, on what amounts to a lottery basis, to its own retail clients. Result? Most Wit clients never get in on the deals that everyone wants—whereas the ones they *can* participate in are the ones no one wants to be involved with in the first place.

Another Web site with IPO underwriting pretensions is run by William Hambrecht, the co-founder of the Hambrecht & Quist outfit that helped Morgan Stanley take Netscape Communications public. Located at www.wrhambrecht.com, this company is similar to the Wit Capital Corp. outfit except that it uses what is known as a Dutch auction format to come up with offering prices for shares.

The format invites anyone who wants to buy shares in one of the Hambrecht offerings—from the smallest individual to the biggest hedge fund—to log on to the Web site, fill in a registration form, then enter a bid price and a specified number of shares. At the end of the auction, W. R. Hambrecht & Co. will type up a long list with three columns.

In column A will go the price-per-share bids, ranked from highest to lowest. In column B will go the numbers of shares bid to be bought at that price. In column C will go the name of the bidder. The underwriter, W. R. Hambrecht, will then start at the top of column B and, moving downward, tally up all shares until the total reaches the amount offered in the IPO. According to Dutch auction rules, the price to be found in column A opposite the lowest bid included among the tallied-up bids, will become the selling price for the entire offering.

The way these things work, such an arrangement means that the price being bid (and not the number of shares offered to be bought) will determine who gets into the deal and who doesn't . . . which means that individuals and institutions alike will be placed on an equal footing in getting an "inside price" for the IPO.

But that in turn means that, with everyone being invited to bid as insiders, no one will be left to drive the price skyward in the aftermarket . . . which means there will be utterly no point in investing in any of its IPOs as speculative, day trading plays. Instead, the only reason to buy the shares at all will be as long-term holdings, and with all the action at the opposite, momentum-driven end of the market, the Web site just isn't attracting the deals Hambrecht had hoped for.

As of this writing, W. R. Hambrecht has been in operation as a Web-based Dutch auction site for a bit more than a year, and to date its offerings have been largely small and obscure companies that have generally performed poorly in the aftermarket. Its best-known offering—for a cultural and commentary "Webzine" outfit called Salon.com—raised $26 million in June of 1999 at $10.50 per share, but the stock opened below even the offering price and as of the summer of 2001 was selling for twenty-five cents per share.

As I warned in an article in *Business 2.0* magazine in March of 2000, in time there will assuredly be a price to pay for this wholesale looting of the market by Wall Street's IPO underwriters. The capital has been raised too fast, too impulsively, and with too little attention to the underlying fundamentals and business prospects of the companies being financed. As a result, a painful readjustment now seems all but inevitable for the companies involved, for their shareholders, and ultimately, for the economy as a whole.

Since 1996, more than 400 dot.com companies have sold stock to the public via Wall Street's IPO market, raising $22 billion in start-up capital for everything from switch-and-router manufacturers to grocery delivery services. That $22 billion is the tip of a $500 billion dot.com iceberg that now sits in the portfolios of mutual funds, hedge funds, bank trust accounts, Keogh and IRA accounts, and individual trading accounts of investors large and small, all over the world.

Because the demand for dot.com IPOs has been so hot, venture capitalists have been willing to invest in almost anything viewed as "in" on Wall Street. There's been little perceived risk in doing so, either, since the days are long gone when a venture fund might have been expected to sit for years through various rounds of financings before attempting an IPO. No sooner do the funds put their money on the table nowadays than they're gearing up to snatch it right back again through an IPO.

Thus, to cite but one of innumerable similar examples, New York–based Flatiron Partners pumped $10 million into the money-losing TheStreet.com financial Web site start-up in May of 1998 and within twelve months the company was selling stock to the public—on financials that showed trivial revenues, colossal losses, and an accumulated $12.4 million deficit that has since nearly tripled. Thereafter, the stock lost more than 80 percent in value from an opening day high of $70, and at latest look was selling for less than $1.50 per share.

That is something few investors in the dot.com boom seemed to expect. A view seems to have taken hold that in some way no one can quite articulate but everyone seems fervently to believe, the business cycle has been repealed and this time stocks really will rise to infinite heights.

In the 1960s, the New Frontier economists who gathered around John F. Kennedy believed they could micromanage growth to keep the economy in a state of permanent expansion. These days the belief seems to be that the "New Paradigm" of a digitized, interactive global economy will accomplish the same thing, creating a giant feedback mechanism that will keep productivity increasing, prices declining, and living standards rising for as far into the future as the mind of man can foresee.

But after the New Frontier of Kennedy came Lyndon Johnson and the Vietnam War and not a peep was heard about permanent prosperity for the next twenty-five years. Meanwhile, the high-flying "Nifty Fifty" stocks of the era—the ones that everyone thought, like the Internet stocks of today, were the only ones worth buying because they could only go up—went down instead just as the dot.coms began to do in early 2000. And of course, the ones that rose the highest and the fastest—namely, the superstocks of the dot.com IPO craze—are the ones that fell the furthest. In other words, with IPOs as with everything else on Wall Street, beware. If you're prepared to lose 80 percent of your money on a quick-hit roll of the dice, then go ahead. If not, stay far away from this gamblers' alleyway.

chapter eleven

Successful Investors Bet on the Jockey, Not the Horse

In the end, it all comes down to management. After the Bollinger Bands and the Stochastics charts, after the day trading gurus and the IPO opening day pops, what you're left with in the end is whoever runs the company. Does he know what he is doing? Is he an effective leader who runs a tight ship? Does he see the opportunity in situations before his competitors do, and take action ahead of his rivals? Ultimately, this is all that successful long-term investing is really about: the ceaseless pursuit of the effective boss.

So let's look at what the Web offers to help us in the hunt. How, for example, it can show us how individual companies perform against their peers in those areas of corporate behavior in which management can mostly directly assert its will: operating efficiency, inventory control, cost containment, and the like. To that end, we'll explore a number of management-related research tools on the Microsoft MoneyCentral Web site (www.moneycentral.msn.com) that measure the efficiency with which management runs its business. These include revenue and income per employee, receivables and inventory turnover, and asset turnover.

There's also a Web site—www.10kwizard.com—that lets you see, for example, what it is that the man or woman who runs the company looks for when he or she invests *his* personal money in the stock market. We'll pay some attention to just how much money the boss has invested in the company he runs—and whether it is really his own money or just some phony-baloney "loan" from the company so that he might be able to have an equity stake in the business without actually having to invest any of his personal funds at all.

The Web also lets us peek inside the world of insider trading—the *legal* kind—to glean some advance intelligence into what the top people who run companies see coming down the road to affect their businesses. The key documents in this regard are Form 144 and S3 filings, which either the holders of unregistered shares or the companies themselves must file with the SEC before the shares can be sold on the open market. We'll look at where to find these filings for free (on the Microsoft Investor Web site) even though other Web sites such as www.edgar-online.com charge for certain of them.

The Web also lets us unearth, rapidly and with minimum fuss, the composition of boards of directors, with an eye toward seeing whether the company we're thinking of investing in has a board composed of people who will actually represent the interests of the shareholders, or whether they appear to be yes-men who know little of the company's business and have simply been picked by management to do the boss's bidding.

Additionally, the Web lets us delve into the murky but revealing topic of executive compensation, with an eye toward taking the cut of the CEO's jib by seeing exactly how much he thinks he's worth to his own shareholders.

• • •

First, however, let's stop and consider the basic and perhaps most obvious reason of all as to why the quality of management should be so critically important to a prudent investor: Simply put, the sheer cost of these people is so damned high. If you're going to invest in a company that spends $14 million per year on the salary, bonuses, and other compensation perks of its top five executives—as Barry Diller's USA Networks did in 1999—then you at least ought to get your money's worth, especially when you consider that in the case of USA Networks, that $14 million was equal to 50 percent of the company's entire net profit for the year.

Buying or selling stock solely on the basis of trend lines, charts, moving averages, and all the other tools of momentum investing is simply to deny that management has any importance whatsoever in the course of stock prices. And if that is so—if stocks rise and fall merely because crowds of investors chase each other in and out of various investments—then what is the point of paying management seven- and eight-digit annual salary-and-perks packages, or indeed even employing them at all? Why not just eliminate the jobs altogether and stick the savings on the bottom line? That is especially relevant when one considers that, in many cases, compensation plans for top management are tied to the market performance of their company's stock, so if we may say that the shares of such a company rise for reasons other than how well the top brass do their jobs, then why should they get a free ride in their pay envelopes?

The fact is, of course, that no reasonable person can imagine any company—large or small—being able to function in business for any length of time without someone in charge. The only real question is whether the person in charge is delivering the goods for the people who employ him, namely the shareholders. When you find such a person—someone with both an impressive track record behind him and some years in the corner office still ahead of him—well, generally speaking, that's a stock you should investigate further as a promising long-term investment.

By contrast, all the earnings growth or EBITDA growth, or any other kind of growth you can imagine won't mean very much over the long term if it turns out that the gains have come by way of financial engineering, dealmaking, and fast talk from a grandstanding CEO with a knack for rhetorical waltzing at press conferences. Sooner or later the economy will turn down, or otherwise change in some way, and the company's corner office Harold Hill will find that the audience for his artful spiel has left the theater (Donald Trump of Trump Hotels and Casino Resorts). Or it might turn out that the company's impressive track record was concocted out of too aggressive accounting, with the result that eventually it gets rolled back and undone, and years' worth of earnings wind up vanishing in an instant (Henry Silverman of Cendant Corp.). Or the accounting can be downright fraudulent, with cooked books, phony inventory records, and whatnot, and the boss can wind up going to jail (Barry Minkow and ZZZZ Best).

Finding out how much money the top people at any particular company are paid takes a few seconds at most on the Web. Simply log on to your favorite Web site for EDGAR filings from the Securities and Exchange Commission—for example, www.edgar-online.com—and search the company's listed SEC filings for the latest shareholder proxy statement (Form DEF 14A). This document, which virtually every public company in the country must file at least once a year, typically asks shareholders to vote in favor of the management-nominated slate of corporate directors at the next annual meeting. There's thus often a lot of information about the directors themselves in these filings—things like their professional résumés, the compensation they receive for turning up at board meetings, and so on.

But there's also a section that deals with the company's five highest-paid employees—that is, the company's top management. Under a section that is normally entitled "Summary Compensation Table," you'll find, for each of the five top-paid employees in the corporation, a listing of how much they received in each of the previous three years by way of salary, bonuses, stock and option grants, and benefits such as health and life insurance, company-paid housing and transportation, and so on.

Though these compensation packages can run to staggering amounts, there is no agreed-upon yardstick for what is excessive compensation and what is not, since every industry is different, and performance benchmarks can vary widely from one sector to the next. But it is important that the CEO be compensated for something more than merely turning up for work in the morning—and most proxy statements spell out exactly what the compensation guidelines are. If it's not there—under a section that might be called "Compensation Philosophy" or something similar—then this is all the evidence you need that management is not really being paid to do much of anything except draw a paycheck.

And when those paychecks run to a measurable percentage of the total administrative and payroll overhead of the company, well, is this the sort of place where you want to be parking your money? What's "measurable"? Here's one way to answer that question: Are the top executives at the company being paid more—as a percentage of total "General and Administrative" overhead—than the top execs at the competition? If so—and if both companies are in most other respects pretty much on a par—then it's a no-brainer that the shareholders of the company you're looking at just aren't getting their money's worth from the hired help.

How do you tell if the boss is doing a good job? Since an elevated stock price is not necessarily evidence of anything but an overpriced stock—and certainly not evidence that the man in the corner office knows what he's doing—we have to look elsewhere for the answer.

The best site I know of on the Web for that purpose is, once again, Microsoft's Investor Web site, located at www.moneycentral.msn.com. Go there and click on the link labeled "Investor." This will take you to the "Investor" home page we've visited so often in these chapters. Now, we're ready to make use of the extraordinarily comprehensive research this site actually offers. Like the human brain, 95 percent of what's in this site goes largely unused, but if you've read this far in the book you're equipped to know just how valuable the research actually is.

What we're after in this case is a comprehensive "Company Report" on a company in which we're considering investing. Let's use Dell Computer, the Texas-based assembler of desktop computers to consumers and business. As this is being written, in the spring of 2000, Dell has been trading in a range of between roughly $40 and $50 for the last eighteen months—this following a five-year surge that had lifted it from barely $4 per share as recently as the start of 1997. In other words, the stock went through a huge run-up, then plateaued. Has management lost its grip on the business? The tools available on the MoneyCentral Web site will help us find out.

In the "Symbol" window on the "Investor" home page, type the letters for Dell's symbol, which conveniently happen to be DELL. Up will come a detailed quote of the stock's behavior in the market that day, plus some brief summary data about the company's fundamentals—things like the price/earnings ratio and earnings per share.

Down the left-hand side of your screen you'll see a list of further links, featuring such things as SEC filings, financial results, and so on. At the bottom will appear the words "Print Report." Click on that link and you'll get a complete, highly detailed report of what's in every link on the list . . . a really quite spectacular—and as of this writing, uniquely comprehensive and sophisticated—presentation of investment information, culled from numerous different research sources on the Web, then assembled for you in graphically easy-to-read form.

Once you get the report on your screen, scroll down to the section labeled "Management Efficiency." This is as near to one-stop shopping as you can get on the Web for finding out whether the people who run the company are doing their jobs well. The section compares how much revenue—and income—the company generates, *per employee*, as against its industry peer group and even the 500 largest companies in the country. In Dell's case we can see that the company's chairman, Michael Dell, runs a tight ship: His company gets 50 percent more revenue out its employees—and two and one half times as much net income—than the average of its industry rivals. The gap is even wider with the 500 largest companies in the country as measured by the Standard & Poor's 500 index, which also appears in the table.

You can likewise see that the company's "receivable turnover" is much better than industry averages. Receivable turnover refers to how long it takes for the company to collect the money that is owed it by customers. The ratio is calculated by dividing the company's total revenues by the receivables showing on the current assets portion of the balance sheet. If you mentally divide the result that appears on the report (in the case of Dell: 9.5) into the number 52 (representing fifty-two weeks in the year), you'll get how many weeks of credit the company is extending, free of charge, to its customers before forcing them to pay up. In Dell's case, customers are getting a free ride, on average, of six weeks whereas the average for Dell's rivals is seven and a half weeks. Since time is money, and the faster you can get paid the better it is for your business, receivables turnover is an excellent measurement for determining whether management is doing a good job. Dell is doing significantly better than its rivals by this measure.

The "Management Efficiency" section uses roughly the same calculation to determine how fast the company turns over its inventory. Control of the company's inventory is one of the premier responsibilities facing any management. When inventory control is fine-tuned effectively, tremendous amounts of money can be added to the bottom line. When inventories are mismanaged, the entire company can be destroyed.

Inventory control is where Dell really stands out. Since Dell doesn't assemble a computer for a customer until it gets an order—and only stockpiles an absolute minimum of components and subassemblies in the warehouse in the meantime—Dell's inventory turns over every six days whereas the average for its rivals is closer to two weeks. And for the S&P 500? Closer to two months.

These numbers alone tell us that Dell is a terrific candidate for further research, no matter where the stock price might be—because the company's management is doing such a first-rate job.

At the opposite extreme, let's look at Compaq Computer, another Texas-based outfit in the business of building and selling desktop computers. As was the case with Dell, Compaq had been a Wall Street darling until the beginning of 1999 when its stock price fell from $50 to the mid-$20s after having risen by close to 600 percent in the previous four years. So once again the same question we asked with respect to Dell: What happened; had management lost control of the business? The answer, it turns out, is an emphatic yes. Pull a Money-Central Investor report on Compaq—symbol CPQ—and you'll see.

In the "Management Efficiency" section we can see that Compaq's top brass are getting 20 percent less revenue per employee out of their workers than are the company's rivals—and one third the net income. One major reason: Compaq has a slower receivables turnover—and a *much* slower inventory turnover—than its peer group rivals enjoy. So bad did Compaq's problems get—largely as a result of the company's misguided acquisition of another computer company, Digital Equipment, in early 1999—that the board ousted the president and CEO, and spent months before finding a replacement. As it happened, the new man hasn't done much better.

Though MoneyCentral Investor reports don't label them as such, there are at least two other measurements contained in each report that reflect directly on how well management does its job: return on equity and return on assets.

These are found under the section labeled "Investment Return." Return on equity (ROE) measures whether management is delivering the bacon for shareholders in terms of earnings. You calculate it by taking the company's latest twelve months of net income from the operating statement and dividing it by the company's shareholder equity from the balance sheet. The result is a percentage that shows, in effect, the earnings yield that management is able to get from each dollar of equity invested by the shareholders.

For example, in the spring of 2000, Dell's balance sheet showed shareholder equity of $4.3 billion and its income statement showed trailing twelve-month earnings of $1.46 billion. Dividing the equity into the earnings gives you a return on equity of nearly 34 percent. That is terrific by any standard, and almost ten times better than Compaq's ROE of 3.8 percent. If a company's ROE is no better than, say, 7 percent to 8 percent or so, then what's the point of owning the stock at all since you can get just as good a return from buying a risk-free U.S. Treasury bond—and wind up with actual cold cash, in the form of a twice-yearly interest payment, in your hand.

You don't want to put too much importance on ROE numbers though, since they can be greatly inflated if the company simply borrows a lot of money—the venerable management tactic of "leverage" (what the Brits call "gearing"). For example, when you borrow money and invest the proceeds in the business in one way or another, both your assets and liabilities go up, so the difference between the two—shareholder equity—remains the same. But if you borrow the money at, say, 10 percent, and are able to get an earnings yield of 15 percent on the investment, your return on equity will naturally rise even though the increased yield is coming by way of borrowed money.

You can factor out the possibility of leverage distortion by looking instead at return on assets—the second measurement of management effectiveness in the "Investment Returns" section of the report. This measurement says, in effect, I don't care whether the money is borrowed or not—all I'm interested in is how much of a yield management is getting on the investment. (Some investment professionals will tell you a better measure is return on investment, which is calculated slightly differently, but this is just hair-splitting, since the basic principle in both cases is the same.)

In any case, both these measures—return on equity and return on assets—show that Compaq is currently performing at roughly one third the level of its industry peers, whereas Dell is performing roughly three times *better* than its peers . . . yet another reason to view Dell's management as doing their job well.

Another way to see what top brass thinks of the company's prospects is to check on how much of its money is parked where. Has management got so much of it in various other companies that they're arguably as absorbed with *that* company's prospects as with their own?

You can do this by checking the SEC EDGAR database to see if the CEO (or anyone else in whom you might be interested) holds a 5 percent or greater equity stake in any public company. If so, such a person must, by law, file a Form 13-D with the SEC. Several sites will allow you to search the EDGAR database for free, using keywords or the names of individuals, but for my money the best is

www.10kwizard.com.

Go there and type in the name Michael Dell and up will come sixty-eight different EDGAR filings. Scroll down through the list and you'll find that nearly all of them involve his role as the head of Dell Computer. As of the spring of 2000, this technology billionaire had no 5-percent-or-greater investments in any companies except Dell, and sat on almost no corporate boards other than his own.

Let's compare that to the holdings of Wall Street financier Ronald Perelman, who has major stakes in dozens of different companies and controls many of them outright, most notably Revlon, his crown jewel. How can one man be six places at once . . . do half a dozen jobs at the same time . . . and still deliver the goods so far as his shareholders are concerned? The answer is, he can't.

No matter how good a manager Perelman might be, no one is capable of simultaneously running the world's second-largest lipstick and makeup company, the world's largest camping goods company, a cigar company, a comic book company, a sporting goods company, a kitchen appliances company, various banks, and who knows what else—and do a good job of it with each of them.

And if you were to see how things have been going for Perelman as an actual operator of businesses as opposed to simply being a clever Wall Street dealmaker, well, the answer is, not great. Three of his companies are by now either bankrupt or out of business, one is the subject of an avalanche of shareholder lawsuits for inventory fraud, and the remaining one, Revlon, has crashed from a high of more than $55 per share in the spring of 1998 to a price two years later of $6.75.

This would, however, have come as no surprise to anyone who bothered to call up a MoneyCentral Investor report on Revlon even at the moment when the stock was selling for $55 per share. The report would have shown that Revlon was struggling with, among other things, a receivables turnover half that of its peer group—meaning that it was taking twice as long for Revlon to collect money owed to it from its customers as rival cosmetics companies took. Revlon also showed a lackluster inventory turnover rate, and a return on equity number buoyed up almost totally by the company's incredible debt load—$1.6 billion of debt on its own balance sheet, plus billions more that Perelman had squirreled away elsewhere in his empire.

Now, with the stock at barely $6.75, nothing much has changed. Revlon is bringing in roughly 50 percent less revenue per employee than its rivals, while losing $34,000 per employee at the bottom line even as the rest of the industry is in the black to the tune of $15,000 per employee. Meanwhile, the receivables and inventory turnover rates remain terrible.

Another source of information about how well (or poorly) management is doing its job can be found in Form 144 filings. These documents, which can be obtained from www.edgar-online.com for a fee, but are free to anyone using the www.moneycentral.msn.com site, must be filed with the SEC by individuals seeking to sell previously unregistered shares to the public. Management can come by unregistered shares in a variety of ways—when they are paid in stock instead of cash, when they invest in a start-up before it goes public and receive back stock in the company, for example.

What's important for our purposes is not that management and other corporate insiders (board members, say) may sell small amounts of stock from time to time. Rather, we're interested in zeroing in on companies in which large numbers of insiders—or key top officials, such as the CEO—appear out of nowhere and begin selling large amounts of stock. This often is a very good indication that management knows something about the company's darkening future prospects that the general public itself doesn't yet know.

There are conflicting schools of thought as to what a sudden bump-up in insider selling foretells. One investment adviser, William Valentine, likens a rise in insider selling to a sneeze, meaning that it might by symptomatic of a cold, and then again it might not, so you shouldn't buy or sell shares solely on the basis of a rise in insider selling.

But we're not interested in using this information as a "sell signal" in the first place. All we're interested in is what it tells us about the nature of the company's management—people who apparently are more interested in their personal financial circumstances than in the prospects of the company, people who would rather skirt the edges of SEC insider trading violations than put their investments at risk while trying to turn the situation around. These are not the sorts of people in whom you want to entrust your money; after all, were the situation to arise when they might be forced to choose between their interests and yours, they've already told you who will come first.

Consider the instructive case of a company called CyberShop, an Internet retailing outfit that got into trouble when it refused to cut its prices to match the competition from the likes of Amazon.com, Value America, Egghead.com, and other online retailers. Deciding not to match the competition was a management decision, and the wrong one as things turned out, because, in the highly competitive Web environment, sales instantly collapsed. But the top man at the company, Jeffrey Tauber, tried to paper over his mistake with a public relations stunt designed to prop up the stock until he could cash out his own personal stake in the business before the news of the company's troubles leaked out.

The story began to unfold in November of 1999 when Tauber appears to have dealt with the pending collapse of his business by having CyberShop erupt in all directions with happy-faced press releases about how fantastically well things were going—even as he was quietly dumping roughly $7 million worth of his stock on the market, knowing full well that, in reality, the business was a shambles. Nor was he alone in that effort, for as it now turns out, two other top officials at the company were also dumping stock. Altogether, a total of nearly 1.3 million insider shares, representing close to 14 percent of the total CyberShop shares in existence—and fully 25 percent of the stock's day-to-day public float—poured onto the market in this way during the last two weeks of November, helping send CyberShop's share price careening from a high of $14.75 on November 29 to a year-end low of $5.12 four weeks later. Thereafter the stock sank even further and by the summer of 2000 it was selling for 10 cents per share.

Does this sound right or fair to you? On February 1, 2000, with CyberShop's stock in a tailspin and selling for a mere $5.37 per share, the company issued a press release proclaiming—on the basis of unaudited financials prepared by the company itself—that its just completed September–December period had been the biggest and most successful quarter in the company's history, with net revenues of $4.2 million.

The people at CyberShop put out this press release because they knew that inexperienced and naive Internet investors often mistake these PR releases for actual news, and frequently buy or sell stock based on what's in them. That's why they released it to the public at precisely 9:22 A.M. Eastern Time, which is to say, just before the market opened for trading and the release stood the best chance of getting noticed, giving the stock a badly needed lift.

It is also why the company managed to leave out the single most important fact any investor would have needed to know in order to evaluate just how things were going at the company. What the release did *not* point out, or even hint at, was the truth behind that $4.2 million revenue number. The number was a mere 23.5 percent growth in sales over the year-earlier period when rival retailers like

Amazon.com and Buy.com were racking up year-over-year quarterly gains of anywhere from 167 percent for Amazon.com to 197 percent for Buy.com.

Ten days later, on February 10, the company issued another press release, which surely would have seemed baffling to anyone who'd read and believed the February 1 release. The February 10 release announced that the company had decided—for reasons that were apparently not worth going into—to sell off its Internet retailing business and redeploy the proceeds to become an investment holding company for Internet start-ups.

Now why, we may well ask, if things had been going so great only ten days earlier, had the company now suddenly decided to do a complete about-face and get out of the online shopping business entirely? The answer, of course, is that the first press release was ridiculous. Contrary to its claims, the business wasn't going great at all; in fact it was collapsing.

CyberShop's deteriorating financials could have come as no surprise to Tauber, or his backers, or anyone else at the company, probably from as far back as last September, and certainly since mid-November when Tauber dumped his stock. The only people kept in the dark through it all were the public shareholders, who, on all the available evidence, appear to have been intentionally misled to think that everything was going great at the company when it wasn't.

In that regard, the final shoe dropped on February 29 when the company released its 1999 full-year and fourth-quarter financials, and the numbers didn't look anything like what the company had said they were back on February 1. Instead of net revenues of $4.2 million the company actually took in net revenues of less than $3.99 million, meaning that year-over-year revenues hadn't grown even 23 percent but less than 17 percent. By Internet standards, that is so slow a growth rate as to amount to no growth at all.

Meanwhile, Tauber and the other insiders had already dumped millions' worth of their shares when the stock was still selling as high as $14-plus per share, and before the world at large knew just how horrid the company's prospects really were.

All this could have been easily spotted by simply going to the MoneyCentral Investor Web site and pulling up a report on Cyber-Shop, known these days as Grove Strategic Ventures. Among the information such reports provide, you'll find at the bottom of each a listing of all SEC Form 144 filings by corporate insiders over the past twelve months—and right there, on November 26, 1999, you'd have seen Jeffrey Tauber selling $7 million of his personal stock in the company, an amount equal to nearly double the company's annual sales for the previous twelve months. The point is not that this was a sign to outsiders to sell their shares too—though as things turned out it certainly was—but rather that it was reason aplenty to be skeptical of management's true motives when, after the truth about the company's prospects leaked out, the company announced that it was changing its name to Grove Strategic Ventures and getting into the then trendy business of becoming an "incubator" of Internet start-up companies.

Inevitably, Tauber and his company were soon deluged with class action lawsuits from angry investors claiming they'd been misled. Such lawsuits are commonplace when corporate managements get in trouble through arguably misleading press releases. Defending them is yet another source of distraction to cause management to pay less attention than it should to the day-to-day business of actually running the company. There is a terrific Web site, run by the Stanford University School of Law, that lists just about every securities fraud lawsuit currently pending against every publicly traded company in America. It is located at http://securities.stanford.edu and it is well worth checking when investigating management competence at a company.

• • •

What about the men and women who sit on corporate boards—whose interests are they serving, yours or management's? Corporate law places a direct fiduciary responsibility on board members to represent the interests of the shareholders, who, under the law, in fact actually *own* the company. But it is management that nominates the members of the board. True, the shareholders vote at the company's annual meeting—either in person or by proxy through the mail—for the ones they want. Yet in practice, management often controls the overwhelming majority of votes—either because they themselves own the shares, or they've cultivated cozy relationships with big institutional shareholders like mutual funds.

This in turn means that in almost all cases, boards of directors turn out to be handpicked by management. And therein lies the problem because board members can only be assured of being renominated—and thereafter relected—to their seats if they stay on good terms with management. Meaning that when management's interests diverge from those of the shareholders, the board members are often put to a crucial test: Whose interests should they look out for, their own or their shareholders'?

To check out the composition of any company's board of directors, go to www.edgar-online.com (or any other SEC document-retrieval service) and call up the company's latest proxy solicitation statement—Form DEF 14A. This will tell you all you need to know about the board—and by using a little deductive reasoning, much of what you need to know regarding the management that selected it.

We begin with the fact that although boards have a legal responsibility to look after the interests of the shareholders, they can also play a valuable role in providing counsel to management and bringing business contacts—and contracts—to the company. Thus, to return to our earlier example of Dell Computer, a quick look at that company's board shows that Michael Dell, the company's chairman and largest stockholder, has clearly selected board members who have expertise in the broad areas of business that are of interest and importance to his company. In the spring of 2000, the ten-person board contains a banker from Citicorp, the head of American Airlines (an important customer of Dell's), two people involved in investment banking, a woman who holds seats on several other boards of companies doing business with Dell, an ex–top official at AT&T who now heads a rapidly growing telecommunications start-up venture, and so on. Generally speaking, this is the sort of board one should look for when making a long-term investment in a company—people who can clearly benefit the company with their own expertise and contacts.

You should also check, in the DEF 14A filing, to see what these people are paid for their services. They should get enough money to make it worth their while to do the job—but not enough that risking losing it would crimp their lifestyle. Each director at Dell draws $40,000 a year for his or her work, which seems about right.

Let's compare all that to Trump Hotels and Casino Resorts, whose nine-member board consists mainly of Donald Trump's own employees at the company. These are people who cannot possibly disagree with Trump on the management of the company since they actually work for him. As we discussed in Chapter 7, Trump's stock was changing hands at more than $30 per share in the spring of 1996; four years later it was selling for $2.75. Yet the same faces who were gathering at board meetings in 1996 were still sitting across from each other in the spring of 2000—a period during which Trump himself raked off millions in salary and benefits from the firm.

Still another management fact to investigate is how much the top brass is paid, and who decides. This too can be determined from DEF 14A proxy statements, or, if you can't find the information there, then from the company's latest 10-K. You can get the documents from www.edgar-online.com, www.freedgar.com, and any other such place.

Within one document or the other you will find a table called "Executive Compensation," which will list the salary, bonus payments, stock option grants, and any other compensation received by the company's top five employees in each of the past three years. My grandfather used to say that you can tell a lot about a man from the condition of his shoeshine, but in this age of celebratory excess, when self-worth is often measured by the size of one's stock portfolio, I think you can tell a lot more about a man—at least about a CEO—from how much he is prepared to pay himself for the work he does.

Consider a fellow like Richard E. Snyder, the ex-head of Simon & Schuster, who left in a corporate shake-up and eventually landed as head of Western Publishing, the publishers of the Golden Books series of books for kids. To have been ousted as head of what was, at the time, the largest book publishing company in America, only to land, after two years in the wilderness, as head of a struggling company one tenth S&S's size, was clearly a major step down for Mr. Snyder. But here was a man who seemed to value himself not by what he did so much as by how much his employer was willing to pay him to do it. So Snyder began work, in the winter of 1996, with an annual salary, bonus, and options package worth more than $14 million.

The best part of the deal was how he managed to turn it into something resembling a real-life version of Monopoly, in which players are handed "starter money" simply to get them in the game. In that spirit, Snyder was handed 599,465 shares of Western Publishing common stock—representing 2.77 percent of the total outstanding—so that he could hold his head up high at board meetings and claim to have "a stake" in the company.

In fact, he had no real stake at all, and that's because the shares were actually nothing more than a present to him. Technically, he had to pay for the stock: $4,795,720, or $8 per share. But on the day he got them—January 31, 1996—the shares were actually selling for $9.87, so he got them at an 18.9 percent discount to the market price. Yet that's the least of it because, in reality, he didn't have to pay a dime since the company in fact lent him the whole purchase price—all Snyder had to do was pledge back the acquired shares as collateral on the loan!

Some deal: You're already $1.87 per share "in the money" coming out of the gate so that every penny the stock goes up represents pure profit to you personally. By contrast, if your game plan for the company fails and the stock crashes, you lose nothing because you invested nothing in the first place. (What was that part again about entrepreneurs "assuming the risks" of a business or enterprise?)

So, having thus set himself up like the publishing world equivalent of the Duke of Bedford, Snyder promptly proceeded to lead the company, rechristened by him as Golden Books Family Entertainment, directly into bankruptcy.

It was one of the most embarrassing—and highly publicized—media world flops of the decade, as the company's stock undertook a three-year swan dive that carried it down from a 1996 high of close to $15, to a bankruptcy low of 3 cents per share. Yet through it all, from one business stumble to the next, Snyder continued to draw his outrageous salary package—an amount so huge, relative to the company's dwindling size, that were Gerald M. Levin, the chairman of Time Warner, the largest media company in the world, to have been paid on an equivalent scale, he would have taken home more than $1.2 *billion* a year during the period.*

In fact, even after a bankruptcy reorganization wiped out all the

*Levin was actually paid "only" $9 million in cash, plus about $60 million in stock annually during the years in question.

company's creditors and gave them back stock instead of the actual cash they had lent the company in the first place, Snyder remained at his post, drawing his stupendous salary—now with the terms rewritten so that he got an annual "base salary" of between $750,000 and $850,000 plus rights to a "bonus" that could total as much as $1.7 million annually, plus a "signing bonus" of nearly 500,000 free shares in the new company. And don't forget, this largesse was for the man who presided over the company's downfall in the first place. And here's the best part of all: Remember the $4 million-plus the company lent him to buy his hold-your-head-high shares in the company back in 1996? Well, since thanks to Snyder the shares had become worthless, the company (which is to say, Snyder, since he was, and as of this writing continues to be, the man running the show) simply told him to forget about repaying the loan, ever.

Let's compare Dick Snyder to a CEO who has gotten an absolute avalanche of negative publicity over the years: Martha Stewart. She's been called suburbia's Queen of Mean, a control freak boss who publicly berates and abuses her employees, who masquerades as a latter-day Betty Crocker when she's actually, in her business affairs, more like Leona Helmsley.

But mostly the charge is baloney, for in real life Stewart turns out to be an extraordinarily hardworking and dedicated business executive, who has built her business into one of the most profitable and fast growing retailing and media companies on earth. In every way that management performance can be evaluated, her company, Martha Stewart Living Omnimedia, stands out as best in class. Check out MoneyCentral Investor and you'll see. The company gets seven times the revenue per employee as do its rivals, and three times the net income. Its inventory and receivables turnover are better, it has a 50 percent better return on equity, and twice the return on assets.

The company went public in an IPO in the autumn of 1999, and as of this writing, more than six months later, insiders have done nothing but buy more shares. Her company's board of directors is composed almost totally of well-placed executives in investment banking, finance, advertising, and Internet commerce—all fields that are central to her company's long-term growth. They are paid only $20,000 per year to serve as board members. Martha Stewart herself draws a salary and bonus, as of this writing, of $1.3 million—in media world terms, a relative pittance. All stock and option awards go to her employees, not to herself.

There are risks in this company, to be sure, beginning with the obvious fact that the company's fortunes are inescapably linked to her own public image—and unlike names such as Betty Crocker and Aunt Jemima, Martha Stewart is an actual living and breathing human being who could, at any minute, drop dead. Then what for her stockholders?

The investment problem presented by her company—and the only significant one at that—is not just what would happen to the company and its stock if, let us say, Stewart were to be run over by a truck, but what will happen to her brand-name appeal as she moves into old age. Because she is an actual, real person with an actuarially determinable lifespan on this planet, the day will inevitably come when her lifestyle hustle will be reduced to coming up with new and exciting ways to pretend she's not wearing Depends. And who's going to want to spiff up the sitting room with a collection of four-color coffee-table books on *that* subject?

· As of the spring of 2000, Stewart's business consists of two magazines (*Martha Stewart Living* and *Martha Stewart Weddings*), a Martha Stewart TV show, twenty-seven Martha Stewart books, a Martha Stewart radio show, a Martha Stewart newspaper column, and a Martha Stewart Web site. She makes an absolute bucket of money from all that, boasting a 12 percent net profit margin, which for a media company is utterly heroic. Most media companies are so leveraged with debt that they don't have any profits at all. Stewart's total debt load is a mere $15 million, amounting to barely 12 percent of her assets. This is a balance sheet to die for.

But to be successful over the long term as a public company, Stewart is clearly going to have to start scaling back on the intense personalization of her lifestyle message and start capitalizing on the name Martha Stewart instead of the person behind the name. As a public company, she's sooner or later going to have to go the licensing route—much more aggressively than she has until now. She's going to have to start flogging Martha Stewart wicker furniture, and Martha Stewart microwaveable hors d'oeuvres, and Martha Stewart mucking-about-in-the-garden boots. And how about a Martha Stewart signature edition of the Lincoln Navigator? And hey, if Ralph Lauren can sell house paint at Home Depot, how about a line of Martha Stewart signature vinyl siding from Georgia-Pacific?

The fact is, Martha Stewart is smarter than I am, and if I can see the need for something like this, she's probably already working on it. That's what smart long-term investing is all about: picking the right jockey, then being patient long enough to let him (or her) win the race. The Internet can help you identify such a person, but in the end, it is you, the investor, calling on the experiences of your life, who will have to make the call.

chapter twelve

On Not Becoming
the Greater Fool

When I first began thinking about writing this book, in the summer of 1996, the Dow Jones Industrial Average stood at 5600, the NAS-DAQ composite index stood at 1080, and in the air you could catch the faintest whiff of a distant and approaching fire. Yahoo had gone public that April at $13 and had jumped on its first trade in the after-market to $24.50 per share. The next day the *Los Angeles Times* carried the headline, "Yippie For Yahoo! IPO Spurs Trading Frenzy As Shares More Than Double." The story went on to note that the IPO's success was all the more remarkable because the company was little more than a start-up, with no track record in business. But that was apparently not very troubling to investors in the shares, who, according to the article, were mainly "individual investors eager to get in on the Internet craze, rather than the institutions that normally dominate initial public offerings."

Eighteen months passed, and by the time I signed a contract with my publisher, the smoke from that distant fire had begun to envelop Wall Street in a day-long haze that made getting one's bearings difficult even at high noon. During those eighteen months, the Dow Jones Industrial Average had climbed by 41 percent and stood at just over 7900. The NASDAQ composite index had risen even more—by fully 50 percent in fact—and stood at 1619. As for Yahoo, well, its shares had already undergone a three-for-two stock split and now stood, adjusted for that split, at nearly $80 per share.

Meanwhile, Wall Street investment firms, mesmerized by the success of Yahoo, had begun cranking out dot.com IPOs the way Mickey Mouse directed the parade of buckets and broomsticks in *Fantasia*— a colossal Wall Street tsunami of investment treasure, poured not into medical research or education, or the biosciences or pharmaceuticals, but into companies bearing names like Cyberian Outpost, Peapod, Gadzooks, and CDnow Online . . . all of them rushed to market by Wall Street underwriters anxious to pocket the fees on deals for companies that, for the most part, had no hope of surviving even one full cycle of the economy, from expansion to recession and back again.

During this time it seemed that scarcely a week would go by without Federal Reserve chairman Alan Greenspan turning up on TV, addressing some conference or another to warn of "irrational exuberance" on Wall Street, and to hint that interest rates would be going up if the speculation didn't cool down. But no one seemed to listen to him anymore, and stock prices just roared higher. And as each new deal came to market, more and more investors would clamor for the shares. It was the absolute definition of an investment bubble in the making. I began, on an irregular basis, to publish a provocatively entitled "Internet Suckers Index," designed to track the soaring market values of companies that, on any fundamental basis known to Wall Street, had no value at all. In April of 1998 I wrote, "These aren't investments, they're financial toys for speculators." I fully expected the bubble to pop any minute. In fact, the wildest surge still lay ahead.

Between the time I began writing this book, in October of 1998, and when the manuscript was completed in March of 2000—roughly a seventeen-month period—the NASDAQ composite index rose 138 percent in value, to 5048 at its peak on March 8, 2000. The Dow Industrials rose "only" 47 percent. It is doubtless a measure of just how blinded people had become to the real performance represented by that number—a growth rate more than twice the average of the Dow in just the previous ten years, let alone any longer time frame—that many on Wall Street had by now begun openly dismissing the Dow Industrials as a barometer of the "old economy" and hardly worth paying attention to anymore.

Embedded within that NASDAQ number, in fact, was a level of speculation not seen on Wall Street in generations, indeed maybe ever. In his delightfully readable *Ponzi Schemes, Invaders from Mars and More Extraordinary Popular Delusions and the Madness of Crowds,* Joseph Bulgatz revisits the famous tulip bulb speculation that bankrupted Holland in 1636, and chronicles in amazement how people—frantic to pay any price for the presumably precious flower bulbs in the belief that they'd be more precious tomorrow—bid up the price of one species of bulb by 1,166 percent during a single nineteen-month period. Compare that to an Internet company named Xcelera.com, which soared more than 72,000 percent between February of 1997 and February of 2000, on little except press-release fueled momentum trading and statements by its chairman that the company would be the world leader in an obscure and technically complex corner of the Internet business. At its peak, in March of 2000, this company, with seven employees and sales of a mere $3 million—and a corporate address consisting of a post office box in the Cayman Islands—carried a market value on Wall Street of more than $7.5 billion.

Xcelera.com-type situations were but one of many consequences of the speculation. As the speculation in IPOs intensified, opening day pops of 300 percent in the aftermarket became the norm, with investors complaining loudly when their shares rose by a "mere" 50 percent on opening day. The level of expectation grew so extreme—and perceptions so distorted—that people no longer seemed to think it odd or unsustainable when each new IPO produced a whole new crop of instant mega-millionaires in the person of twenty*something* youngsters who had invested a few thousand dollars and a year of sweat-equity into launching a Web site, then took the business public and overnight found their shares worth $100 million, $200 million . . . and in many cases a lot more even than that.

No young men seemed more to epitomize this New Paradigm route to instant riches than Todd Krizelman and Stephan Paternot, who founded theglobe.com while they were still undergraduate students at Cornell University in 1994. Having caught the eye of a Cornell alumnus named Michael Egan, who in turn had a contact on Wall Street, they were able to take their company public in November of 1998 (see Chapter 10). Thanks to their company's opening day pop of 900 percent in the aftermarket, the two young men, who had no business experience of any sort, found themselves each instantly worth more than $700 million. Within hours, they were giving interviews to the media from their offices, which upon inspection had the look and feel of college dorm rooms, with empty take-out food containers, Coke cans, two-day-old pizza slices, and clothing lying everywhere. This was headquarters of a company that investors—in the grip of a speculative fog so deep they could no longer see the noses on their own faces—now valued at more than $8 billion.

It is in the nature of investment bubbles that one never knows he's in one until he tries to get out—until he becomes what is known on Wall Street as the Greater Fool, the fellow who keeps the game going. I have researched the matter thoroughly, and I must confess that I cannot establish with certainty—or even generally—who it was who first coined the term Greater Fool. Nonetheless, in one guise or another, he is the character who has allowed every bull market in history to become "overextended." He is the fellow who willingly pays more than he knows something is worth in the belief that he'll be able to resell it for even more tomorrow, to an even *greater* Greater Fool.

The Greater Fool doesn't explain everything about Wall Street, but he explains a lot, especially in late-bull-market cycles when prices have been rising not just for months but for so many years that rising prices become a kind of default expectation . . . the basic condition that people remember when they consider their own life experience. As Mark Twain is said to have remarked, history may not precisely repeat itself, but it does seem to rhyme a lot. So if all you remember are rising investment values, then rising investment values are pretty much all you're going to expect in the future. The Greater Fool is the fellow who finances that expectation when the *reasons* for rising prices no longer prevail. He's the buyer you sell to so that you don't have to answer the question of what it was that caused you to hand over your money in the first place—so that *you* don't get stuck with the dunce cap as the Greater Fool.

It is greed that invites the Greater Fool onstage, to be sure. But what causes his exit is one of life's most baffling questions, like how come thousands of fish can be swimming in one direction, then simultaneously all turn and head off on a new course with no uberfish at the head of the school leading the way. How come fish and birds know to change direction? How come 10,000 money managers can stand up from their desks at the same exact nanosecond and announce, "I think it's time to sell . . ." then go out for coffee and a Danish, and the market drops 400 points before lunch? I don't know why things like that happen, but they do.

You just never know when the Greater Fool will disappear. All you can know for sure is that when he does, investment values will return with a thud to where things stood before he arrived. It's what happens when the music stops.

Unfortunately, it is simply not possible to anticipate the Greater Fool's departure since he always exits when the weather seems sunniest, when the reasons for continued optimism are most compelling. It is the very fact of his departure that causes the sky to darken. Said Irving Fisher, the distinguished Yale economist, on the eve of the October 1929 stock market crash, "In a few months I expect to see the stock market much higher than today."

Here is how economist Hernan Cortes Douglas sums up the euphoric view of the future that often foretells the Greater Fool's departure:

> Before every collapse, economists say the economy is in the best of all worlds. Everything looks rosy, stock markets go up and up, and macroeconomic flows (output, employment, etc.) appear to be improving further and further. This explains why a crash catches most people, especially economists, totally by surprise. The good times are invariably extrapolated linearly into the future.
>
> "This time is different" is euphoria's motto . . . the rallying cry of "cognitive dissonance"—the denial of the warning signs, the rationalization of risky decisions, and inaction. We do not want to see, we do not want to know; we rationalize and justify the unjustifiable. Buyers of stocks confidently expect to sell to someone else at an even higher price. If they cannot, they lose. In financial circles, this is called the "Greater Fool Theory." And again history teaches us that this theory makes its grand entrance, time and time again, before a crash. (The Collapse of Wall Street and the Lessons of History, monograph, Friedberg Mercantile Group, 1998).

History is filled with examples of ruinous financial speculations: The aforementioned tulip bulb bubble of seventeenth-century Holland, when virtually the entire wealth of the nation was poured into a wild speculation in flowers that seems idiotic in retrospect but must have made perfect sense at the time; the South Seas bubble of eighteenth-century Britain, when investors behaved similarly over some worthless shares in an exploration and development venture; the nineteenth-century bubble deals of William Franklin Miller (aka 520 percent Miller), the "Napoleon of Finance."

And now as I write in the spring of the year 2000, the evidence is mounting that we are in the midst of another one. The major indexes and averages of the stock market are falling further, faster, than at any time since the Crash of 1987. Tomorrow the averages could reverse course and begin surging up again, to be sure. But the tech sector in general, and the dot.coms in particular, look to be more seriously wounded. Many of these stocks have seen 70 percent, 80 percent, and even 90 percent of their values wiped out in weeks and even days. Market commentators opine that the collapse occurred because investors developed a collective fainting spell from the nosebleed heights to which the market climbed, and that people are returning to the tried-and-true principles of value investing.

Maybe that is what is happening, and then again maybe it is not. When you're climbing up the outside of an eighty-story building, it doesn't help matters to look down—and the higher you get the more sense it makes to keep looking up. But with each step upward, the gravitational tug of history pulls harder in the opposite direction, forcing us to concoct ever more convincing reasons to deny what seems obvious. These days the belief seems to be that the New Paradigm of a digitized, interactive global economy will create a giant feedback mechanism that will keep productivity increasing, prices declining, and living standards rising for as far into the future as the mind of man can foresee.

But as my colleague Andrew Tobias has pointed out in his marvelous book *The Only Investment Guide You'll Ever Need*, in 1972

Avon was selling for $140; two years later you could buy it for less than $19. During the same period, Coca-Cola fell from $149 to $45; Walt Disney collapsed from $200 to $30; Polaroid fell from $149 to $14. Prices of terrific companies can and do decline precipitously.

The difference today is that it's not just professionals who are at risk on Wall Street, it's everyone. One way or another, more than 75 percent of all American families now have money in the stock market. The Internet has opened the gates to an increasingly level playing field between the pros of Wall Street and the amateurs of Main Street, and millions upon millions of people are streaming through those gates.

What sorts of people are they? As an Internet columnist and financial radio show host, I'm in as good a position as anyone to answer that question, at least anecdotally. Every day I get dozens of e-mails from people, people I don't know, in places I've never been, asking me investing questions of such breathtaking naïveté it's almost frightening. Here's one I received not long ago, from a man in Australia.

Dear Chris, I am very interested in learning about stocks . . . and how they work. Could you please take the time to recommend a book or a Web site within Australia which will inform me what I need to know? Thank you.

To which I can only say this: No, I can't offer you the sort of advice you want. But I can tell you something you need to know. Only hindsight is 20/20 perfect, yet based on the history of Wall Street to date, I'd say that you and the millions of others like you who are eyeing this market as first-timers are at grave risk. Simply put, you stand a good chance of becoming Greater Fools—those last-in-line chumps who stand there with their hands outstretched to do the buying when everyone else decides to sell.

• • •

No one can know what the future will hold—except perhaps to say that history has a way of mocking the affairs of man, and that just when the sun shines brightest is when the sky begins to darken . . . the coup in Mexico that pushes the price of oil to a new and permanently higher plateau; the Congress that stampedes itself into a four-year spending spree that sends consumer prices soaring; the prostate cancer or heart attack that strikes down the chairman of the Federal Reserve and spurs a global stock market panic; the Chinese attack on Taiwan; the Russian reoccupation of Georgia. It could come from anywhere, at any time, and only after the fact will we know it's come at all—the McGuffin that wanders onstage when no expects it and sends the affairs of man careening off in a direction that no one foresaw.

The advent of the Internet is now giving everyday investors the tools they need to compete in this minefield with those who buy and sell stocks for a living and a career. The guiding purpose of this book has been to help you find and use those tools, not so that you can become a professional investor too, but rather to help you avoid becoming the person without whom the pros cannot prosper—the Greater Fool.

On Wall Street it takes luck to grow rich, but one need only have common sense to keep from growing poor. With common sense, and the hyperlinks and lessons in this book, you can make money—maybe not *all* the money, but enough money—and you can make it four seasons a year, through bull markets and bear markets alike, through periods of rising and falling interest rates, and expanding and contracting economies . . . and along the way you can have a life that is full in other measures than simply the endless search for fulfillment in a stock portfolio. And isn't that what you really wanted all along?

Some of My Favorite Financial Web Sites (and a couple that are very overrated)

If the only reason you bought this book was to get a list of useful financial Web sites, here's your list. This list is not meant to be complete, or even to cover all the major topics discussed in the book. But the thirty seven sites listed below will augment concepts discussed in the book and give you quick access to many of the financial tools that professional money managers pay thousands of dollars yearly to receive. On the Web you can get the same thing, in most cases, free.

> Mega-sites:

www.dailystocks.com If all you're looking for is a site that links to other sites, you can't do much better than this one. The whole world of investing is organized into seventeen super-categories (news, commentary, IPOs, and so on), each with several—and in some cases, dozens of—links to other Web sites specializing in one aspect or another of the super-category's topic.

www.superstarinvestor.com This is a variation on the DailyStocks theme, with slightly different super-categories. Worth inspecting.

http://cbsmarketwatch.com The best of the "original content" sites, this gives you most (but not all) of what you'll find on DailyStocks and Superstar Investor, but with the added bonus of very good original commentary and analysis by staff writers and outside contributors. The site is constantly being improved, so it pays to check it often for new offerings.

www.moneycentral.msn.com The best technical and momentum-angled research tools you'll find anywhere on the Web. Also the best and most sophisticated portfolio-tracking software. If you want to take the trouble to key in all 5,000-plus stocks in the NASDAQ composite index and on the Big Board you'll be able to track them against dozens of different categories of trade-related information—something that not even the Bloomberg service offers to its own subscribers, who pay $12,000 per year for a connection.

www.yahoo.com Sign up for the service, which is free, and Yahoo will stick a little thingie on your browser's toolbar so that, whenever the spirit moves you, you can type in a stock symbol and instantly be deluged with quotes, charts, and plenty of associated fundamental and technical research data. One handy plus: With one click you can see what's being said about any stock on Yahoo's message boards.

www.bigeasyinvestor.com This site offers an ingenious software package that is downloaded onto your hard drive and becomes a portfolio-tracking instrument containing every technical and fundamental analysis tool you can think of. The site sends out useful daily e-mailed tip sheets to help you get the most out of the package. Very good offering, and as of this writing, unique on the Web.

www.quicken.com The asset allocation tool is a standout; the rest is pretty ordinary.

www.thestreet.com A kind of low-rent version of CBS MarketWatch, the site is struggling financially, and by the time you read this it may be out of business or merged into a healthier rival. To keep its head above water, the company recently split itself into two sites—a free one, and one that costs $9 or so per month. The free site is worthless, and there's not much to commend the premium site except its stand-out contrarian commentator, Herb Greenberg. For the rest, forget it.

> Economic and Government Data Research Sites:

www.sec.gov You can get EDGAR filings here, though curiously enough, they are sometimes days late in being posted online. Also, the servers are slow and buggy (your tax dollars at work, right?). The one good thing about the site is its press release page, which often lists disciplinary actions against brokers and other SEC rules violators.

www.federalreserve.gov Just about every monetary and interest rate statistic you can think of can be found here.

www.minneapolisfed.org If the Federal Reserve servers are down, go to this site and you can find most of the same stuff.

www.bea.doc.gov One-stop shopping for nearly all macroeconomic statistics involving the United States.

www.bls.gov Where to go for employment statistics.

www.oecd.org Where to go for economic statistics on countries around the world.

> **News:**

http://interactive.wsj.com Why subscribe to the print version of the paper when you can get the same thing online for a mere $29 per year?

www.nytimes.com Ditto, and the online paper is totally free to boot.

www.bloomberg.com A quick rundown, in summary form, of what Bloomberg's paid subscribers are learning from the Bloomberg News Service. Caution: The information on this site is delayed from what goes out on Bloomberg's wires, which means that by the time you see it here, Bloomberg subscribers have already read it and, presumably, acted on it.

www.nytimes.com/aponline This will get you breaking business news from the Associated Press, as supplied to the *New York Times.* Cool or what!

http://moneycentral.msn.com/investor/news/breakingnews.asp This will get you Reuters business news, as supplied to Money Central.

www.cbs.marketwatch.com/headlines/headlines.asp?source=htx/ http2_mw&slug=headlines This will get you all business headlines, from all sources received by CBS MarketWatch.

> Stock Exchanges:

www.nasdaqtrader.com Here you can get up-to-the-minute information on any NASDAQ-listed stock. You can see if the stock is available for short sale, which stocks have had trading halted and why, and (my personal factoid favorite) which market makers account for how much volume in individual NASDAQ stocks. You can use this data to determine whether a stock is being moved by institutions or perhaps just day traders.

www.nyse.com This is a crummy, PR-type site with very little useful information about what's actually happening on the Big Board day to day. Don't bother.

> Penny Stocks:

www.otcbb.com This site is run by NASDAQ and contains the most up-to-date information anywhere on the trading status of individual penny stocks.

www.topstock.com Getting historical charts on penny stocks can be difficult. This site provides them by way of links to a data supplier named Telescan.

> Off-Hours Trading:

http://island.com As time passes, it becomes possible to trade stocks more and more hours of each day. This site will give you premarket quotes, constantly updated, of the Top 20 NASDAQ stocks being traded on the Island Electronic Communications Network. It doesn't necessarily give you a full view of the entire world of premarket trading, but the Island ECN, which is used by a number of day trading firms, gives you a pretty good idea of what's hot in the premarket.

www.marketxt.com Another good source of premarket quotes.

www.instinet.com Delayed quotes on the premarket—so delayed, in fact, that they're worthless.

> Futures Quotes:

www.cme.com You know that little box that appears on CNBC showing the S&P and NASDAQ prices in the premarket? These are prices on futures contracts that trade on the Chicago Mercantile Exchange. Here is the site where you can get them if you want to know how the market is likely to open at 9:30 a.m. Eastern Time and you don't have access to a television. Caution: Interpreting this data is trickier than you'd think.

www.cbot.com Here is where you can get quotes on interest rate futures contracts—not that you'd want to buy or sell them (though you might), but simply because knowing whether demand for the contracts is strong or weak will tell you what professional investors think is likely to happen to interest rates down the road. If the current Federal Funds rate (the Federal Reserve's favorite interest rate lever to control economic activity) is 6.5 percent and the six-month futures contract for Fed Funds is 93060, it means investors think that in six months' time the rate will stand at 6.94 percent; you get this by subtracting the quoted price—93060—from 100000.

> Historical Stock and Market Data:

www.globalfindata.com Want to know what the price/earnings ratio of the Standard and Poor's index was in 1871, or any point thereafter? Or similar data for the Dow Industrials? Here's the site that can tell you.

www.e-analytics.com One-stop shopping for every factoid imaginable about the Dow Industrials. Here you can learn, for example, the original stocks in the Average, and each date on which the composition of the Average was changed, and how. A better source of information about the Average than the site maintained by Dow Jones itself.

> Legal Research:

http://securities.stanford.edu The Web's most comprehensive collection of securities class action lawsuits. A must-visit site if you're considering investing in a stock that has a controversial history in any way. Chances are some securities fraud law firm has filed a class action against such a company. Here's where to go to see if a case exists and what its status is.

www.lawschool.cornell.edu/lawlibrary The best Web site for research into the law itself. Check it out.

> Corporate Earnings:

www.thomsoninvest.net/FirstCall/rpttin.sht Nearly all comprehensive financial sites provide earnings estimates of one sort or another.

Here is the site that supplies them. From this site you can learn which companies are expected to report earnings in the coming days, the date on which the report is due, and what Wall Street analysts are expecting to hear. If the reported number comes in higher than the forecast, look for the stock to rise. Neat game to play: Look for stocks that are due to report earnings that day. Then check premarket trading in the shares. You can often spot leaked insider information in this way. Then file a complaint with the SEC. If your information pans out, you'll get a bounty under an SEC program.

www.earningswhispers.com What analysts say when, figuratively speaking, they gather at the office water cooler forms the Wall Street "whisper number" about a company's upcoming earnings. The whole idea seems a little fishy to me, but investors nonetheless pay attention to these numbers, so here is where you can find them.

> Intraday Market Behavior:

http://finance.yahoo.com Just about everything there is to know regarding the performance of the markets during regular trading hours can be found on the Yahoo finance site. The most active stocks by volume, the biggest gainers, the biggest losers—it's all there, well organized and available at the click of a mouse.

http://moneycentral.msn.com/investor/home.asp Has the same type of data as Yahoo Finance. The big plus is the unparalleled portfolio-tracking software MoneyCentral offers. The only negative is that the site's servers are slower than Yahoo's. You make the choice.

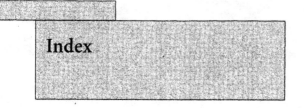

Index